HI/MIS
High Impact
Manufacturing Information
Systems

Automation in Manufacturing Titles from Van Nostrand Reinhold

---

HI/MIS
High Impact
Manufacturing Information
Systems

Norman D. Klapper

VNR **VAN NOSTRAND REINHOLD**
New York

Copyright © 1992 by Van Nostrand Reinhold

Library of Congress Catalog Card Number 91-44595
ISBN 0-442-00845-7

Printed in the United States of America.

Van Nostrand Reinhold
115 Fifth Avenue
New York, New York 10003

Chapman and Hall
2–6 Boundary Row
London, SE1 8HN, England

Thomas Nelson Australia
102 Dodds Street
South Melbourne 3205
Victoria, Australia

Nelson Canada
1120 Birchmount Road
Scarborough, Ontario MIK 5G4, Canada

16 15 14 13 12 11 10 9 8 7 6 5 4 3 2 1

Library of Congress Cataloging-in-Publication Data

Klapper, Norman D.
    HI/MIS: High impact manufacturing information systems / Norman D. Klapper.
        p. cm.
    Includes index.
    ISBN 0-442-00845-7
    1. Production management—Data processing.   2. Manufactures—Management—Data
processing.   3. Management information systems.
I. Title.
TS155.K642   1992
658.5'0285—dc20
                                                                          91-44595
                                                                          CIP

To: Kristin, Sarah, and Aaron

Special thanks to *M.A.K.—Network Software Inc.* for the use of their *Click-Net*™ product. Several of the network diagrams appearing in this book were produced with the help of this excellent tool.

I also wish to acknowledge Ray M. Shortridge, Ph.D. for his insightful contributions to the early stages of the manuscript.

CONTENTS

Information Request Form

Please have vendors send me information on the following:

_____ **CIIM**, Interactive Information Systems, Inc.

_____ **Expandable/MRP**, Expandable Software, Inc.

_____ **Macola Manufacturing Software**, Macola, Inc.

_____ **MFG/PRO**, qad.inc

_____ **Minxware**, Minx Software, Incorporated

_____ **MPS***plus*, Bridgeware, Inc.

_____ **SYMIX**, Symix Computer Systems Inc.

_____ **THE JIT ENTERPRISE RESOURCE SYSTEM**, JIT Resources Int'l., Inc.

_____ **Additional** *HI/MIS* products

_____ **Additional** *VNR* books in this field

_____ **Other** related products and services

Name: (Mr./Mrs./Ms.) _____

Title: _____

Company: _____

Address: _____

_____

City/State: _____ / _____

Country/Zip: _____ / _____

Phone: (___)_____ (optional)

Is your need...   immediate ___
                    within 1 year ___
                    for information only ___

A completed copy of this request form should be sent to:

HI/MIS Product Information
P.O. Box 41095
San Jose, CA 95160

PREFACE

Until just recently, the dream of a fully functional, integrated information system serving the needs of manufacturing, finance, and marketing was beyond the reach of smaller businesses. The application software was too expensive, the required investment in computer hardware too great, and the costs to implement, maintain, and support the system were exorbitant.

Businesses either did without or made due with substandard systems, putting them at a significant disadvantage relative to their larger competitors. This problem was especially severe for manufacturing enterprises that needed good information system support for reducing costs, controlling inventory, planning material requirements, improving quality, and implementing World Class Manufacturing methodologies such as JIT (Just-in-Time).

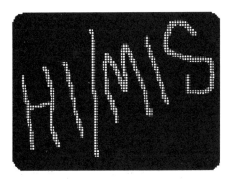

HI/MIS \'ach-i -em-i-es*noun* (ca. 1991): Any of several fully functional, high-performance, integrated information systems serving the needs of manufacturing, finance, and marketing that are based on advanced technologies and are available at a cost that is within the reach of small and medium-size companies.

Beginning several years ago, and accelerating during the last few years, the realization of this dream has become possible. Driven by advancements in several key technologies and the introduction of a new generation of software products, it is now possible to provide high performance, sophisticated, fully functional systems at a cost that is within the reach of small and medium-size companies. This unprecedented level of performance-for-price, plus the unique characteristics and challenges associated with these systems put them within their own distinct classification. I call this new generation of products *HI/MIS*—High Impact Manufacturing Information Systems.

According to recent studies, the majority of future innovation and new jobs will come from the small business sector. It is important that these entrepreneurial companies are given every advantage to compete and succeed in the global marketplace. Effective, affordable information systems can help them do this.

There are products out there that *can* do the job for smaller businesses. A lot more companies could benefit from these systems if they only knew that they existed, believed that they could work for them, and knew how to select and implement them. That is the purpose of this book.

The following sections explore:

- WHO is a candidate for an *HI/MIS*
- WHAT are the important components of an *HI/MIS*
- WHY companies are moving to *HI/MIS*
- HOW to evaluate, select, and implement an *HI/MIS*

PART 1—WHO CAN CAPITALIZE ON *HI/MIS*?

Chapter 1, *HI/MIS* Candidates, examines the various types of companies that can benefit from *HI/MIS*. These companies include:

Entrepreneurial businesses, which need inexpensive, easy to implement, easy to maintain, powerful systems to compete with their larger rivals.

High growth and start-up companies, which need to conserve capital to fuel growth, but at the same time must acquire the functionality necessary to manage the much larger, more complex company they will become.

High technology companies, which need sophisticated control and excellent tactical information to manage the challenges of new product introductions and engineering change activities.

Divisions of large corporations, which wish to decentralize operations or enable individual business units to utilize systems that are most appropriate for their unique needs at minimal cost.

Manufacturing and distribution enterprises, which need a high level of information system support for standard production and inventory management activities such as Manufacturing Resource Planning (MRP-II), Distribution Requirements Planning (DRP), Master Production Scheduling, Capacity Requirements Planning, and Shop Floor Control, and to support their efforts to employ World Class Manufacturing techniques such as Just-in-Time (JIT) and Total Quality Management.

Multinational operations, which need specialized support for transactions with foreign suppliers and customers, financial control and reporting of foreign subsidiary operations, and need to affordably automate globally dispersed sales or operating units without incurring excessive telecommunication costs.

Chapter 2, *HI/MIS* Illustrative Cases, provides brief examples of business situations that demand *HI/MIS* solutions. Three examples are presented:

Case 1 is a high-technology, start-up company seeking their first system.

Case 2 is a rapidly growing entrepreneurial company attempting to enter new markets.

Case 3 is a large company with multinational operations venturing to decentralize their information systems.

These cases illustrate the demanding combination of information system needs, operational constraints, and financial limitations that make finding an acceptable solution difficult. *HI/MIS* can then be judged in the context of providing solutions to these challenging business situations.

PART 2—WHAT IS *HI/MIS*?

Chapter 3, Components of an *HI/MIS*, explores the fundamental elements that constitute an *HI/MIS*. The discussion of these elements helps to define *HI/MIS* and demonstrates that they exhibit both important advantages (benefits) and potential disadvantages (caveats). The functionality, cost, and vendor characteristics associated with *HI/MIS* are explored, as described below.

Functionality

Software capabilities are surprisingly—even astonishingly—good, often including in excess of 90 and sometimes 95 percent of the capabilities of software 10 times as costly.

Software ease-of-use is very good, at least in the relative sense, due to the incorporation of more modern techniques at the user interface level.

Report writing is typically very capable and easy enough to operate so that end users can write their own reports; it is often based on standard third-party report writers and languages that utilize SQL.

Operating systems are principally local area networks or shared processor (minicomputer) systems and are sophisticated enough to handle all necessary functions, while at the same time remaining relatively less complex to support.

Source code is frequently *not* included with the software, can usually be purchased at additional cost, and can almost always be escrowed, but sometimes is totally unavailable.

Software modifications are sometimes entirely unavailable or available only from a very limited number of sources.

Cost Factors

Initial software costs are often only a fraction of those for the more traditional, non-*HI/MIS* products.

Initial hardware costs are dramatically less, due to several recent technological advancements and the extremely competitive environment created by multiplatform operating systems.

Ongoing operational costs normally stay in line with the initial software and hardware costs, and range from 10 to 18 percent per year, exclusive of internal support personnel costs.

Vendor Characteristics

Vendor size is usually very small, with only a handful of the vendors numbering over 100 employees.

Vendor support is typically provided through phone-in response centers and remote dial-up access to client systems.

Vendor distribution channels are likely to be varied, with multiple methods employed and varying levels of quality found within different geographic regions.

Chapter 4, *HI/MIS* Technologies, explores the enabling technologies that make *HI/MIS* possible. The discussion covers advancements in microprocessors, channel and bus designs, hard disk storage, language compilers, and database environments. This information will assist in evaluating the limits on the size of business, the number of users, and the operating environments that can be supported with current *HI/MIS* products. It also provides a basis for understanding the future, where it is expected that:

- New *HI/MIS* products will emerge.
- Existing *HI/MIS* products will be significantly enhanced.
- More *HI/MIS* products will become available as established minicomputer and mainframe products continue to migrate downward to lower-cost hardware platforms.

Chapter 5, Capabilities of an *HI/MIS*, provides details on the depth of functionality that exists in current *HI/MIS* software products. The discussion is broken into separate sections and modules for each of the common functional areas:

Section	Modules
Manufacturing and Distribution	Bills of Material
	Capacity Requirements Planning
	Distribution Requirements Planning
	Engineering Change Control
	Inventory Control
	Job Costing
	Lot Tracking
	Master Scheduling
	Material Requirements Planning
	Operations Routings
	Product Costing
	Purchasing
	Shop Floor Control
	Yield Reporting and Analysis
Marketing	Sales Order Processing
	Sales Quotations
	Sales Analysis
Financial	Accounts Payable
	Accounts Receivable
	General Ledger
	International Operations
	Payroll
Other	Field Service
	Process Control / Data Acquisition Interface
	Report Writing
	EDI (Electronic Data Interchange)

The capabilities selected for discussion are some of the most advanced, complex, problematic, difficult to find, or otherwise most notable capabilities. *HI/MIS* software products are shown to be capable enough to be considered seriously as solutions for a wide range of business situations.

Chapter 6, *HI/MIS* and World Class Manufacturing, examines the ability of *HI/MIS* products to support the specialized needs of companies attempting to implement World Class Manufacturing (WCM). WCM methodologies that have a direct impact on information systems, such as Just-in-Time (JIT) and Total Quality Management (TQM), are discussed. The chapter describes the software functions required to support these key WCM methodologies and how *HI/MIS* provides that support.

Also discussed is the overall relationship between *HI/MIS* and Word Class Manufacturing. The two schools of thought regarding the role of information systems in the attainment of WCM status are presented, along with a more specific discussion of the potential role of *HI/MIS*.

PART 3—WHY UTILIZE *HI/MIS?*

Chapter 7, *HI/MIS* Costs, examines the typical costs incurred when acquiring and operating an *HI/MIS*. The analysis also contrasts these costs with traditional, non-*HI/MIS* systems. Three cases are presented to demonstrate the factors affecting the cost of an information system.

> Case 1 is a relatively small company (around five million dollars in annual revenue) with a small number of users located at one site.
>
> Case 2 is a medium-size company (about 20 million dollars in annual revenue) that operates in a more complex situation, with several users located at two sites.
>
> Case 3 is a large organization (approximately 100 million dollars in annual revenue) that has a fairly large number of users. This case also demonstrates the costs stemming from international operations.

Chapter 8, *HI/MIS* Benefits, explores the value that can be obtained from implementing an *HI/MIS*. Important benefits are identified that directly affect a company's ability to vie with its competitors and improve its overall financial performance. The benefits that are presented include:

- Improvements in customer service, through better support of order promising, order status tracking, and reductions in lead times.
- The use of MRP-II, JIT, and other advanced manufacturing management systems that are necessary to compete successfully in today's marketplace.
- The ability to measure, monitor, improve, and control quality through the availability of reliable production and field information, and the ability to statistically analyze this data on a real-time basis.
- The rapid identification of developing problems and the ability to take corrective actions before the problems result in scrap, obsolescence, or rework.
- The ability to identify opportunities for cost reductions and process improvements through the availability of reliable costing information.
- Reduction in inventory levels, which will improve the availability of capital, improve ROI (return on investment), and reduce inventory carrying costs and floor space requirements.
- An increase in the efficient use of personnel, which allows for business growth with minimal increase in headcount and enables existing personnel to refocus their energies on improvement activities.
- Significant reduction in ongoing operating expenditures for MIS, which can be used to immediately increase bottom-line profitability, or can be invested back into the business to obtain competitive advantage.

Chapter 9, Caveats Associated with *HI/MIS,* covers some of the unique challenges, potential problem areas, and valid reasons to *not* attempt the implementation of an *HI/MIS.* Among the topics discussed are:

- The company's internal systems support capabilities. All systems, including *HI/MIS,* require adequate internal support from both the technical and application standpoints. While this requirement can be significantly less with an *HI/MIS,* it is still a critical item that is often overlooked by smaller companies.
- The company's ability to implement *any* fully functional, integrated manufacturing, marketing, and financial system, regardless of software ease-of-use considerations. This is always a big job, requiring significant resources. It is particularly difficult for small companies to dedicate the proper level of resources to this task.
- The size of the vendor, which for *HI/MIS* products is typically very small. This has implications on the vendor's ability to stay in business over the long term and its ability to provide comprehensive system support and training.
- The availability of source code, which is frequently not included with *HI/MIS* products, and the availability of software modifications, for which there may be a very limited number of sources. This has implications on a company's ability to adapt the software to its changing needs and on its ability to ensure the viability of the system in the event of a failure on the part of the vendor.
- The presence of certain specialized needs that may not be satisfied with standard *HI/MIS* products.

PART 4—HOW DO COMPANIES ACHIEVE *HI/MIS?*

Chapter 10, Evaluating and Selecting *HI/MIS* Products, presents proven methodologies to use in the process of choosing an *HI/MIS* product. Among the concepts discussed are:

The initial definition of requirements. Why this is a critical first step and how interviewing techniques and checklists can be used to improve the process.

High-level systems planning. Why this is necessary to limit the range of solutions to be considered and to ensure that the long-term, strategic factors are properly taken into consideration.

The use of automated software selection products. How they can streamline the selection process and important limitations and potential problems in their use.

The use of formalized, printed "Requests for Proposals." Some questions on the validity of this method, associated problems, and the explanation of a modified approach that yields better results.

How to use "cut criteria" to streamline the process and allow more time for comprehensive evaluation of the best candidate products.

Selecting the right internal personnel to participate in the evaluation process and how to use *structured* product demonstrations to improve the quality of the evaluations.

Site checking. Why it is critical, how to do it, and the right questions to ask.

Getting the proper hardware configuration to support the chosen software. How to avoid being oversold or undersold.

Evaluating vendor contracts. What to expect in the typical contract and what to watch out for.

Negotiating with the vendor. Practical techniques to use in acquiring the chosen product at the right price.

The use of outside consultants to assist in the process. Where they can be useful and how to evaluate their competence.

Chapter 11, Leading *HI/MIS* Products, introduces several of the top *HI/MIS* products available today. The section on each product begins with one page of general vendor and product background information. Following these introductory pages are several screen images of the actual products. These images were obtained by using screen capture software to take an electronic snapshot of the products as they were running. This brief, visual examination will help the reader develop some understanding of the high level of functionality and advanced user interfaces found in *HI/MIS* products.

All of the *HI/MIS* product vendors have agreed to make additional information available. An *Information Request Form* is included to facilitate the acquisition of this material.

Chapter 12, Implementing an *HI/MIS*, presents proven methodologies to use in the implementation of an *HI/MIS*. Among the concepts discussed are:

The implementation planning process. Why it is a necessary first step and the key considerations to be included in the plan.

What a typical implementation will require in terms of resources and elapsed time.

How to set priorities in order to accomplish the implementation and begin realizing benefits from the system as soon as possible.

How to form an internal team to lead the implementation process, and methods the team can use to facilitate and control the process.

When to obtain product training, and methods to maximize its effectiveness.

Why good operational procedures are critical and at what stage they should be developed.

The use of the "pilot" technique to test and validate implementation alternatives.

How to decide on the use of system cut-over alternatives such as parallel processing and "cold-turkey."

What to do when the system needs to be implemented yesterday, along with some accelerated methods that can be used in this situation.

How to evaluate the results of the implementation in order to ensure that the expected benefits are obtained.

The use of outside consultants to assist in the process, where they can be useful, and how to evaluate their competence.

In conclusion, this book is intended to be a practical guide for identifying, evaluating, and successfully implementing *High Impact Manufacturing Information Systems*. This is an exciting new domain that offers tremendous opportunities.

I hope this book will help companies recognize these opportunities and use them to their advantage.

part 1

WHO CAN CAPITALIZE ON *HI/MIS*?

1

HI/MIS Candidates

What types of companies are candidates for using *HI/MIS?* The best way to answer this question may be to look at some examples. Let's examine the typical information system needs of seven different categories, or classes of companies.

> *Class 1*—Entrepreneurial businesses
> *Class 2*—High-growth companies
> *Class 3*—Start-up companies
> *Class 4*—High-technology companies
> *Class 5*—Divisions of large corporations
> *Class 6*—Manufacturing and distribution enterprises
> *Class 7*—Multinational operations

CLASS 1: ENTREPRENEURIAL BUSINESSES

Definition. Privately owned businesses under $50 million in revenue.

Needs. The information system must be relatively inexpensive. These are relatively small companies, with correspondingly small budgets for information system expenditures. It is simply not economically feasible for these companies to spend one million dollars (or anywhere close to that amount) on an information system.

The system must be relatively easy to implement. Entrepreneurial businesses are typically thinly staffed and dependent on a small number of key people. Often, these same key people must lead the effort to implement the system. An entrepreneurial business cannot feasibly send key people off-site for several weeks at a time for training, and it cannot feasibly have its key people devote a great proportion of their time to the implementation process.

The system must be relatively easy to maintain. These smaller companies typically lack the internal resources necessary to support a complex operating environment. Larger companies have the internal personnel. Systems analysts, application programmers, hardware specialists, operating system specialists, communications specialists, network administrators, data base administrators, computer operators, and MIS managers perform the critical support tasks necessary to maintain the more complex systems on an ongoing basis.

Entrepreneurial businesses need powerful systems in order to compete successfully with their larger rivals. The concept of using information systems for competitive advantage is becoming a reality in many industries. In the future, not just the largest companies, but companies of all sizes will be using information systems to provide enhanced services to their customers. Entrepreneurial businesses unable to employ these advantages may find their market share diminishing and their long-term viability in question.

CLASS 2: HIGH-GROWTH COMPANIES

Definition. Rapidly expanding companies, experiencing or projecting greater than 20 percent growth per year.

Needs. Companies experiencing this rate of growth will almost always be capital and/or cash-starved. This is because the growth cycle usually progresses according to the following scenario.

Successive Steps	Financial Effect
Increase capital equipment to expand production capacity	Decreases available capital
Increase raw material inventories	Decreases available cash
Increase direct production costs, e.g., labor	Decreases available cash
Increase work-in-process inventories	Decreases available cash
Increase product shipments and accounts receivable	No immediate effect

This scenario is highly simplified. For example, increases in good inventory, receivables, and profitable sales will have some impact on available capital. But the dominant effect is that increased levels of cash and capital must flow out for a long period of time before increased cash flows in. The system must therefore be relatively inexpensive to conserve the capital and cash that will be in short supply.

At the same time, the company will be under pressure to expand the functionality of its current information systems. The increased volume of production, shipping, and administrative activities may strain the limits of the systems. New classes of products, new distribution methods, and important new customers may demand entirely different types of information system support. The system must be capable of handling the increased volume of business and necessary new functions.

CLASS 3: START-UP COMPANIES

Definition. Newly formed companies, anticipating or just starting shipment of products.

Needs. Again, the system must be relatively inexpensive. Start-up companies typically have a limited amount of initial capital, and seeking additional capital can be extremely expensive. Prototypes of new products may have been produced, but shipments and revenues may not have started yet. Cash supplies decrease steadily each month, according to the "burn rate."

There is an old saying that the funding a start-up receives in its early stages will be "the most expensive money" it ever spends. Start-up companies are often backed by venture capital firms or other similar investment sources. These backers will initially provide the start-up with funds to finance the company through the research and development stage. In return for this, the company founders will typically give the backers an ownership interest in the company.

Funding a start-up is a very risky business. Investors justifiably demand a very high rate of return to compensate for this extraordinary risk. A request by the company's founders for additional funding may mean that additional equity in the company must be forfeited. When shipments start and a revenue stream begins, alternate, much less expensive financing will become available. Since money becomes "cheaper" through time, anything a start-up can do to delay expenditures is advantageous.

Another factor relating to risk is that the backers will want to delay major expenditures until the successful future of the start-up becomes more certain. It is typical for start-ups to lease everything possible, such as office space, furnishings, equipment, etc. Unfortunately, it is very difficult for a start-up to obtain lease financing for computer hardware and virtually impossible to obtain on software.

If the start-up fails, as a high percentage do, the backers want to minimize their downside risk. A brand-new $500,000 machine used for production may seem to make economic sense. But if the company is not yet shipping product, the backers may be unwilling to take this additional level of risk. They know that in the event of failure, the machine would likely be sold at auction for $200,000, generating an additional $300,000 loss. A $500,000 nontransferrable software license will be seen as an even riskier proposition. Its salvage value would be zero.

The dilemma facing start-ups is obvious. There are very strong demands to keep expenditures at the minimum level and to delay them as long as possible. But product shipments may be imminent and a functioning information system is absolutely required. Faced with this situation, start-ups will often delay their decision on, and acquisition of, an information system until the last possible instant. This leaves them in the difficult position of having to then implement a system in an impossibly short amount of time.

Some start-ups choose to implement a less than fully functional system. Because funds are limited, they settle for a system that may service the company for the initial year or two, but will run out of gas as the company continues to grow. There are several problems associated with this approach:

1. It is very costly to change systems in midstream. The cash outlay for the initial system may have been small, but the total effort invested by the company's personnel in implementing it will have been large. For the most part, this investment will be wasted.
2. The change-out process can be very disruptive to operations. The company will have grown, and now a much larger number of internal personnel will have to deal with the change. Also, the company's established methods of doing business with vendors and customers may need to be modified.
3. It does not necessarily get easier. Two years from now the company will probably be in an even steeper portion of the growth curve, facing the same, if not even more difficult, challenges. Funds will still be tight, and personnel resources will be stretched even further.

Start-up companies as they prepare to become fully operational, must begin building the necessary infrastructure. The information system itself is, of course, an integral part of this infrastructure. But the early implementation of a fully functional information system can also help to identify and develop the corollary operational business procedures that are also needed. It forces the implementers to ask questions such as: "How will we promise a delivery date to a customer?" "What is the procedure for credit approval on distributor shipments?" and "Who will be responsible for cash collections?"

CLASS 4: HIGH-TECHNOLOGY COMPANIES

Definition. Technology-based companies in industries that see rapid and continuous product changes and very short product life cycles.

Needs. The system must be sophisticated. These companies are in a very dynamic environment, where information must be provided, analyzed, and acted upon quickly. Accurate costing information must be supported. The company cannot rely on age-old standard costs that change minimally year to year. Actual costs change constantly and dramatically.

The fast pace of business in these industries poses significant challenges to management. Existing products are always being upgraded, enhanced, or produced with new techniques. New products are always under development, being tested, or starting pilot production for imminent release.

The high level of engineering change activity poses additional challenges.

Managing production, distribution, and customer support within this environment without making serious mistakes is difficult. It is very easy to use a wrong version of a component in production, order more of an obsolete part, or be short of a critical component needed for a new production run. Also, in industries where product support must be provided to customers, keeping track of precisely what was shipped to each specific customer may be required.

Many high-technology companies are also faced with sophisticated requirements specific to their industry area, such as:

1. Biotechnology companies must comply with FDA lot tracking requirements.
2. Some firms sell directly to the DOD and other U.S. government agencies that require very specific cost-tracking methods.

Class 5: Divisions of Large Corporations

Definition. Plant sites, operating departments, and subsidiaries of larger entities that conduct their own autonomous planning and control functions.

Needs. The advantages of decentralized management of subsidiary operations are well known. By also using a decentralized approach to information systems, many companies have obtained additional advantage. Among the benefits of implementing independent systems for subsidiary operations are:

1. Each subsidiary operation is allowed to use the information system best suited to its particular needs. Consider the case of one large company that has three divisions, a small operation performing chemical processing, another producing high-volume/low-cost items to stock, and yet another that is a job shop producer of very high-cost items. Each operation has specialized needs, and forcing one information system to service all three would necessitate serious compromises in functionality.
2. Parent corporations like their decentralized operations to be "detachable." The sale, or spinoff, of subsidiaries is certainly made easier if the management infrastructure is already in place to operate the business autonomously. An important related factor is the detachability of the subsidiary's information system. If the subsidiary is timesharing on its current parent's system, the acquiring company will typically want to sever this arrangement as soon as possible. Confidentiality, if not cost, will be the primary reason. The acquiring company must therefore find a way for the subsidiary to process its own data. If this will be difficult and expensive, the subsidiary is going to be less attractive as an acquisition.

Although parent corporations may be large enough to be able to spend megabucks on their overall corporate information system, the individual systems for the subsidiary operations must be relatively inexpensive. It is not unusual for a large corporation to have in excess of 50 separate operating units. Implementing an autonomous (and expensive) information system for one operation, at a cost of perhaps $500,000, is not a problem. But if the corporation were to attempt to provide an autonomous system for all 50 of its operations, the total cost would be $25 million—a sizable sum, no matter how large the corporation.

CLASS 6: MANUFACTURING AND DISTRIBUTION ENTERPRISES

Definition. All companies, of all sizes and varieties, that engage in manufacturing, assembling, processing, or distribution activities.

Needs. The system must have a high level of functionality. All enterprises of this type need good support of their critical production and inventory management activities—it is a prerequisite to being competitive. A generic financial-only system will not be adequate.

In addition to the basic level of functionality needed by all manufacturing and distribution enterprises, companies in many industries require still more specialized functions. Examples of these functions include:

1. Manufacturing Resource Planning (MRP-II): the "explosion," aggregation, and time-phasing of material requirements, the integration with order processing activities, and the coordination with financial subsystems to "close the loop."

2. Master Production Scheduling: the primary coordinating element of an MRP-II system that attempts to harmonize the various factors of forecast product demand, actual customer orders, firm production plans, and provides a look into the future by projecting capacity loads, inventory levels, value of production, and the available-to-promise quantities that are used to quote realistic product delivery schedules for new customer orders.

3. Distribution Requirements Planning (DRP): the coordination of supply and demand between branch warehouses and production facilities, the proper tracking of in-transit (pipeline) inventory, and flexible, site-oriented purchasing and customer order processing.

4. Capacity Requirements Planning: the function that attempts to balance the limited capacity in production departments, key workcenters, individual machines, outside subcontractors, and related resources with the current and scheduled load by reporting projected overload conditions, identifying bottleneck operations, and, in more sophisticated systems, attempting to optimize work plans to maximize throughput.

CLASS 7: MULTINATIONAL OPERATIONS

Definition. Businesses that buy or sell goods internationally, and businesses that control foreign subsidiaries.

Needs. Increasing numbers of companies are entering the global marketplace. As trade barriers come down, companies are finding large new markets for their products and are teaming with foreign suppliers or opening their own offshore production facilities to enhance their manufacturing capabilities. Unfortunately, the complexity of doing business internationally is still very challenging.

Buying from foreign vendors and selling to foreign customers often involves numerous transactions in foreign currencies. The proper accounting, risk management (hedging), and gain/loss recognition associated with these transactions is time-consuming and difficult. If the volume of these transactions is significant, the system must be able to provide automated support.

The local laws of foreign countries often make the creation of separate foreign registered subsidiaries a requirement. For example, let's say our U.S.-based company wants to sell directly into the European market. After researching the specific legal and tax requirements, we find that it will be a practical requirement that we set up small subsidiaries in England, Germany, France, and Italy.

The accounting for each of our European subsidiaries must be conducted in the home country's local currency, so our system must support pounds, marks, francs, and lira. In addition, the French tell us that we must use their standard chart of accounts, which is significantly different from our own. And in the United States (in order to be in accordance with GAAP, U.S. generally accepted accounting procedures) we must gather each and every subsidiary's data on a monthly basis, perform a complex semihistorical translation of currencies, and consolidate the financial results for final reporting in U.S. dollars. Unless we want to significantly increase our accounting staff, the system must provide automated support.

Assuming we find a system sophisticated enough to handle this area, we have another problem. How do we provide affordable access to the system for each of the subsidiary operations? If the system is physically located in the U.S., each subsidiary will most likely connect to it via international data (or standard telephone) lines. But the telecommunication charges to provide online access in this manner will be excessive. Another alternative is to locate self-sufficient copies of our chosen system in each of the subsidiaries, allow them to process their day-to-day transactions locally, and then perform a single, inexpensive transfer of data to the U.S. at the end of each month. For this alternative to be feasible, the chosen system must be relatively inexpensive.

SUMMARY

Seven categories or classes of companies that are likely candidates for using *HI/MIS* were examined:

Class 1—Entrepreneurial businesses
Class 2—High-growth companies
Class 3—Start-up companies
Class 4—High-technology companies
Class 5—Divisions of large corporations
Class 6—Manufacturing and distribution enterprises
Class 7—Multinational operations

Many companies will actually share the needs associated with two, three, or more of these classes. While the needs of the different classes are varied, generalizations can be made:

1. The information systems for these companies serve specialized, critical needs, and therefore must be highly functional.
2. For the majority of these companies, the cost of the information systems is also of primary importance.

For these reasons, all of the above classes of companies are good candidates for *HI/MIS*.

$\overline{\underline{2}}$

HI/MIS Illustrative Cases

This chapter will provide examples of business situations and the associated problems that require *HI/MIS* solutions. These illustrations will help the reader gain an understanding of the challenging business dilemmas that *HI/MIS* can help resolve.

The companies in the three cases that follow are composites of several real companies. By using these composites, more of the individual company's characteristics and business dilemmas can be introduced in a condensed manner. This also allows the direct and candid illustration of the typical problems, limitations, concerns, and motivations commonly found, without the worry of bruising egos or unintentionally showing an actual company in a negative light. While the business situations illustrated here are hypothetical constructs, I'm sure that experienced system implementors will recognize and identify with many of the challenges presented.

The three composite, illustrative cases are:

> *Case 1*—A high-technology, start-up company
> *Case 2*—An entrepreneurial company experiencing rapid growth
> *Case 3*—A large company with multinational operations

CASE 1—A HIGH TECHNOLOGY, START-UP COMPANY

The company was formed two years ago and until just recently has been in the development stage. Their product is a diagnostic system used to perform a battery of common medical tests. The system is dependable, very accurate, inexpensive, and easy enough to use that it can be located in the doctor's office.

The concept of the product is that the nurse initially obtains a drop of blood from the patient. The diagnostic unit then processes the sample in just a few minutes. The results are printed out and available to the doctor by the time the patient examination begins.

The company was funded by a venture capital group, which initially invested four million dollars. This group now owns 40 percent of the company.

The president is a brilliant research scientist with advanced degrees in both medicine and chemical engineering. He and two close associates are the original founders and have controlling interest in the company.

Things have been going well for the company recently. The product finally received approval from the Food and Drug Administration (FDA). A new vice president of Operations has just been hired to prepare the company for live production and shipping operations.

A few days into the job, the new VP of Operations discovers that there is no current information system in place and no activity occurring to acquire one. By checking with the company's controller he finds out that she is currently using a simple financial package and spreadsheets.

This system was perfectly adequate when all they had to do was keep track of expenses. But the VP knew that a fully functional information system was needed now that the company would be buying, processing, and shipping millions of dollars worth of materials each month. He realizes that the company has a serious problem and that he needs to talk to the president. He calls the president and a meeting is scheduled for the afternoon of the same day.

The president is working with a set of numbers for the upcoming round of financing. The president and the venture capital group had always anticipated that cash requirements would increase as the company ramped up to produce and ship product. At the time of initial funding, they had agreed that when the company met the milestone of FDA approval, the venture capital group would contribute up to another $2.5 million. It was also agreed that the company would grant an additional 1 percent equity for each $200,000 contributed at this stage.

The president had a preliminary estimate that another one million dollars would be required. He was considering whether it would be a good idea to have the venture capital group contribute a little more than this, to provide a cushion for unexpected events. A quick calculation shows that the one million dollars will cost the president and the founders another 5 percent of the company's equity.

Giving up even 1 percent was distasteful to the president. He could see that the company's future profitability would be excellent. Each reduction in ownership diminished his share of these future profits. He began to wonder if there wasn't some way to avoid the need for additional funds. But he realized that it was necessary—there was just no way around it.

As the president finishes his thoughts on this matter, the VP of Operations arrives for their afternoon meeting. After an exchange of greetings, the discussion starts.

(VP of Operations)   "I was surprised to see that we don't have any information system support for the manufacturing and order processing functions. We're going to need a good, functional system to support us as we start volume production and shipping.

"The spreadsheets and simple financial programs worked fine when all we had to do was keep track of expenses, but now we will be buying, processing and shipping millions of dollars worth of materials each month. And this is going to start very soon. We need an information system up and running, well . . . yesterday."

(President)   "I see what you are saying. We do have to be able to keep track of and control these activities. Actually, we knew this a long time ago and had planned on eventually getting a new system. I think that with all the redesign work we had to do and the concentration on getting FDA approval, it must have gotten lost in the shuffle. But you're certainly right. I realize we should put a system in place immediately."

The president thinks to himself, "We have that million dollars coming in. We can just use funds out of that, so the only challenge should be the timing."

He asks, "How long to get one installed?"

(VP of Operations)   "Well, it's not quite that easy. Before we install anything we must select a system, and before we select one, we need to define exactly what we need."

(President)   "How long then, will all of that take?"

(VP of Operations)   After thinking for a moment he answers, "Too long. At another company I worked with, we took six months to go through the decision process. We're starting production here in 60 days. That's not even long enough to do the installation."

(President)   "Well, we don't have time to optimize our decision. Remember, we hired you because of your previous experience with companies like us. What were they using at your last company?"

(VP of Operations)   "It was an okay system. It was kind of hard to use. There were parts of it they never did get working."

(President)   "But it did work, didn't it? It took care of all the basics? It must have. They're a one hundred million dollar company."

(VP of Operations)   "Yes, it did work."

(President)   "Then I suggest, given our time constraints, that we go with what they're using."

(VP of Operations)   Uneasy with the decision, but with no other apparent alternative, answers, "You're right. I'll call an old friend who's in charge of their MIS department and get in contact with the product vendor."

The VP of Operations leaves the president's office to begin work on acquiring an information system.

(President)   The president, a brilliant research scientist, doesn't have much experience with information systems. He thinks to himself, "Gosh, that was simple. I hope our new vice president doesn't get stuck on easy problems like that very often, or I'm going to be helping him out a lot."

(VP of Operations)   The VP of Operations, who has had quite a bit of experience with different information systems, thinks to himself as he walks to his office, "The president really doesn't understand the wide difference in quality in information systems. It's not that easy. But in this case it's not worth arguing about. He was right. We don't have time to do anything else."

The VP made contact with his old company and then with the vendor. The vendor prepared a proposal. The software cost was $500,000 and the hardware cost was another $500,000. Recognizing that this was a lot of money, he checked again with his friend at his old company. His friend assured him the quote was reasonable and was actually surprised at how much the hardware prices had dropped. Their company had spent over a million and a half to-date on hardware.

The VP's friend also reminded him that he should budget for the other involved costs. They had 12 people on staff to support their system. But their company was larger and had been shipping product for quite a while. Based on additional details his friend gave him and his own past experience with information systems, the VP felt that a skeleton staff of just three employees should be able to support the system initially.

The VP felt confident, he had all the information, he had the plan, and he was ready to report to the president and get started. Another meeting with the president is arranged.

(VP of Operations)   The VP explains how he got the information and hands a copy of the vendor's proposal to the president. As the president is reading the proposal the VP begins to further explain, "We will need three additional employees . . . "

(President)   At this point, the president pulls a pad of paper from his desk and begins writing some numbers on it. In a slow, deliberate, somewhat shaky voice, "Three additional employees will add about $200,000 to short-term funding. So, along with this proposal, this means that we would need another $1.2 million from the venture capitalists for this." (The VP noticed how pale the president had turned and figured this was not happy news.)

The President, fighting an urge to panic and start screaming, said in a calm voice, "We can't afford this. I can't believe we need a system this expensive."

(VP of Operations)   "Well, a project team of six people spent six months researching all the available products at my last company and that's the best alternative we could find. We looked at all the available software products. There were actually very few that could handle our needs."

(President)   Incredulous that there could be so few choices and that they are so expensive, asks "You sure about that?"

(VP of Operations)   "I think so. I am sure there are cheaper products. The

problem is that in our industry, we need a pretty sophisticated system. I remember the process we went through at my last company to find the best product. We obtained the names of all the possible software products from talking with the major mainframe and minicomputer hardware vendors. We looked at probably 10 or 15 packages, and as I mentioned, only a few were real candidates. All of the serious products were in the same price range."

(President)   Thinking to himself "I guess if six intelligent people worked for six months, their conclusions are probably unarguable. I guess I'll have to accept that as fact. But let's see what other alternatives might be playable."

He asks "What if we go with a cheaper, maybe not quite as good system to start with, and then go with a better one after a few years? We should be in a much better position to afford it then."

(VP of Operations)   "That's exactly what we did at a previous start-up company I worked for. I've got to tell you, it was a terrible experience. First, we spent a tremendous amount of time developing workarounds for stuff that the software didn't do correctly. Everybody hated the system. We couldn't get the reports we needed. It was a mess trying to manage the manufacturing operations. Within a year we decided that the system had to go, and we decided to replace it with the exact same system we are talking about here."

(President)   "But you were able to survive with it for a year?"

(VP of Operations)   "Yes, but what I am saying is, if we had known what we were in for, we would have gone with the right system from day one. We wasted a lot of money and an awful lot of effort on the first system. In addition to what the first system cost, we invested a lot in operating procedures, user training, setting up files, loading data, and so on. Almost all of this investment was wasted.

"When we finally replaced the system, it really upset some of our operations. People had to be retrained on the new system and learn new procedures. We even had to adjust some of the mechanics of how we did business with our vendors and our customers."

(President)   The president, hearing the VP's arguments and believing that they made sense, began to feel better about at least one point. The VP they had just hired did indeed have relevant experience that would be valuable in helping them avoid costly mistakes.

(VP of Operations)   "In hindsight, it's easy to see that we made a mistake in assuming that it would be easier to implement the right kind of system a few years down the road. I don't know if it will be different here, but at that company, cash was still scarce a year later. We were shipping, but we were continuing to grow. We still needed cash to finance our expanded production. And, in terms of personnel, we were even more stretched for time. I know it seems like it's tough now, with everyone wearing several hats, but it really doesn't get easier in the first several years. Changing systems after a year, while we had volume production going on, was a miserable experience."

(President)   "OK, we definitely don't want to do that. What if, instead of implementing an inadequate system, we wait a while, until we get a decent revenue stream, and then implement the right system?"

(VP of Operations)   The VP imagines for a moment what it would be like to try and manage the company's operations without any system at all. The picture is ugly. So ugly, in fact, that he begins to feel a sharp pain in his stomach.

He answers, "I just don't think that's feasible. Not only would we lose control of activities, but I don't see how we could comply with federal requirements. If we get visited to make sure we're complying, and we don't even have a system in place, I think we're going to have a problem. Also, I really need to be working right now on developing and implementing good operating procedures. I understood that the primary reason I was hired now was to start putting together the infrastructure we need to actually start building and shipping a large volume of product. Getting an information system really dovetails with this. It would help us identify and develop the operating procedures we need. We really can't delay doing this. We must have decent procedures in place before we're swamped by all the production, distribution, quality, cash collection, and other issues that are going to be hitting us as soon as we start shipping."

(President)   The president agreed with the VP. He didn't understand all that the VP was saying about operating procedures, but it was clear that simply waiting and running for a while without any system was not a sound alternative.

Remembering that there was more funding available from the venture capital group, the president began to wonder if this expenditure was just an inevitable cost of doing business. If so, then it made sense to go ahead and make the investment in the most propitious manner. In this case, it apparently meant making the investment now and spending what was necessary to get the right system the first time.

"OK, let me get with our financial people and the other founders. I'm not disputing that we need to do this. But we're going to have to do a lot of communication and preparation before we invest that kind of money. I'll get back with you soon, but in the meantime I want you to start preparing a presentation on this for our next board meeting."

(VP of Operations)   The VP, sensing that the meeting is being brought to an end, seeks assurance that the company will follow his recommendations. "How do *you* feel about this?" he says, pointing to the vendor's proposal on the president's desk. "Do you think we should do this, now?"

(President)   "It's not that simple. It's just not that simple. I heard your arguments and I think they make sense. But I need time to digest this and talk with the other founders. I'll get back with you as soon as I can." The president pushes his chair back from his desk to signify that the meeting was indeed over.

(VP of Operations)   Picking up on this clue, the VP is still somewhat disconcerted and manages only a meager "Okay, thanks" as he leaves the room.

Back in his own office, the VP thinks "These people just don't understand. If we don't get a decent system, really quickly, we are in serious trouble. I don't want to fight a battle with top management during my first few months on the job, but there is no way this company can start volume production and shipping without a decent system. No way."

(President)   The president, still sitting at his desk, thinks, "Ouch, that was an expensive meeting. If I have to take more money from the backers, it's going to cost me . . . let's see . . . $1,200,000 for the information system plus the one million we already planned, for a total of $2,200,000."

He begins to write some additional figures on the pad of paper. After factoring in the 1 percent equity that must be given for each $200,000 and the venture capital group's current holdings of 40 percent, the president now begins to feel a sharp pain in *his* stomach.

He thinks "That means instead of giving up another 5 percent of the company, we'll have to give up another 11 percent. And worse than that, the venture capital group will then own 51 percent and we will own 49 percent. We lose control of our own company. I don't know what the alternative is, but there is no way we are going to spend $1,200,000 on this. No way."

CASE 2—AN ENTREPRENEURIAL COMPANY EXPERIENCING RAPID GROWTH

Our Case 2 company produces precision machined parts for the Department of Defense. The president has operated the company for more than ten years. During this time the company has sustained growth to its current level of $15 million in annual revenue.

The president felt that the improving relations among the superpowers would lead to reductions in defense spending. He also believed that his competition would become more aggressive in bidding on the smaller contracts. As a consequence, he decided to reorient the company towards the commercial market and away from a total reliance on defense work.

In repositioning the company, the president recognized that he needed to reduce costs in order to compete successfully in the more price-sensitive commercial markets. Also, the company would be dealing with a wider range of products. Each product would have its own cost structure and customer base. The president's decade of experience in justifying the costs for his defense contracts convinced him of the need for a sophisticated information system. He understood that the pressures of the commercial marketplace would place demands on the existing system that it had not been designed to handle.

The company has already made its initial moves into the commercial market and the results have been quite good. Several large orders have been booked and volume is increasing rapidly. Projections call for revenue growth of at least 40 percent over the next 12 months.

The current information system is viewed as being totally inadequate. It is over five years old and barely hanging on. Response times are poor. Even with only six people currently using the system at a time, they are waiting up to a full minute between transactions. The increasing volume of business will kill the system. No further expansion of the existing computer hardware is possible. Something must be done.

At the same time, the engineering department has identified a new machine to help accomplish the needed cost reductions. They feel that this machine will reduce the number of rejected parts due to out-of-tolerance problems. The new machine is computer-controlled and has the flexibility necessary to substantially reduce setup time. This will be of particular advantage since the larger array of parts being produced is expected to result in shorter production runs and more setups.

Today is the weekly staff meeting. The president makes his way to the conference room. Already seated in the conference room are the company's vice presidents of Engineering, Sales, Marketing, Manufacturing, and Finance. The VP of Finance also represents MIS. The president begins the meeting by reiterating the company's goals in entering the commercial market.

(President)   "Good morning. As you know, we will be spending the first portion of our regular staff meetings discussing progress on all of our tasks related to expanding into our identified commercial markets. This is probably the biggest, most important move our company has made in its history, and I want to remind you that I need everybody's support in this.

"We are already showing positive results. We can definitely produce revenue, but now my concern is whether we can bring that success down to the bottom line, and whether we can handle this new business without plunging into total chaos."

The phrase "plunging into total chaos" brings a light round of laughter from the group as the president continues to explain.

"So we have identified two initial, critical challenges. First we must concentrate our efforts on achieving cost reductions. Remember, increased revenues are great, but if we can't translate that to the bottom line, then what's the point? We'll hear a report on progress in this area in just a minute.

"Our second critical challenge is that we need to make improvements in our information system to support our growth and what is going to be a more complex operating environment."

Before the president could even finish his sentence, there was a round of groans, signifying the group's displeasure with the current information system.

"Okay, obviously this is a popular subject, but let's start by hearing about our progress on cost reductions." The president nods to the vice president of Engineering, indicating that it is time for his report.

(VP of Engineering)   "We identified our biggest opportunities for cost reduction to be the elimination of scrap and a decrease in our setup times. By scrap I mean the number of parts that are rejected for quality purposes. We already spend too much time on machine setups and it's going to get a lot worse when we have many, many more products being produced and many short run quantities. We think we have found a solution, however, that solves both of these problems."

"We are recommending that we purchase a new computer-controlled machining center. The one we picked out can consistently keep tolerances twice as tight as the best of our current equipment. This should almost entirely eliminate our out-of-tolerance rejects, which is the biggest component of scrap. And the setup is a breeze. Ninety percent of the time you use a set of standard fixtures and the unit is flexible enough that it picks the right tool from its magazine, orients it properly— and highly accurately I might add— and then away it goes. All of this is computer-controlled, of course."

At this point, the VP of Engineering pauses to gaze around the room to see what kind of response he is getting from the group. He begins to smile broadly as he sees the look of wonderment in the group members' eyes. That is, until he looks at the VP of Finance, who seems to have a somewhat different expression on his face.

(VP of Finance)   "That sounds really impressive. How much does one of those cost?"

The VP of Engineering, who is a bright individual, surmises the obvious in the few seconds before he responds. The VP of Finance must have megabucks he wants to spend on his project. This could be the opening battle of a war.

(VP of Engineering)   He responds "Well, that really depends on a number of things. There are several different models. They handle different numbers of tools and there are a lot of options on how we accomplish the programming . . ."

(VP of Finance)   "Ballpark."

(VP of Engineering)   "Okay . . . the base unit—I'm talking about the most likely model we would go with—is about $650,000." Before he can look around the room again to gauge reaction, the VP of Finance continues with another question.

(VP of Finance)   "Does that include the costs for new tooling, new fixtures, training of operators, training of however many people on your staff to write programs?"

(VP of Engineering)   "No . . . since we haven't made a definite decision on the model, we don't know how many and exactly what type of new tools would be needed. And you're right, there are other associated costs. We haven't ignored these, but it's too early in the process to say exactly what the total cost will be."

(VP of Finance)   "Ballpark."

(VP of Engineering)   At this point the VP of Engineering is noticeably uncomfortable. He tries to answer the question as nonchalantly as possible. "Maybe a million."

(President)   The president now senses that a conflict between the two vice presidents is developing. In an effort to ease the situation he offers "Okay, we're prepared to make an investment if we need to, but I also recognize the need to understand exactly how big that investment will be."

(VP of Finance)   "Right, I'm not disputing the investment. I just want to get a handle on how large it's actually going to be. I still have a few major questions to ask. Is this one machine big enough? I mean, does it have the capacity to handle all of the parts that we would like to run on it? Are we going to get another request for a second machine six months from now or even a third machine?"

At this point, the group shifts their attention to the VP of Engineering. It is apparent that he is irritated. But before he can speak, the VP of Finance continues his questions.

"I think another major question is to make sure the cost is really justified. The depreciation and operating costs on a million-dollar machine will cost us at least a couple hundred thousand dollars a year on our bottom line. Will we save that much, given this machine will only handle a portion of our total production?"

Again the group shifts their attention to the VP of Engineering. The president, noticing that the VP of Engineering is now obviously angry, decides that more discussion is indeed required, but that this is not the best forum. He decides to interrupt the process.

(President)   "OK, some good issues have been raised here, so here's what I want you two to do. I want you to get together and evaluate these issues. By that, I mean how much the initial investment will be, whether one machine will be enough, and the cost justification. That's going to require both of you to work together. I'll arrange a separate meeting between the three of us prior to the next staff meeting to go over this."

"In the meantime, we need to move on with this meeting, so let's hear about progress on our information systems situation." The president relaxes, knowing that this should be an easier discussion. After all, everyone hates the current system.

Meanwhile the VP of Engineering is thinking to himself "I bet I'm right, he's going to want to spend megabucks on his project, which means its his project or mine."

(VP of Finance)   "I think everyone here is already painfully aware of the problems with our current system. Obviously the system is slow and seems to be getting progressively worse. This is not a new problem. About six months ago, we obtained a quotation from our hardware vendor for new equipment. Unfortunately, our current model is at its maximum. There is nothing else we can do to it to improve its performance."

"So the vendor gave us a quote on the next model up. With a trade-in allowance, the cost would be about $200,000. But based on what my MIS people tell me, it would probably be better to go two models up in the line to really get to the performance level that we need. That would cost about $400,000. And yes, we have to stay with the same hardware vendor. Our software only runs on that brand of hardware. Which leads me to why we didn't go ahead and upgrade the hardware."

"We believe that we need new software, with better functionality than the system we currently have. I visited, along with a few people from my department and a few people from manufacturing, another company that produces similar products that are being sold to the same commercial markets we are targeting. They are using a much better system. We were all really impressed. You would be amazed at all the things that software could do. And the reports they had available . . ."

(VP of Engineering)   The VP of Engineering was unable to contain himself any longer. He comments "That's great. Is their system affordable?"

(VP of Finance)   "It's not cheap. It's a top of the line system. We may not go with that particular one."

(VP of Engineering)   "So how much does that particular one cost?"

(VP of Finance)   "The software would cost, depending on the hardware platform we would choose, about $500,000."

(VP of Engineering)   "That's just for the software? You mean we would have to get completely new hardware? How much would that cost?"

(VP of Finance)   "Well . . . with this particular package, we would have to get new hardware. My MIS people tell me that a realistic figure for the hardware would also be about $500,000."

(VP of Engineering)   "A million dollars total, and what do we get for that? I mean other than faster speed which we could have for $200,000 with our current system."

(VP of Manufacturing)   The VP of Manufacturing, who has so far sat quietly through the meeting, begins to speak "We get a lot. And we need a lot. Our current system won't support MRP the way it needs to run. We also need a master scheduling function and better costing information. To reduce costs, improve lead times, and make us more competitive we are going to be adopting some JIT practices in the next year. Our current system has no support at all for this."

(VP of Engineering)   "That's great. But I don't see how you can reduce costs by spending a million dollars on an *overhead* item. Let me guess, I suppose this new system will need more MIS people. Somebody has to be making all those reports that you liked so much.

"But the biggest problem I see is not the money. This sounds like a major project in terms of effort. I imagine a $500,000 piece of software has to be really complex. How long is it going to take to get it implemented? How many people are going to have to work on it?"

(President)   Sensing that the atmosphere in the room has reached the boiling point, the president again decides to interrupt the process. He breaks in: "Okay, again we have some good issues that have been raised. I think we certainly must do something to improve our information system."

"But I do also share the concerns that were raised. I don't mind making an investment, but I have to admit that buying an overly expensive information system does not seem to fit well with the concept of overall cost reductions. We should be looking for ways to streamline our operations, including the overhead areas. And I do need my managers to focus on restructuring the company to be more competitive. I don't want them distracted by implementing an overly complex information system."

"Let me say that I believe in *both* projects. Both are extremely important to us. I think that's why the discussion has been so . . . lively. But this is not a situation where we are going to do just one or the other. We are going to improve our information systems *and* we are going to improve our manufacturing to reduce costs. Period."

"But the answer is not to throw money around. It can't be. We have limited resources and these are just the first of what will be several projects." Then, looking directly at the VP of Engineering, he continues: "I want you to come up with alternative methods to get the cost reductions . . . and," now looking directly at the VP of Finance, "I also want you to come up with an alternative."

"We'll take up discussion on these projects again at our next meeting."

The president continues on with the rest of the meeting while the VP of Engineering and the VP of Finance reflect on the challenges that have been presented to them.

The VP of Engineering is thinking to himself, "Oh great, I'll just have my people spend a bunch of time calibrating the old machines twice as often as they do now, do a bunch of work redesigning fixtures to improve precision and reduce set-up time. I'll probably have to set up more organized preventive maintenance and, and . . . gee, it sure would have been more fun and less effort to just go out and get those new machines."

At the same time, the VP of Finance is thinking "Oh great. I'll just have to make a silk purse out of a sow's ear. I haven't the slightest idea what to do. I wonder if there's any possibility that my MIS Manager might be mistaken. Maybe there are less expensive solutions that would be just as good . . . No, that's probably just wishful thinking."

CASE 3—A LARGE COMPANY WITH MULTINATIONAL OPERATIONS

The company is a conglomerate with $1.4 billion in annual revenue. It has 32 operating business units, each of which has individual revenues in the range of 5 to 100 million dollars.

The company's strategy has been to acquire an underperforming firm, bring in new management if necessary, and then help the firm become a leader in its market niche. After the firm, which is now a subsidiary, has grown near the $100 million revenue level, it is typically spun-off. This provides additional capital for the acquisition of new firms.

The individual operating units of the company are quite autonomous, and each General Manager is held accountable for their unit's performance. There is currently a corporate staff of around 300 to support the business units. Senior management wants to drive that number down to less than 200 people. In conjunction with this, the CEO decided that the information systems should be decentralized. Senior management also recognized the fact that the salability of the operating units would be enhanced by making their individual information systems detachable.

The corporate Director of Information Technology was asked to develop the new direction for information services. Currently, most of the operating units receive all information services from the corporate data center. The Director of IT supervises the Central Data Processing Group, which operates the Data Center and provides systems development services. The Director is aware of senior management's goal to drive down the number of corporate staff. Decentralizing the information systems would certainly accomplish this in her area.

It is decided that the Director of IT will visit three of the company's operating units to discuss this concept with the local management teams. Upon her return, the feasibility of the project will be evaluated and implementation planning would begin. These three units would most likely be the first to deploy their own decentralized systems.

(Director of IT)   As the Director of IT is on the plane to the first site, she is thinking "I don't cherish the thought of having to downsize my staff, but management is dead-set on doing this. I guess it does make good business sense."

"I can see some of my staff being redeployed to particular operating units. Those remaining at corporate would still have plenty to do. Not only would they continue to provide support for the corporate level applications, but the divisions would really benefit from having centralized support available."

"Each operating unit is going to need help implementing its new systems and will probably need a fair amount of ongoing technical support. If any modifications are needed, I don't want them done at the units. I think we should continue to provide modification services centrally so that the quality can be controlled. If one of these operating units has a catastrophe, it's still going to be seen as my responsibility."

"We need to have a set of standards. I know these operating units are supposed to be autonomous and are being given the charter to run their own systems, but we will need at least a basic set of corporate standards."

"What if all 32 units pick different software and hardware? It would be impossible to provide any centralized support. How would we coordinate information between units and back up to corporate for consolidation? It can't work that way. The operating units can have their own systems on site, but we'd better find the one best package that will take care of all of them. Everybody can standardize on it and then we'll be able to support them."

The Director of IT arrives at the first operating unit, a $10-million-per-year job shop manufacturer of brake assemblies for heavy construction equipment. The operating unit's Controller meets with her.

(Controller) "We're really doing okay with the current system. Your people do a great job of support. We asked for some changes to the job estimating program and really liked what they came up with. I guess we're not exactly looking forward to losing that support. My biggest concern is that if we go with different software, would it match our business adequately? We're a job shop. There are certain features in your system that we couldn't do without. I don't see how we could replace the job estimating program I just mentioned. We also like the way actual job costs are reported. We can buy specialized materials and they get charged directly through to the job . . . Is it possible that we could use your system and just run it locally?"

(Director of IT) "Yes, it's possible. But I'm not sure how practical that is."

(Controller) "What do you mean?"

(Director of IT) "It runs on a mainframe. There are smaller versions of the mainframe that can run the same operating system and therefore the same software."

(Controller) "How much do they cost?"

(Director of IT) "The smallest units are really inexpensive. They cost only a few hundred thousand dollars."

(Controller) "Actually, we would view that as kind of expensive. Remember, we're only a ten-million-dollar business."

(Director of IT) "Then you're really not going to like the software price. Its purchase price is about $500,000, depending on which particular modules you would need."

(Controller) "There is no way we could spend that much."

(Director of IT) "I don't know. Top management is very committed to this project. If you made the right case . . . "

(Controller) "Then let me ask you this. How much would it cost to operate on an ongoing basis? Would we have to hire a person to run it?"

(Director of IT) "Realistically, you couldn't run it with just one person. The operating system is too complex. When you figure in the database technology that would need to be supported plus adequate support at the applications

level, I think it is more realistic to expect that a handful of people would be required."

(Controller) "Forget it. We might get corporate to okay the initial expenditure to purchase it, but I can tell you that our unit's General Manager would be dead-set against it. We've already had discussions on this and he is adamant that this decentralized system project is not going to add to his overhead."

"I think he's under a lot of pressure to improve our bottom-line performance. So we're under tight cost controls. There is no way he would allow additional headcount or absorb large monthly expenses to operate our own system. He just won't go for it."

(Director of IT) "Well, I don't have an answer for you today. But that's all-right. The purpose of my visit wasn't to reach any conclusions, but to gather data. I think I've gained an understanding of your needs. I'm sure we'll have quite a bit more discussion on this before we find an acceptable solution."

The Director of IT is now off to the second operating unit, a $30-million-per-year highly repetitive manufacturer of anticorrosive gaskets. The operating unit's Materials Manager meets with her.

(Materials Manager) "We are actually kind of glad to see this decentralization project going on. We really hate the current system. It doesn't fit our operations at all. The best we can tell, it might be a fit for a job shop type of operation. We don't even use the manufacturing parts of the system. The only part we use are the financials so that our results can be consolidated by corporate."

"We sure get charged an awful lot of money for that. I forget what the Controller told me the charge was, but it was something ludicrous. I mean, it was in the tens of thousands of dollars per month."

The Director did not know what to say. The Materials Manager's point about the system not being appropriate for their operation may have been valid, but his comment that the monthly charges allocated out from her department were ludicrous did not sit well.

(Materials Manager) "We already have an MRP package about half-way installed. It runs on a microcomputer and it only cost us a few thousand dollars. We bought it out of our own departmental budget. You should see it. It even does backflush transactions, you know, to support our JIT production lines for the standard gaskets."

The Director really doesn't know what in the world a backflush transaction is, but she knows she is looking at the early stages of a very high-risk situation. She had prior experience with other operating units that had gone behind corporate's back and put in cheap microcomputer products. Every single one had turned into a problem. The software was buggy or the vendor couldn't support it or the operating unit personnel did not treat it seriously enough. Some of those units were still not even performing regular system backups.

(Materials Manager)   "I'd like to talk with you more, but I've got to get to a quality control group meeting. I'm in charge of this week's meeting, so I couldn't get out of it. Sorry."

(Director of IT)   "That's okay. Thanks for spending time with me."

As he leaves the room, the Director thinks to herself, "That may have just been an excuse to end our meeting. I know it's been difficult to get this operating unit to accept any of our advice or services in the past. They are probably going to block any effort on our part to give guidance to their project. If they try and run this $30 million operation on some ill-supported bargain-basement micro-computer system, with no procedures, no controls, and no internal support . . . it's a recipe for disaster. We definitely have a problem here."

The Director of IT arrives at the third operating unit. This is a $70-million-per-year manufacturer and distributor of electronic switching devices. A large portion of their revenue comes from international sales. This operating unit's General Accounting Manager meets with the Director of IT.

(Accounting Manager)   "I've got mixed emotions about this decentralization project. I don't think we have the internal staff to support ourselves right now. On the other hand, the possibility of getting a new system that would better take care of our needs is appealing."

"The current system is OK, but it doesn't address the financial areas. You see, we're a subsidiary of corporate, but we also have several subsidiaries under us. We market our products throughout North America and part of Europe, so we had to establish small, separate subsidiaries in Canada, Mexico, Great Britain, France, and Germany. Besides the three different versions of VAT we have to support, our biggest problem is that the subsidiaries' books are kept in the home country's local currency. We're dealing with Canadian dollars, pesos, pounds, francs, and marks. We can handle it, but it takes a lot of effort."

(Director of IT)   The Director, seeking to determine how important an issue this actually is, asks "How much of an effort is it? How many people perform this task?"

(Accounting Manager)   "We have two people who spend basically full time on this. It would be a lot more, but we have this accounts payable clerk who is really good with spreadsheet software. You should see what she put together. It does currency translations, revalues receivables, and even calculates unrealized gain/loss. It's really slick."

(Director of IT)   The Director thought she had better evaluate whether this was just a nice little productivity tool, or something that they might be putting an over-reliance on. She asks, "How long would it take to do the job without it?"

(Accounting Manager)   "Oh gosh, it's tough to say. We've grown dependent on it. We couldn't close our books each month without it. If it weren't for those spreadsheets she developed, we would probably have to hire two more full-time people."

(Director of IT)   "Can anyone else on your staff make changes to the spreadsheets when required?"

(Accounting Manager)   "No, not really. I remember when she went on vacation a few months ago. We were in the middle of a closing cycle and we started getting some numbers that looked a little funny. We tried and tried, but nobody could figure out what was going wrong. It was something to do with a macro being called by a macro, or something like that.

"Anyway, we finally tracked her down and she fixed it over the phone in about 15 minutes. The only hard part was finding her. She was on a scuba-diving trip in the Caribbean."

(Director of IT)   The Director is thinking to herself "This doesn't do much for my confidence level. This operating unit's ability to close their books on time is dependent on a shaky spreadsheet application, put together by an accounts payable clerk who's likely to get eaten by sharks. What's going to happen when these divisions start to manage their own complete systems?"

The Director of IT is on her way back to corporate headquarters. While on the plane, she has time to reflect on her three visits.

"It looks like I have problems at each of these sites. How am I going to find one system, or even just a few systems, that are going to satisfy all the specialized needs I saw? This is a Catch-22 situation. All of the sites want sophisticated systems, but they don't want to spend much money. And they obviously don't have the internal support necessary to maintain a complex operating environment.

"Well, the solution is obvious. All I have to do is find software that is very powerful, very inexpensive and very easy to run. And it can't run on a mainframe or even a large minicomputer. The operating units won't spend that much. So just to make it completely impossible, the software would have to run on a microcomputer or maybe a small minicomputer.

"Well, enough feeling sorry for myself. What am I going to tell the CEO when he asks for my plan?"

SUMMARY

This chapter presented illustrative examples of three challenging business situations. The cases covered:

- A high-technology, start-up company seeking their first system
- A rapidly growing entrepreneurial company attempting to enter new markets

- A large multinational company venturing to decentralize their information systems

These composite companies were used to illustrate the demanding combination of information system needs, operational constraints, and financial limitations that often make finding an acceptable solution difficult. Does a product or class of products exist that can help companies like these?

The thesis of this book is that this class of product *does* exist today. But, the reader should be the ultimate judge. The following chapters will help in making this judgement.

part 2

WHAT IS *HI/MIS?*

3

Components of an *HI/MIS*

The purpose of this chapter is to provide the reader with an understanding of the fundamental elements that constitute an *HI/MIS*. Subsequent chapters will further develop this understanding by exploring the associated technologies, range of capabilities, and benefits and caveats associated with *HI/MIS*.

Many factors contrast *HI/MIS* from other, more traditional systems. The specific *HI/MIS* elements that will be discussed here are:

Functionality

- Software capabilities
- Software ease-of-use
- Report writing
- Operating systems
- Source code availability
- Software modifications

Cost Factors

- Initial software costs
- Initial hardware costs
- Ongoing operational costs

Vendor Characteristics

- Vendor size
- Vendor support
- Vendor distribution channels

FUNCTIONALITY

Software Capabilities

The most important dimension of an *HI/MIS* is the capability of the software to serve the critical needs of companies in complex, sophisticated environments. How good are current *HI/MIS* systems at doing this? They are surprisingly— even astonishingly—good, often including in excess of 90 and sometimes 95 percent of the capabilities of software several times as costly.

This is the key message. If this book accomplishes nothing else, I hope it at least convinces the reader that the *HI/MIS* products are capable enough to be given serious consideration as solutions to their needs. Because of the importance of this message, an entire chapter (Chapter 5) is devoted to exploring some of the more essential capabilities of *HI/MIS* products.

However, the capabilities of current *HI/MIS* software products are limited in a few areas. They are not geared for use as the primary system in extremely large corporations. The infrastructure and methods used to conduct business are too different from a smaller operation.

As an example, let's consider a multibillion dollar aerospace/defense company. The purchasing cycle for this company will, of necessity, be very complex. It will involve several successive layers of review and approval procedures. I won't bore you with the details of the individual steps, but in summary, a purchase order may go through ten steps, produce six hardcopies, and pass through the hands of five people in four different functional departments before it is finally released. Support from an information system can help to streamline some of these burdensome tasks; there are some non-*HI/MIS* systems geared towards this.

Another area of limitation in the capabilities of current *HI/MIS* software products is their support of some of the very specialized needs of companies in certain industries. (Chapter 9 discusses this in greater detail.)

As an example, let's look at a semiconductor company. The unusual nature of the semiconductor fabrication process, and the difficulty of planning production in the presence of factors such as binning and fan-out, require unique support techniques. There are a handful of non-*HI/MIS* systems that have been specially designed for this specific industry.*

Software Ease-of-Use

New hardware and software technologies enable *HI/MIS* systems to provide the user with advanced techniques for interfacing with the software. These features make the system easier to use and make the user more efficient in working with the system. User interface features commonly found in *HI/MIS* products include:

---

*Note: Even with these unique requirements, several semiconductor companies have recently opted to implement *HI/MIS* systems (due to their other advantages), and internally develop the necessary add-on functionality.

Menu-driven control. Users can navigate throughout the system by choosing the action they want from a menu. This basic level of functionality is still not present in some traditional systems.

Menu shortcutting. Some users prefer a nonmenu (command line) method of choosing actions. Someone who remembers the commands can invoke the action more efficiently than one who chains up and down the menu hierarchy. Some *HI/MIS* systems support short-cutting methods that allow the user to choose an action directly from any place in the menu structure. This provides the option of using either the menu or the command line for choosing an action.

Full-Screen Editing. HI/MIS systems typically permit the user to edit an entire screen of information, freely moving the cursor to any field on the screen for editing. After editing, the system updates the full record in the file.

This method is more efficient than the line-at-a-time editing used in many traditional systems. To edit an existing record in the line-oriented method, the user must first tell the system the precise field to be edited; the system then opens the field; the user makes the change; then the user repeats the sequence again for any other fields in the record that require editing.

Look-ups. Anyone who has ever used a business computer system has experienced the frustration of being in the midst of a transaction, needing to know an exact part number, vendor name, customer code, or account number, and not being able to remember it. In many traditional systems, the user has to cancel the transaction, perform an inquiry to find the answer, and then start over. The more modern interfaces found in *HI/MIS* products typically allow the user in the middle of a transaction to perform a quick look-up of the necessary information, without disrupting the processing of the transaction. Common look-up methods include:

- Simple scrolling, where the user can press a key to successively view the alternative values that are possible for the particular field.
- Tables, where a table of acceptable values (or records from a related file) appears, and the user can then indicate which of the table entries is desired.
- Partial key search, where the above two methods are modified by starting the scrolling or limiting the table to values that match the specified partial value. For example, a user knowing that the needed account number falls in the 5000 range could first specify "5" as the partial search key. This eliminates the need to scroll past all the account numbers before 5000.

Pop-ups. Most *HI/MIS* products have the ability to pop-up help information, notes, or inquiries. For example, the user presses a key that pops-up an inquiry window displaying current inventory on-hand quantities at various stocking locations.

Context Sensitive Help. When the user pops-up help information, most *HI/MIS* products are smart enough to remember the function the user is currently performing and deliver help information specific to that function.

Windowing. Some *HI/MIS* products allow windowing, or switching, from one system function to another and then back again. For example, a user is entering a large, new purchase order and receives an urgent request to check the status of another order. By immediately opening a window, the user can make an inquiry to find the other order number. Another inquiry could then be made to check the order's status, and perhaps yet another inquiry to see if there may be any other orders due to come in for the same material. After obtaining this information, the user simply closes the window. The system then returns the user to the original place in the new purchase order for completion of processing.

Customizing. HI/MIS products typically permit the user to tailor the user interfaces to meet specific needs. The change can be modest, such as selecting a different color scheme for the screens. More substantial changes can be created through macros, which are collections of system functions that are assigned to a specific macro name or special key combination. Macros are frequently used by a user who wishes to automate a series of steps that are routinely made while operating the system. The macro contains a record of the keystrokes involved in the steps. The user can execute those steps by invoking the macro.

Report Writing

The report writing functions of *HI/MIS* systems are generally very easy to use. Usually, they are menu-driven and allow the user to perform convenient look-ups of the necessary file and field names. Standard report and screen formats can usually be generated automatically by the system, and output can be directed to the user's display, printers, or disk files.

HI/MIS report writers are typically powerful and allow inquiry against all files and all fields within the entire system. They also allow the user to select and sort output based an any field. Some of the more advanced systems allow users to utilize existing (and sometimes establish new) relationships between multiple system files. The report writers can usually export system information in multiple standard formats, such as DIF and other popular spreadsheet and database formats. Many *HI/MIS* products take advantage of popular third-party report-writing products. These report writers were developed by other vendors and have been adapted to work in an integral fashion with the file structures of the *HI/MIS* product. Certain *HI/MIS* products utilize advanced environments such as:

- Fourth Generation Languages (4GL)
- Relational Database Management Systems (RDBMS)
- Structured Query Language (SQL)

Users of these products can take advantage of the underlying environment to provide advanced ad-hoc inquiry and report-writing capabilities. For example, a user wants to produce a listing of any inventory items that show a negative quantity in the system. If the HI/MIS product supports the use of SQL, the user could easily produce this listing with the following simple SQL statement:

"Select partnum, partqty from partfile where partqty < 0."

That's it. That's all that would be required to produce the report in a suitable format. The user would have to know that the file was called "partfile" and that the fields were called "partnum" and "partqty". But in some systems, even this information can automatically be pulled from look-ups.

Operating Systems

The operating system environments that support *HI/MIS* products consist principally of local area networks (LAN), such as Netware 386 from Novell, Inc., and shared-processor (minicomputer) systems, such as SCO XENIX System V from The Santa Cruz Operation, Inc.

A LAN, in this context, is made up of multiple microcomputers that cooperate to perform the overall workload of the system. This is known as a *distributed processing architecture.* The applications actually run on the user's PC. Other PCs perform centralized functions, such as managing shared peripherals and transferring information to and from centralized data storage.

In a *shared processor architecture,* a single computer (or a few connected computers) perform essentially all of the system workload. All of the users' applications run on this centralized computer. The processing power of this single unit must be great, since it is being shared by all of the system users. But the higher cost of this requirement is offset by the use of lower cost computers at each user station. The users' PCs need only the modest power required to perform terminal emulation. In fact, the users could be supplied with inexpensive terminals if there were no other requirement for their own PC.

The *HI/MIS* supporting operating systems in both the LAN and shared processor environments will typically be less complex than most of the non-*HI/MIS* supporting operating systems. They are still fairly complicated, but they require less tuning, ongoing maintenance, and specialized knowledge.

An important advantage of the *HI/MIS* supporting operating systems is that they can run on a wide variety of hardware. This enables companies to choose the best price-performance hardware platform available. Many of the non-*HI/MIS* operating systems are proprietary, running on only one brand of hardware.

The power and capabilities of *HI/MIS* supporting operating systems are very good. They provide for adequate system security and ample hard disk storage.

(Chapter 4 discusses these issues more fully.) The systems also do a good job of managing shared peripherals, such as spooled printers.

Source Code Availability

Many companies find it desirable to obtain source code in order to modify the software to meet their unique needs or to integrate with other information systems. Even if no modifications to the software are contemplated, it is still beneficial to have access to the source code. (See Chapter 9 for problems that can occur when source code is not available.)

Unlike the majority of non-*HI/MIS* systems, source code is often *not* included with *HI/MIS* products. The *HI/MIS* vendors have expressed the following reasons for this:

- Most of their clients are smaller companies that tend to not perform their own modifications.
- Clients who might want to perform their own modifications generally lack the resources to do it properly and therefore cause difficult support problems.

While these concerns are understandable, the fact remains that it is still beneficial to at least have source code available, should a future situation necessitate its use. Several of the *HI/MIS* vendors have addressed this by making the source code available for an additional cost, and almost all have standard escrow arrangements for the source code to cover certain contingencies. (See Chapter 9 for comments regarding the effectiveness of escrow arrangements.)

Software Modifications

Not all *HI/MIS* software vendors provide for modifications of their products. In a few cases, modifications are entirely unavailable. The reasons for this include:

- The strategy for long-term product development requires that all users have the same system. Having a wide array of modified systems in the user base would make upgrading the product much more difficult.
- The primary mission of the vendor's software development staff is to upgrade and enhance their product to keep it competitive. Diverting that resource to modifying the product for individual users would impede making advancements in their product.

In other cases, modifications are available only from the vendors directly or from a very limited number of other sources. The reasons for this include:

- Vendors may be concerned that some of their proprietary technologies will be compromised. They are therefore reluctant to turn their source code and development tools over to another party.

- The vendor may be (justifiably) concerned regarding the quality of the modifications that will be performed by another party. A poor job in coding or documenting the modification will eventually create problems that wind up requiring additional support from the original vendor.
- The vendors may view the modification business as a profitable part of their operations and simply want to keep the profits for themselves. (See Chapter 9 for an important caveat regarding this situation.)

COST FACTORS

Software Costs

One of the most obvious distinctions between *HI/MIS* and non-*HI/MIS* systems is the sharp difference in the cost of the software. Before *HI/MIS* products became available, it was the standard assumption that the cost of fully integrated manufacturing software would be measured in hundreds of thousands of dollars. Today, *HI/MIS* software products are available at only a fraction of this cost. (See Chapter 7 for a more complete discussion of software costs and specific examples.) Fully functional, integrated manufacturing software can now be purchased at a very affordable cost. You can still spend a few hundred thousand dollars on software, but with *HI/MIS* software, this would be for one of the top systems, with the software license sized to support 100 or more concurrent users. The cost of a similar non-*HI/MIS* software product, also sized to support 100 or more concurrent users, could approach or exceed one million dollars.

It is interesting to note, almost without exception, that the *HI/MIS* software products are new systems. They are next generation, successor products to their older, non-*HI/MIS* predecessors. There was no gradual evolution of the older systems into *HI/MIS* systems. The older systems did not drop in price each year, eventually costing only a fraction of their former cost. Because there is often a tendency to equate cost with value, it is useful to consider some possible reasons for the continued wide disparity in costs between *HI/MIS* and older systems.

- The older, non-*HI/MIS* software required huge investments in their original development. Developed before the availability of newer, more productive software technologies, the products required more person-years of effort and expense to be completed. Their higher price may reflect the desire to recover this initial investment.
- The vendors have continued to invest substantial resources in maintaining and enhancing these older products. Again, hampered by older technology, the costs of this ongoing maintenance and enhancement is large and must be recovered through sales revenue.
- The older products typically were designed to run on mainframe and large minicomputer hardware. The market accepted a software price of several hundred thousand dollars when the hardware platform cost around a million dollars. However, the market does not appear

too receptive to paying several hundred thousand dollars for a software product that operates on a $20,000 platform. This may be one of the reasons the older vendors do not always jump at the chance to move their products to newer, lower cost hardware platforms.

- Reducing software product prices can be seen negatively in the marketplace. Potential customers may view this action as an attempt to salvage market share that is being lost to other, perhaps better products. In addition, the software company's investors may oppose a price reduction that would have a negative effect on short-term financial results.

- The older vendors have developed infrastructures geared to support big systems at big sites. The vendors have very large support staffs, and some have offices staffed with internal personnel throughout the world. They use marketing and sales methods geared for large-ticket sales. A product demonstration meeting at a customer site may involve as many as 10 vendor personnel, all flown in specifically for the meeting. If the vendor's product prices were reduced to only a fraction of their current levels, it would simply be impossible for the vendor to support this type of infrastructure and conduct business in the same manner.

Hardware Costs

Another characteristic of *HI/MIS* systems that has a significant impact on cost is the class of hardware that they run on. As a result of improvements in technology, it is now possible for large, sophisticated systems to run successfully on microcomputers and small, affordable minicomputers. (See Chapter 4 for a review of these technologies and Chapter 7 for a more complete discussion of hardware costs.)

The choice of operating environment, whether a microcomputer-based LAN or a single small minicomputer, will have some effect on overall system hardware costs. It is possible, however, to construct a rule-of-thumb approximation of hardware costs expressed as dollars per user. Based on technology and hardware product pricing at the time this book was written, the hardware rule-of-thumb for *HI/MIS* systems is approximately $1,500 to $2,500 per user.

The desired responsiveness of the system will, of course, affect the cost of the required hardware. Users who are accustomed to large systems and relatively slow system response times will be happy if the new system provides two- or three-second response time performance. Users who are accustomed to having their own stand-alone desktop microcomputer and relatively instantaneous response times will want the new system to provide sub-one-second response time performance.

Satisfying user expectations of system response time performance is important, but even more significant is ensuring that the chosen hardware environment can support the future growth and demands that will be placed on the system. Increasing the number of users accessing the system, increasing data file sizes, and increasing the number of transactions being processed will require ever-increasing levels of system performance.

Current *HI/MIS* systems, running on properly configured hardware environments, have shown impressive performance. It is difficult to discern exactly where the theoretical limit is on the maximum system size that can be supported with characteristic *HI/MIS* hardware, but the practical limit must be at least as high as the largest existing sites that are currently running *HI/MIS* systems. To date, there are sites running in excess of 100 system users and processing over 40,000 transactions per month.*

Ongoing Operational Costs

The costs involved in buying the software and hardware are only part of the total cost of an information system. Once the system has been installed, the business incurs ongoing costs as it operates the system. These operating costs, discussed in greater detail in Chapter 7, include:

- Depreciation/amortization of the initial investment
- Maintenance of the hardware and support services for the software
- Direct operational expenses, such as internal support personnel and telecommunications charges

Clearly, the ongoing depreciation and amortization expenses will be significantly less with *HI/MIS* systems due to their much lower initial purchase cost. The savings in monthly depreciation and amortization will be proportional to the difference in purchase costs between the *HI/MIS* and non-*HI/MIS* systems.

Two rules-of-thumb exist that define the approximate relationship between initial system costs and the costs of ongoing maintenance. Currently, the rule-of-thumb for the cost of ongoing maintenance for the hardware components of a system is an annual charge of approximately 9–13 percent of the hardware purchase price. The rule-of-thumb for the cost of ongoing maintenance/support for the software is an annual charge of approximately 10–18 percent of the software purchase price.

Fortunately, these ratios stay fairly consistent across both non-*HI/MIS* and *HI/MIS* hardware and software products. This produces a significant savings in monthly operational costs for the *HI/MIS* systems. The savings is directly proportional to the difference in purchase costs between the *HI/MIS* and non-*HI/MIS* systems.

A company's internal support costs can also be significantly different with an *HI/MIS* system. *HI/MIS* systems run within relatively less-complex environments and therefore require relatively less support resources.

Non-*HI/MIS* systems require more internal support. A multitude of support staff are needed with traditional systems: systems analysts, application programmers, hardware specialists, operating system specialists, communications

---

*Caution: The specifics of your application may require extra processing capacity, which may cause your performance limit to be below this level.

specialists, network administrators, database administrators, computer operators, and MIS managers may be required to provide the ongoing support necessary to maintain the more-complex operating environments of non-*HI/MIS* systems. Certainly most companies will not need all of the personnel mentioned above. But even an addition of just one or two full-time personnel can have a noticeable impact on smaller companies.

The last factor that affects ongoing operational costs is the difference in telecommunications requirements. *HI/MIS* systems, due to their lower costs, can be physically located at the remote plant sites, warehouses, branch offices, or other subsidiary operations. This reduces the need for telecommunications to a minimal level.

Non-*HI/MIS* systems will tend to be centralized. To enable on-line access to the system, remote sites must be connected to the large, central system via telecommunications (or other costly methods). In this situation, telecommunications charges can quickly become a significant portion of the company's total ongoing costs to operate the system.

VENDOR CHARACTERISTICS

Vendor Size

HI/MIS vendors are typically smaller in size than the leading non-*HI/MIS* vendors. For example, the typical profile of an *HI/MIS* vendor might reveal that it has been in business for six years. The company is financed by internally generated funds and annual revenue is at approximately five million dollars. About 50 employees work for the company.

The typical profile for a vendor of traditional information systems is somewhat different. This company may have been in business for 12 years and is sufficiently mature to be a publicly-held corporation. The company generates $25 million in annual revenue and employs about 250 people.

Very few vendors, even the vendors of mainframe-based products, have software-only revenues above $100 million. But clearly, the typical *HI/MIS* vendor is smaller than the vendor of traditional systems.

The size of a software vendor can affect its ability to provide support, finance growth, and advance its products. More importantly, size has implications on the company's stability and staying power. (Chapter 9 covers these issues in greater detail). However, the software industry is a volatile one, and size alone does not ensure future success.

Vendor Support

As mentioned above, the depth of support available from *HI/MIS* vendors may be limited by their size. Currently, *HI/MIS* vendors provide some combination of the following methods to support their product:

- *Telephone hotline.* Product support personnel, usually a location, answer telephone calls from the users and ass the problems. Hotline support is typically available during working hours or extended working hours (to accommodate time zone differences). Twenty-four hour, seven-day-a-week coverage is usually *not* available.
- *Dial-up access.* The vendor connects via phone lines to the user's computer system. This method allows the vendor to see exactly what the user sees and leads to a quicker and more accurate diagnosis of problems.
- *Product training.* The vendor provides formal training on the software. The options for where training occurs varies by company and include: the vendor's office, selected regional locations, or the user's site. The frequency and availability of regularly scheduled training classes also varies by vendor.
- *Consulting services.* The vendor assists the client in implementing the system in an optimal manner. The nature of these services requires that vendor personnel work at the user's site.

By contrast, vendors of traditional systems provide all of the above methods, but do so on a more extensive basis. For example, they will typically provide longer hours of telephone hotline support or offer a more extensive schedule at more locations for formal user training.

The larger installed base and larger number of support personnel of non-*HI/MIS* vendors has one additional advantage. A sudden peak in demand for support services will likely represent a smaller percent increase in additional support required.

The smaller vendors do seem to exhibit somewhat more variance in the responsiveness of their support services. They cycle through short periods of relatively slow and relatively fast response times to support questions. The responsiveness of the larger vendors is usually more consistent. Of course, this is no great advantage if their responsiveness is consistently poor!

Vendor Distribution Channels

HI/MIS vendors employ a variety of methods in distributing their products:

- Direct: the vendor is the sole source for the product.
- Dealers: the type of dealership may be a Value Added Reseller (VAR) or a retail storefront.
- Distributors: found usually within international markets.

A vendor might distribute solely through one of these channels or use a combination of them. The method employed will have an effect on the consistency of support service quality.

Vendors who sell direct-only will have the most control over the quality of support. But there can still be considerable variance between geographic regions that are serviced by different branch offices. Vendors who sell through dealers and distributors have less control over quality of support. Correspondingly, there will tend to be even wider variance in quality levels.

The important message is that the quality of support for *HI/MIS* products can vary significantly by geography. A product may have excellent support and a large, happy installed base of clients on the West Coast and at the same time may have inadequate support and a large percentage of dissatisfied clients on the East Coast.

SUMMARY

This chapter outlined the fundamental elements that constitute an *HI/MIS* and the factors that serve to contrast *HI/MIS* from other, more traditional systems. *HI/MIS* have both important advantages (benefits) and potential disadvantages (caveats), which will be explored in greater depth in later chapters.

HI/MIS Advantages

- Software capabilities
- Software ease-of-use
- Report writing
- Software costs
- Hardware costs
- Ongoing operational costs

HI/MIS Potential Disadvantages

- Source code availability
- Software modifications
- Vendor size
- Vendor support

4

HI/MIS Technologies

During the last several years, many technological factors have contributed to the realization of *HI/MIS*. These factors can be organized into five broad categories:

- Hardware
- Architecture
- Operating Systems
- Language Compilers
- Database Management Systems

HARDWARE

The first and most obvious factor that has contributed to the realization of *HI/MIS* is the dramatic increase in performance of low-cost computer hardware. Technological advances have significantly improved the performance capabilities of the hardware equipment components discussed below.

Microprocessors

Often called the "brains" of the system, the microprocessor performs the bulk of the calculation and data manipulation operations. Microcomputers and small minicomputers are typically based on microprocessors. (Figure 4-1, component label <1> shows a microprocessor in a system diagram.)

Software programs are compiled (decoded) into a set of instructions the microprocessor performs. The greater the number of these instructions that a micro-

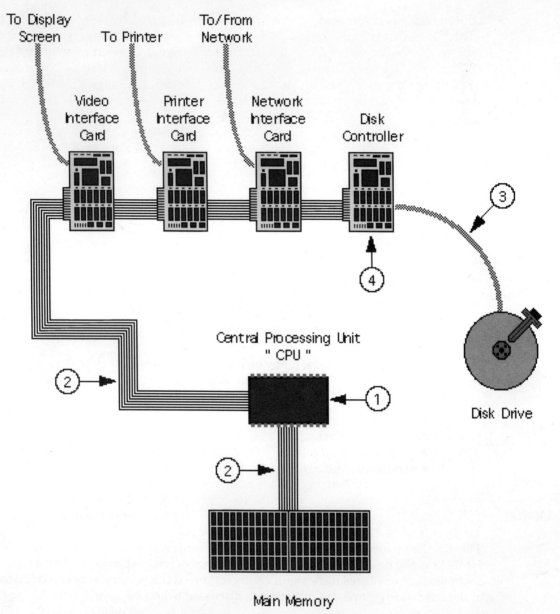

Figure 4-1. System Diagram.

processor can accomplish in a given amount of time, the greater its performance. Microprocessor performance is usually measured in MIPS (million instructions per second). For example, a processor with a rating of five MIPS processes five million instructions per second. While this is an imperfect measure of performance, it does give some indication of performance capability.

Recent advances in the design and manufacture of microprocessors have produced significant increases in their speed while dramatically reducing their cost. The first business microcomputers contained processors that provided performance of less than one million instructions per second. Current microprocessors perform at levels that exceed 45 MIPS. Small computers, based on these high performing microprocessors, perform as well as the midrange minicomputers that were state-of-the-art only a few years ago, and they cost far less to buy and operate.

Finally, systems with multiple microprocessors working in combination have started to become available. Employing up to four or six microprocessors, these systems boost performance to even higher levels.

Data Buses

Data buses are the main highways on which data travels through the central system. The buses transport data to and from the microprocessor, main memory, and other connected devices. (In Figure 4-1 components labeled <2> show the data bus.)

A highway's capacity for automobiles is determined by factoring the number of lanes available for the cars with the speed at which they travel. If you examine the surface of a typical microcomputer system board, you may actually see clusters of parallel lines routed to and from the microprocessor and other components. These are equivalent to the individual lanes in the highway analogy.

Several years ago, technology limited the microcomputer bus to a width of eight data bits. This is analogous to eight automobile lanes on a highway. As a result of technological improvements, current data buses commonly transport 32 bits of data at a time.

The speed of the traffic on a computer's data bus is not measured in miles per hour. Instead, the speed of the clock that synchronizes the flow of the data traffic controls the speed of the data along the bus. The faster the clock cycles, the faster the data moves along the highway. The cycles are measured in megahertz (million cycles per second). The speed of microcomputer buses increased from below 5 megahertz on the early personal computers to current speeds exceeding 20 megahertz.

Channels

A channel is a pathway on which data travels between the central system and a peripheral device, such as a disk drive, video screen, or printer. The channel leads from the bus to a peripheral device, as a secondary road leads from a highway to a small city.

The most important channel connects the central system to the disk unit(s) that store the data. This channel is responsible for the transport of data permanently stored on the disk drive to and from the connection point with the central system's data bus (The component labeled <3> in Figure 4-1 shows the disk channel.)

The capacity of the drive channel is largely determined by the speed and sophistication of the disk controller. (The component labeled <4> in Figure 4-1 shows the disk controller.) The capacity is measured by the amount of data that the disk controller can transport through the channel per unit of time, and is usually expressed in megabytes per second. The disk controllers available several years ago for microcomputers were limited to a sustained speed of about one megabyte per second. Technological improvements have led to current drive controllers that deliver performance in excess of 10 megabytes per second.

Data Storage

The primary method of data storage continues to be hard disk drives. One of the important factors in disk drive performance is how quickly the drive can access the requested data and begin transferring it to the drive channel. This is typically measured by the drive's average access time, which is expressed in milliseconds. The first drives available for business microcomputers had average access time ratings of around 80 milliseconds. Current high-performance drives have average access times under 10 milliseconds.

Physically, disk drives are getting smaller. The form factor for disk drives went from 8 inches to 5.25 inches in the early 1980s. In the later 1980s, the form factor declined to 3.5 inches and now, drives with 2-inch media are beginning to appear.

However, while shrinking physically, disk drives multiplied the quantity of data they stored. Early microcomputers could be connected to just a few disk drives, with each drive containing perhaps 20 megabytes of storage. Current technology enables a microcomputer to connect to many disk drives, each with far larger amounts of storage capacity than its predecessors. Accordingly, the total system storage can now attain levels measured in gigabytes (billions of bytes). Currently, a single system can support more than 50 gigabytes of data storage capacity.

The cost of this storage capacity has dropped steeply over the years. Several years ago, hard disk storage cost in the range of $100 per megabyte. Currently available disk drives provide storage capacity at under two dollars per megabyte.

ARCHITECTURE

There are two basic methods, or architectures, used to provide multiple users with concurrent access to systems. For the purposes of this chapter, these two architectures will be referred to as *Shared Processor* and *Local Area Network* (LAN). An exploration of the mechanics of these architectures will help in the overall understanding of the technologies that support *HI/MIS*.

Shared Processor

In the shared processor architecture, all of the data processing is performed on one central processor. Many traditional minicomputer and mainframe systems employ this technology. The central unit can be a powerful microcomputer or a

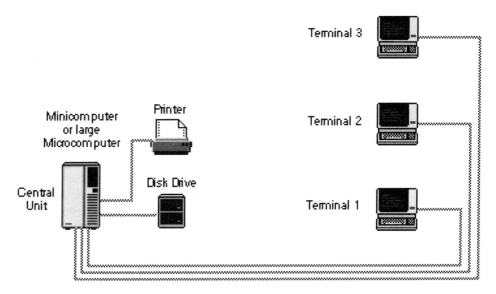

Figure 4-2. Shared Processor Architecture.

small minicomputer. The user operates an inexpensive terminal, or a microcomputer set up to emulate a terminal.

The mechanics of how this architecture works is illustrated in Figure 4-2. In this example, the system is running an integrated software product, called *XYZ*, on a shared processor system. Two people are currently using the system. Brenda is using terminal 1 and is about to process accounts payable checks through the *XYZ* software. She selects this function from the menu of choices appearing on her terminal. The keystrokes for this choice are transmitted from terminal 1 to the central (shared processor) unit.

The *XYZ* software is running on the central unit. *XYZ* processes Brenda's choice and issues commands to the operating system to load the accounts payable check-writing program, *apckwr*. The operating system locates the *apckwr* program on the disk drive and commands the disk drive to transmit the program's contents to the central unit. Then the operating system receives the *apckwr* program into a portion of the central unit's main memory and starts running it.

Scott is using terminal 2 and is ready to enter purchase orders through the *XYZ* software. He selects this function from the menu of choices appearing on his terminal. The keystrokes indicating Scott's choice are transmitted from terminal 2 to the central processor. The *XYZ* software and the operating system deal with Scott's selection just as they did with Brenda's. When the purchase order program, called *prcord*, is loaded to the main memory in the central unit, the operating system begins running it.

At this point, the two programs, *apckwr* and *prcord*, are both loaded in the main memory of the central unit. The single microprocessor concurrently serves both Brenda and Scott; they are sharing the same microprocessor.

However, the microprocessor cannot work for the two of them simultaneously. The microprocessor executes instructions from Brenda's *apckwr* program for a very short time, and then it turns to Scott's *prcord* program. The microprocessor is fast enough that, from Brenda and Scott's perspectives, the two programs are running at the same time.

As other users come on the system, they also share the microprocessor with Brenda and Scott. The microprocessor continues to move quickly from one user's work to another. There is, however, a limit to the number of users that can be served quickly by the microprocessor. As the number of other users approaches that limit, Brenda and Scott will perceive a slowdown in the speed with which the computer responds to their requests.

Local Area Network

The LAN architecture is an example of a concept called *distributed processing*. In this concept, multiple microprocessors, located in multiple machines, work in combination to process the system tasks. Each user needs to have his/her own computer. There is also a central unit, but it performs a fundamentally different role. For the purposes of this chapter, the central unit will be referred to as a *file server* and the user-dedicated computers will be referred to as *workstations*.

Figure 4-3 provides a very simplified illustration of how this architecture works. Brenda and Scott are running the *XYZ* integrated software product on the LAN. Brenda, using workstation 1, is ready to process accounts payable checks. She selects this function from the menu of choices appearing on her workstation.

Brenda's keystrokes indicating her choice are received by a copy of *XYZ*, which is loaded and running on her workstation. The keystrokes are not transmitted to the file server. *XYZ* interprets her keystrokes and decides that the accounts payable check-writing program needs to be run. *XYZ* issues commands to the network operating system requesting the *apckwr* program from the file server.

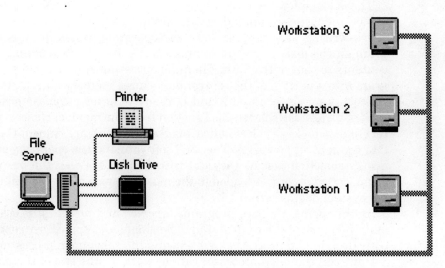

Figure 4-3. Local Area Network (LAN) Architecture.

The network operating system locates the file *apckwr* on the file server's disk drive and commands the drive to transmit the file's contents. Upon receiving the *apckwr* program into a portion of the file server's main memory, the operating system instructs the file server to then retransmit the file to Brenda's workstation. Brenda's computer receives the *apckwr* file, loads its contents into a portion of its main memory, and runs the application.

Scott, using workstation 2, needs to enter purchase orders. He selects this function from the menu of choices appearing on his workstation. His computer processes this input. With the file server working just as it did for Brenda, the purchase order program, called *prcord*, is loaded to the main memory in Scott's workstation and begins executing. At this point, the two programs are loaded in two separate machines. Brenda and Scott can operate their programs simultaneously, with the microprocessor in Brenda's computer executing *apckwr* and the microprocessor in Scott's computer executing *prcord*.

What happens if the programs need the same piece of data? For example, what if both Brenda and Scott need to access the standard payment terms for a certain vendor? The key is that the permanent copy of this data resides in only one place, on the file server. The network operating system controls the file server and coordinates how the users share access to the information they both need.

The amount of communication between devices in a LAN is significantly higher than in the shared processor architecture. When Brenda works on the shared processor, only her keystrokes and the data to be displayed on her terminal screen were transmitted to and from the central unit. For Brenda to begin processing accounts payable checks, perhaps as few as 5,000 characters or bytes of information had to be communicated between her terminal and the central unit.

On the other hand, with Brenda working in the LAN architecture, the entire program that she used was transmitted from the file server to her workstation. This program could easily be 250,000 bytes in size. The total inter-device communication occurring on the LAN was approximately 50 times greater than that for the shared processor.

To move the large volume of data traffic found on a LAN quickly, the connectivity hardware needs a large capacity, or *bandwidth*. Specialized devices, network interface cards (NICs), provide the large bandwidth a LAN requires. The NICs are usually connected to cables that run between the workstations, file servers, and certain other devices that are on the network. The cable might be made of coax, twisted pair, or fiber optic material.*

Another important environment that is emerging and rapidly becoming more prevalent is called client-server. In this environment, multiple machines can share the job of serving up database or application services to multiple client machines. Client-server systems complement the two basic architectures (shared

---

*Note: This is a highly simplified illustration of two basic architectures. It would be a mistake to jump to conclusions regarding their relative performance capabilities. Many other factors will influence their actual performance characteristics, and there are many other nonperformance factors to be considered in evaluating which architecture is best for any given situation.

processor and LAN) described earlier. Their inherent flexibility can provide tailored performance, optimal operating costs, and excellent expandability. (The full discussion of client-server technical issues is beyond the scope of this book.)

OPERATING SYSTEMS

The operating system controls access to the system and information, the sharing of peripheral devices among users, managing data files, communicating among the devices, and administering to the general needs of the information system. Technological advances have significantly improved the capabilities of today's operating systems. Following is a description of the typical functionality found in current *HI/MIS* operating systems.

Security

Users are assigned passwords by a system administrator. The operating system stores the passwords in an encrypted form. When the user logs on the terminal does not display the password. This helps keep a user's password confidential. As an additional aid to confidentiality, the system administrator can instruct the operating system to force the users to change their passwords periodically.

Upon logging-in, the system recognizes the users, asks for and validates their passwords, and enables the users' rights. Based on their predefined rights, the users can selectively be given access to only certain files. Further, the type of access given can be specified as selectively including read, write, modify, or delete capabilities on a file-by-file basis.

Users can be further restricted by being allowed to log-in only from certain terminals or workstations. To prevent off-hours access, the operating system can be instructed to allow user log-ins only during a specified hour range.*

Peripheral Sharing

An example of a common peripheral device that will be shared by the system users is a high-speed printer. In fact, the central system may manage several connected printers of various types. *HI/MIS* operating systems have good support for this complex situation.

The first type of support is called *print spooling*. When a user performs a function that generates printed output, they will be given the option to spool to one of the centralized printers. Instead of sending the output to the small, slow printer connected directly to their terminal or workstation (if they have one at all), the

---

*Note: While all of these capabilities may be available from the operating system, the application software may or may not take advantage of them. Some application software relies solely on its own built-in security capabilities. Be sure to investigate how the particular application software product under consideration interacts with the security features of the underlying operating system.

user can select from the variety of printers connected to the central unit. Further, the user can instruct the system to print a certain number of copies on a certain type of form. While the central unit is busy processing the requested print output, their workstation is released to perform other functions.

The second type of support is called *print queue management*. At the central unit, the operating system maintains the queues of incoming print jobs from the multiple system users. Priorities can be assigned, and jobs can be restarted and switched between available printers. The system will automatically notify the operator if any special forms need to be loaded and if any problems occur during the printing process.

Disk Drive Management

The operating system also manages the system's disk drives and the files stored on them. Earlier versions of operating systems placed a ceiling on the maximum number of bytes of information that a file could contain. Advances in technology have raised this ceiling high enough so that, in practicality, it no longer exists. The operating systems have also advanced in their capability to manage the huge amounts (multiple gigabytes) of total system storage that can be connected.

HI/MIS operating systems have also advanced in their capability to enhance the performance of disk-intensive tasks. A technique called *caching* is used by operating systems for this purpose. The operating system keeps a copy of the most recently accessed data from the disk drive in a cache (an area of the system's main memory). Retrieval of data from main memory is several times faster than retrieval from disk drives. When the same data is needed again, the operating system remembers that it is still available in the system's fast main memory. The data is then retrieved directly from main memory, effecting what can sometimes be a very significant increase in system performance.

The operating systems have become smarter, making decisions about what data to keep resident in the limited amount of main memory available for the cache. This improves the *hit ratio,* or percent of times that the operating system can successfully find the needed data in the cache without accessing the disk drive.

Remote Communications

The operating system also plays a part in enabling remote users to access the system. There are many ways to provide the communications link between remote sites, but the most common is to use the public telephone network. (Figure 4-4 illustrates a standard remote communications environment.)

When standard telephone lines are used, the remote points will most often communicate using an asynchronous, analog method. This requires only inexpensive modems to provide the interface between the computers and the phone network. The communications bandwidth provided by this method is relatively small. The capacity may be limited to approximately 10,000 bits per second. It is important to understand the effect that this limited bandwidth can have on the

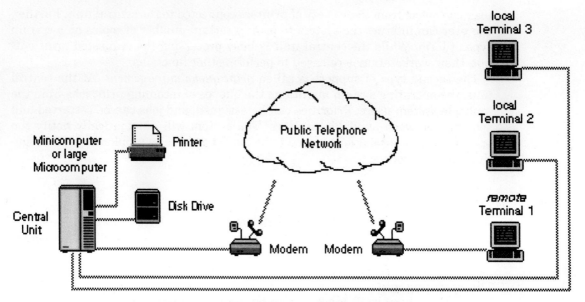

Figure 4-4. Standard Remote Communications.

two different system architectures discussed earlier.

This bandwidth limitation does not usually create a problem for a shared processor system. In the typical situation, the data traffic flowing from the central processor to the remote sites is relatively small. It would consist primarily of the information necessary to update the terminal screens and transfer data to the printers located at the remote sites. Similarly, the data traffic from the remote sites to the central processor is fairly light since it consists only of the data that the users type in on their keyboards.

On the other hand, the limited remote communication bandwidth can present a problem for LAN systems. Delivering entire program files and large quantities of data file records from the central processor to the workstations generates an enormous volume of data traffic. LANs require a wide communication bandwidth to move this data quickly and thereby be responsive to the users.

A typical LAN will utilize network interface cards and cable media delivering performance in the range of five million bits per second. This is 500 times faster than the 10,000-bits-per-second capacity of the typical remote communication link. If a remote user attempts to connect to the LAN, the communications will be forced to squeeze through this remote communications bottleneck. In this situation, an average-size, 250,000 byte program would take over 4 minutes to load and begin executing at a remote user's workstation.

There are solutions to this remote users/LAN bandwidth challenge. The most direct is to utilize another, higher capacity communication method to provide the linkage between remote workstations and the central system. Many different methods are available, but they all share one common characteristic: They are significantly more expensive.

A relatively inexpensive technique has been developed to provide a limited

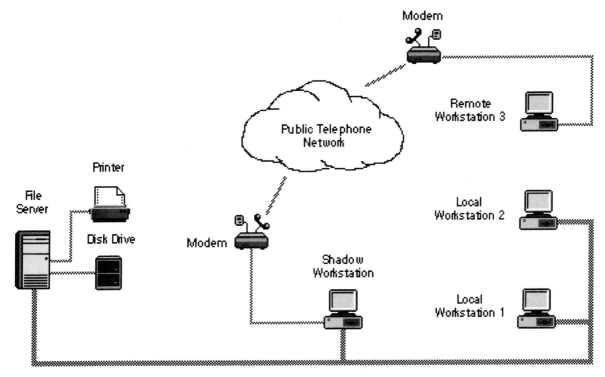

Figure 4-5. LAN Remote Communications.

number of remote users with practical LAN access. "Shadow" workstations can be set up at the central system. (Figure 4-5 illustrates this method.) The application programs actually run on the shadow workstation. Special software running on both the shadow and the remote user's workstation transfer (mirror) the screen images and keyboard input between the linked workstations. This limits the data traffic and thereby reduces the required bandwidth to the same level required for the shared processor architecture. A disadvantage of this technique is that two workstations are required to provide processing capabilities for one user.

Other techniques are available today, and more advanced and affordable techniques to address remote communications continue to be developed. One of the most interesting is the use of hybrid architectures that take advantage of the best characteristics of both the shared processor and LAN technologies.

LANGUAGE COMPILERS

Application software is written in a computer programming language, such as COBOL, FORTRAN, C, BASIC, or Pascal. Many of the words and syntaxes of software written in these languages initially bear some relationship to human language. For example, to instruct the program to execute a task, the language uses terms such as "perform" (COBOL), and "do" (FORTRAN). The programming language is constructed this way to make it easier for a person to understand and write the software code.

All programming languages must then be translated into a language that the computer itself understands before it can execute the instructions. Compilers are the software tools that translate programming language into machine language. The sophistication of the compiler determines how easy or difficult it will be to use a particular computer programming language in developing new systems.

Several years ago, the compilers available on microcomputers did not support the same set of languages that were supported on large minicomputers and mainframes. Even if a particular language was supported, the level of support would typically not be as extensive or complete as the developer needed. Today the situation is quite different. Compilers for practically all of the popular programming languages are available to run on microcomputers. In addition, the sophistication and capabilities of the compilers and associated development tools have improved tremendously. In fact, the situation is now quite often reversed. Many current developers of software for large minicomputers and mainframes now use microcomputers as their primary development platform.

Also fueling the improvement in this area is the appearance of entirely new languages. These "4GLs" (fourth-generation languages) are very efficient environments for the rapid production of new software systems. Using an example from an earlier chapter, let's assume we are a software developer and we need to write a program that produces a listing of any inventory items showing a negative quantity in the system. If we are writing our product in a 4GL, the entire program might consist of this single statement:

```
Select partnum, partqty from partfile where partqty < 0.
```

Obviously, a lot of functionality can be quickly developed in this environment. This capability accelerates the rate at which sophisticated applications can be developed and simplifies the effort required to maintain and enhance them. The 4GLs also have the advantage of shielding the system developer from the intricate details of the involved operating system and hardware. This allows the exact same software to run on multiple types of operating systems and hardware.

DATABASE MANAGEMENT SYSTEMS

A database management system (DBMS) is used by software to store, organize, access, and maintain system data. DBMS technology provides several important advantages. A primary advantage is the use of a data dictionary, which stores, in one place, all of the detailed information that describes the size, type, validation rules, and relationships between all the files and fields in the database.

Development of new software is more efficient in a DBMS environment. All of the descriptive file and field information is already known by the system and need not be repeated. The "calls" or requests to the DBMS for data are typically simple and straightforward to program. The structure of files can be changed and new fields can be added without changing any programs.

Sophisticated database management systems are now available to run in the microcomputer environment. Another advantage often associated with DBMS products is their ability to run on multiple types of operating systems and hardware. This factor enables several of the *HI/MIS* products to run on a wide range of hardware, from microcomputers through large minicomputer platforms.

SUMMARY

The technological changes in hardware, architecture, operating systems, language compilers, and DBMS underlay the development of powerful new *HI/MIS* products. They have also enabled the downward migration or adaptation of pre-existing minicomputer and mainframe products. There are several examples of this. Of the currently available *HI/MIS* products:

- At least two were originally minicomputer-only products. Fortunately, these products were built in a 4GL/DBMS environment. When the underlying 4GL/DBMS could run competently in a micro-computer based LAN environment, two fully functional, formerly minicomputer-only products instantly joined the HI/MIS ranks.

- At least three other products were also originally minicomputer-only. Improvements in the capabilities of available COBOL and C language compilers and the availability of a competent Unix-compatible operating system have enabled these products to also become multiplatform and run on microcomputer-based systems.

The future should see a continuation of this downward migration. Another important trend that is certain to continue is the rapid increase in the performance capabilities of low-cost hardware. This will enable a continually growing percentage of companies to take advantage of *HI/MIS*.

As mentioned earlier in the book, it is difficult to discern exactly where the theoretical limit is on the maximum system size that can be supported with current *HI/MIS* hardware. But wherever this line is today, it is rapidly being pushed upward by technology. (Figure 4-6, on page 56, illustrates this trend.)

In the future, it can be expected that more *HI/MIS* products will become available as established minicomputer and mainframe products migrate downward to less expensive hardware platforms. Furthermore, continuing improvements to the available software development environments will enable new *HI/MIS* products to be developed and existing ones to be significantly enhanced.

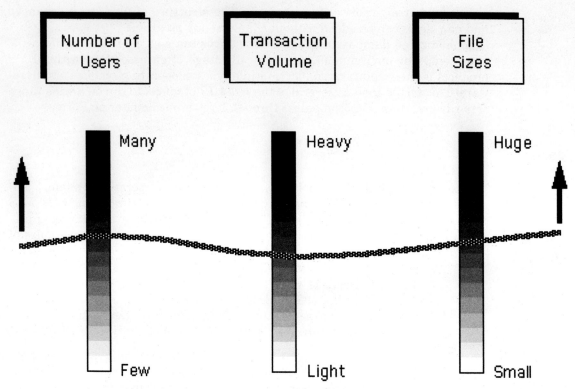

Figure 4-6. Maximum Supportable System Size.

5

Capabilities of an *HI/MIS*

This chapter explores the range of capabilities that exists in current *HI/MIS* software products. The discussion is broken into separate sections and modules for each of the common functional areas:

Section	Modules
Manufacturing & Distribution	Bills of Material
	Capacity Requirements Planning
	Distribution Requirements Planning
	Engineering Change Control
	Inventory Control
	Job Costing
	Lot Tracking
	Master Scheduling
	Material Requirements Planning
	Operations Routings
	Product Costing
	Purchasing
	Shop Floor Control
	Yield Reporting and Analysis
Marketing	Sales Order Processing
	Sales Quotations
	Sales Analysis
Financial	Accounts Payable
	Accounts Receivable
	General Ledger
	International Operations
	Payroll
Other	Field Service
	Process Control / Data Acquisition Interface
	Report Writing
	EDI (Electronic Data Interchange)

This is quite a large number of modules to discuss. But *HI/MIS* products are typically complete, integrated systems that support a full range of business functions. The challenge is in finding a way to present *HI/MIS* capabilities in a concise manner.

The full list of capabilities that are supported in typical *HI/MIS* (and non-*HI/MIS*) software products would easily contain over 2,000 elements. Obviously, it is not practical or even particularly useful to list each one. The vast majority of these 2,000-plus elements are supported by practically all of the products.

A subset of all these elements, perhaps 500 or so, can be used to actually differentiate between products. On these 500 capabilities, there will be some qualitative difference in how well particular products provide support versus other products. But even the discussion of 500 capabilities is not practical in the constraints of one chapter of one book.

If instead we limit the discussion to only some of the *key differentiating* capabilities of the *HI/MIS* products, a concise discussion becomes (barely) possible. In each of the modules, only a few, at most, of these capabilities have been selected for discussion. The capabilities selected represent some of the most advanced, complex, problematic, difficult to find, or otherwise most notable capabilities. Every company considering an *HI/MIS* will have additional key capabilities that should be discerned and evaluated.

In Chapter 10, on how to select an *HI/MIS*, there is considerable discussion on evaluation techniques. One of the important techniques mentioned is the concentration of efforts on the evaluation of a manageable number of capabilities. This enables the in-depth, qualitative review that would otherwise be impossible. If too many capabilities are examined, there will not be sufficient time to develop a true understanding of how the product will perform. In keeping with this concept, the number of capabilities listed in this chapter is small, enabling a somewhat more extensive and qualitative discussion of each.

Each of the capabilities presented in this chapter is discussed in terms of how it is used by businesses and how the capability is typically supported by the software products. Also listed is whether support can be found in almost all, many, or only very few of the current *HI/MIS* products. Finally, evaluation notes are listed that can be used as part of the process of evaluating candidate software product solutions.

Section: *Manufacturing & Distribution*

Module: *Bills of Material*

Capability: **Component Scrap Allowance**

How Utilized:	Users can specify a scrap allowance in determining the quantity of materials required for production. For example, in producing electronic board devices that require several very inexpensive resistors, the resistors are difficult to position properly in the boards and are sometimes destroyed in the process. In this example, a scrap allowance would cause the system to plan for a small extra quantity of resistors to be on hand during production of the boards.
Ways Supported:	The system enables the user to specify a scrap percent that is tied to each component on a bill of material. (This should not be confused with the concept of a yield percent, which applies to the entire assembly.)
HI/MIS % **Capable:**	**Almost All**
Evaluation Notes:	1. A few systems only support the specification of a "scrap" percent tied directly to the component part's master record. This is an inferior method, since scrap rates can vary widely based on the item being produced.
	2. Examine how the system utilizes the component scrap allowance in calculating standard costs.
	3. Examine how the system utilizes the component scrap allowance in calculating quantities for kitting. Should the system automatically request the delivery of the extra components to production, or should the components remain in stock until their need is verified? Can the user specify this choice of action on a bill of material and on a component-specific basis?
	4. If the system automatically requests the delivery of extra components, does it round to the nearest whole unit, or does it request a fractional amount, such as 3.5 extra resistors?

Section: *Manufacturing & Distribution*

Module: *Bills of Material*

Capability: **Support of Date Effectivity**

How Utilized:	Engineering changes can affect the components specified to be used in production. Sometimes these changes take effect immediately, at other times they become effective at a later date. Users need to factor these dates of effectivity into their purchasing plans and production activity.
Ways Supported:	The system enables the user to specify a beginning and ending date during which the component specification on the bill of material is in effect.
HI/MIS % Capable:	**Almost All**

Evaluation Notes:

1. Ensure that the system correctly factors the dates of effectivity into MRP calculations. If component A is scheduled to be replaced next month by component B, MRP should correctly discontinue planning orders for A and begin anticipating the need for B.
2. Examine how the system prints picklists. Are effectivity dates used properly in determining the components that are picked and delivered to the floor for production?
3. Can the system reproduce, based on effectivity dates, the bill of material that was in effect at a past date?
4. Ensure that automatic costing routines work properly when replacement components are listed on the same bill with different effectivity dates. Some systems may incorrectly include the costs of both the original and the replacement components in calculating the cost of the parent part.

Section: *Manufacturing & Distribution*

Module: *Bills of Material*

Capability: **Negative Quantities**

How Utilized:

Production processes often yield coproducts and byproducts. An example of coproducts is a die producing two O-rings with different diameters at the same time, with the smaller ring nested inside the larger. An example of a byproduct is the production of a semiconductor device, such as a microprocessor. The produced microprocessors sort into two different speed ratings. While it might be desirable if the higher speed units were produced 100 percent of the time, it is an unavoidable fact that some of the slower speed units will be produced as byproducts of the process. The slower speed units are not worthless, but they do have a significantly lower value in the marketplace.

Users need to properly plan for the production of coproducts and byproducts. Additionally, the costs of the primary products should properly reflect the value of the associated coproducts or byproducts.

Ways Supported:

A very few specialized software products directly support coproducts and byproducts. The best workaround provided by the more standard software products involves the use of negative quantities in the component specification of the bill of material.

For example, the slower speed microprocessor Y is listed on the bill of material of the faster microprocessor X. A user expecting one Y unit as a byproduct of producing two X units specifies a -0.5 quantity of Y as a component on the bill of material for X. The following bill of material illustrates this example:

Bill of Material for: Unit-X

Component	*Quantity*
Wafer	0.01
Unit-Y	−0.5

The slower Y units should then be visible to users as expected receipts whenever the production of X units are planned.

HI/MIS % Capable:

Many

Evaluation Notes:

1. Ensure that the system will actually allow the entry of a negative amount in the component quantity field.
2. Examine how the system uses a negative component quantity to anticipate and report expected receipts of coproducts and byproducts.
3. Examine how the system uses a negative component quantity to properly adjust the cost of the primary part for the salvage value of the byproduct.

4. Ensure that the kitting and backflush functions of the system are not impaired by the use of negative component quantities.

Section: *Manufacturing & Distribution*

Module: *Capacity Requirements Planning*

Capability: **Product Load Profiles**

**How
Utilized:**
A product load profile defines the amount of work, or loading, that the production of a particular product will place on a company's resources. Users need to evaluate this resource loading to ensure that the necessary resources can be made available to execute their production plans.

The types of resources put on a product's profile can be varied. Labor and machine hours have already been specified on the operations routings. Material dollars can be derived from the bills of material. However, a separate product load profile also allows the user to easily specify the effect of production on resources such as working capital, electrical power, floorspace, etc.

**Ways
Supported:**
The system enables the user to specify a profile or specification of the nature and quantity of company resources that are consumed in the production of specific products. The system then analyzes the company's full production plan, calculates and aggregates the resulting resource loads, and reports accordingly. Since the load profile of products is similar across like products, some systems allow multiple products to share the same profile, thereby easing the data maintenance requirements.

**HI/MIS %
Capable:**
Many

**Evaluation
Notes:**
1. Examine how the system reports the load being placed on resources. Is it time-phased so that it can be determined when the resource loading will occur?
2. Ensure that the horizon, or maximum amount of time into the future, is far enough out that it allows for adequate planning.

Section: *Manufacturing & Distribution*

Module: *Capacity Requirements Planning*

Capability: **Work Center Calendars**

**How
Utilized:**
The productive capacity of a work center may vary over time. Preventive maintenance and other scheduled downtime may temporarily impact capacity. Phasing-in new equipment or retiring old equipment has a more permanent impact on capacity. As new processes are introduced, the natural learning curve will produce a constant change in capacity. Since this variance in capacity can be significant, it is advantageous to factor it into the long-term planning and short-term scheduling of production.

**Ways
Supported:**
The user specifies a capacity for each work center along with a beginning and ending date for the period the capacity specification is in effect. The system then analyzes capacity loads against a more-realistic variable capacity level in the work centers.

HI/MIS %
Capable:
Very Few

**Evaluation
Notes:**
1. Examine the mechanics of how the system maintains the work center calendars. If the method is too cumbersome, this capability may be more trouble than it is worth. For example, ensure that standard workdays, weekends, and shift additions and deletions can be easily maintained.

Section: *Manufacturing & Distribution*

Module: *Distribution Requirements Planning*

Capability: **Multiple Site Inventory Support**

**How
Utilized:**   Companies often maintain inventory at multiple sites. This may be because different parts of the production process are performed at different
plants, or to facilitate the quicker fulfillment of customer orders.
Production planning, customer order processing, and inventory control
functions need to be able to track and determine the status of inventory
at these multiple sites.

**Ways
Supported:**   The system is capable of maintaining and reporting not just one on-hand
quantity, but a separate on-hand quantity figure for each site. Further,
the system should allow for the booking of customer orders and the allocation of inventory tied to specific sites.

**HI/MIS %
Capable:**   **Many**

**Evaluation
Notes:**
1. Some systems support only a limited number of sites. Ensure that this
limit is high enough to cover all warehouses, consignment locations,
plants, buildings, subcontractors, and other locations where inventory
must be tracked.
2. Some systems appear to support multiple sites, but in reality support
only multiple locations. A separate location may be a shelf or bin
somewhere within the primary site.

Section: *Manufacturing & Distribution*

Module: *Distribution Requirements Planning*

Capability: **In-Transit Shipment Tracking**

How Utilized:	At any one time, companies that employ regional warehouses or other similar distribution networks often have a large percentage of their total inventory somewhere in-transit from one site to another. Customer order processing and inventory control functions need to be able to track and determine the status of this pipeline inventory.
Ways Supported:	The system processes the intersite shipment and immediately provides visibility of the in-transit status of the inventory. The system shows the shipment as an expected receipt at the destination site, along with an expected delivery date, and perhaps even carrier information for further inquiry.
***HI/MIS* % Capable:**	**Very Few**
Evaluation Notes:	1. Most systems support workarounds if they do not have this specific capability, such as using intermediate sites to track the in-transit shipments. Ensure that any suggested workaround provides the proper visibility to all interested parties and that the mechanics of the workaround are not too burdensome.

Section: *Manufacturing & Distribution*

Module: *Distribution Requirements Planning*

Capability: **Ship-from by Line Item and Subsequent Change**

**How
Utilized:**
When a company can ship from multiple sites, customers will often want to specify the preferred ship-from location at the time they place their orders. A large customer may order products for use at several of their locations. In this situation, the ship-to and preferred ship-from locations can vary on a line-item-by-line-item basis within the same order. The customer may also prefer to negotiate price terms and book the order now, but may defer specifying the ship-from locations until a later date.

**Ways
Supported:**
At the time the order is entered, the user can specify the preferred shipping site for each line item on the order. The system also allows the user to change the ship-from specification after original order entry, and at the time of actual shipment of the products.

**HI/MIS %
Capable:**
Many

**Evaluation
Notes:**
1. Ensure that the system does not force the user to cancel and reenter the entire order as the only method available to change the ship-from specification.
2. Examine the mechanics of how the system handles the original booking of an order with no ship-to/ship-from specifications, and the subsequent addition of this information. Can the order quantity on a line item be partially split and its ship-to/ship-from specified?

Section: *Manufacturing & Distribution*

Module: *Engineering Change Control*

Capability: **Engineering Change History**

How Utilized:
A company needs to track the revisions to the design and manufacturing specifications of its products and needs to know what specifications are currently in effect. Further, to maintain and service products that have already been shipped, it must be able to figure out when an engineering change became effective and to which products it was applied.

Ways Supported:
The system maintains a history of engineering changes. For each engineering change, the system records the old and new revision designator plus the beginning and ending dates for which the engineering change is effective. The system provides a report of all engineering changes made to a part and a report of all parts that were affected by a particular engineering change.

HI/MIS % Capable:
Many

Evaluation Notes:
1. Examine the amount of descriptive information associated with the engineering change that can be maintained in the system.

Section: *Manufacturing & Distribution*

Module: *Engineering Change Control*

Capability: **Engineering Bills and Routings**

How Utilized:	Before new or changed bills of material and operations routings become effective, they progress through an engineering evaluation and approval process. Bills and routings in this pre-approval status need to be kept separate from the bills and routings that have been released to production.
Ways Supported:	The system is capable of maintaining engineering bills and routings that are separate and distinct from production bills and routings. Changes and what-if scenarios can be tested on the engineering bills and routings without adversely affecting current production or production planning activity. Newly developed bills and routings can be copied over to production upon approval.
***HI/MIS %* Capable:**	**Many**
Evaluation Notes:	1. Examine the ability of the system to simulate the impact that a proposed engineering change will cause. Can the standard cost roll-up routines be run against the engineering bills in order to project the new costs of the parent products? Can the master production schedule be used to determine the aggregate effect of the proposed change on profitability, the need for newly specified materials, and the effect on obsolescence of supplanted materials that are already on hand or on order?

Section: *Manufacturing & Distribution*

Module: *Inventory Control*

Capability: **Maximum Amount and Precision**

How Utilized:

High-volume manufacturers often deal in extremely large quantities. As an example, a company producing small plastic gears through an injection molding process has more than 10 million gears on hand at any one time. The cumulative annual shipment figure for the gears exceeds one billion. On the other hand, the specified quantity of the raw material required to produce a gear is extremely small, only .000125 pounds of plastic. In this situation, the system would need to support nine digits to the left and six digits to the right of the decimal.

Ways Supported:

The most straightforward way to support this requirement is for the system to provide enough digits for the maximum amount and precision required. If this is not supported, the standard workaround is to use different units of measure. Since it is always possible to construct an extreme situation in the future where the maximum amount or precision capabilities of a system would be exceeded, it may be prudent to evaluate how well the system can support this standard workaround.

In the example above, if the system does not provide adequate precision, the raw plastic could be measured in grams instead of pounds. This will work, unless our on-hand quantity or annual usage of raw plastic (now measured in grams) exceeds the maximum amount provided for in the system. Another approach would be to change the unit of measure on the finished gears to 100-count or 1,000-count. This may fix the problem of allowing the company to measure raw plastic in pounds, but it might create problems by confusing its customers and shipping personnel.

The best support of this workaround is for the system to provide multiple units of measures for the same part. This enables the company to order the raw plastic by the pound from the vendor and to specify it on the gear's bill of material in grams. The gear is treated internally as 1,000-count and can be ordered by customers in their familiar quantities.

HI/MIS % Capable:

Almost All (support either extremely large maximum amounts/precision or multiple units of measure)

Evaluation Notes:

1. Examine how the system handles the situation of an on-hand quantity exceeding the maximum limit. Does the system crash, or does it truncate the amount and cause an imbalance, or does it prevent a transaction from occurring that would cause the limit to be exceeded and print an error message?

Section: *Manufacturing & Distribution*

Module: *Inventory Control*

Capability: **Backflush Transaction Support**

How Utilized:

A company manufacturing in a repetitive or JIT environment typically does not want—or need to use—work orders. The traditional work order flow involves creating a specific order for a specific quantity, scheduling the order, checking for the availability of needed materials, allocating the materials, releasing the order to production, kitting the materials, and reporting detailed production activity that occurs as the order is actually processed. In a stabilized, repetitive environment, this is wasted effort. In a JIT environment, materials may be pulled through the system by a method such as kanban, which bears little resemblance to the work order flow described above.

A backflush transaction capability allows the user to simply state the quantity of what was actually produced. There is no need to open a work order or kit materials, which significantly reduces the volume of transactions necessary to be reported in the system.

Ways Supported:

When the user specifies the quantity of the parent item produced, the system automatically creates individual issue transactions for all of the materials that are contained on the parent's standard bill of material.

HI/MIS % Capable:

Almost All

Evaluation Notes:

1. Examine how the system utilizes scrap or yield allowances in calculating the quantity of materials that are automatically issued from inventory.
2. Examine how phantom parts affect the backflush process. Does the system "blow-through" the phantom part and automatically record the issue of the phantom's component material? If there is a positive quantity on hand showing for the phantom, does the system use this quantity first before continuing to record the issue of lower-level components?
3. Check that the system allows the user to specify the location that issued the consumed material. Many companies running in a mixed-mode environment or in the process of implementing JIT will have materials that are used under both backflush and work order control. Typically, these companies will transfer a portion of this common material from the main stockroom to a separate location used to feed the JIT line. The backflush transaction should record the issue of material from this second location, not from the main stockroom.

Section: *Manufacturing & Distribution*

Module: *Inventory Control*

Capability: **Group Component Issue**

**How
Utilized:**

A company manufacturing in a work order environment will typically perform a kitting process in preparation for production of an order. The kitting process involves making sure that all necessary component materials are available and then pulling (finding and collecting) all of them. If the bill of material for the item to be produced is large, hundreds of different items may need to be included in the kit.

Either during or immediately after the kitting process, data must be entered into the system in order to record the issue of the components to the order. If the system does not have a group component issue capability, then the user must record a separate issue transaction for each one of the different components in the kit.

**Ways
Supported:**

The system can record the issuance of an entire kit of component materials to an order upon the input of a single transaction. The individual issue transactions created by the system are based on the standard bill of material for the item being produced.

***HI/MIS %*
Capable:**

Almost All

**Evaluation
Notes:**

1. Ensure that the system also allows for manual overrides of the standard issue amounts. This function is often called *kitting by exception.*

Section: *Manufacturing & Distribution*

Module: *Inventory Control*

Capability: **Physical Inventory Processing**

How Utilized:

Counting, recording, validating, and booking physical inventories is a time-consuming task for many companies. Cycle counting is an effective technique that can be used during the interim periods to measure and control inventory accuracy. Exemplary cycle count results might eliminate the need for a separate full physical inventory. However, if a full physical inventory is required, there are a few software capabilities that are very useful.

One that is beneficial is a system's ability to freeze inventory balances. This allows ongoing inventory transactions to be processed in the system during the days following the count of physical inventory. Without this freeze capability, a company must delay all inventory transaction processing until it has fully validated, approved, and booked the physical inventory, which usually takes several days. The company would be using out-of-date inventory information during this period.

Another useful capability is the support of inventory tags. For a company that has the same component material physically located in many different parts of a stockroom, or perhaps the entire facility, manually aggregating all of the separate counts is very error-prone. With a tag-oriented count, each separate physical location where the component is found can be given its own tag, thereby allowing the system to do the work of aggregating all of the counts. Tag control, tag preprinting, and missing tag reports all contribute to making a tag-oriented physical inventory easier to accomplish and control. The tags do not need to be affixed to the component materials, or even be printed. The key is that a tag-oriented physical inventory process is supported.

Ways Supported:

The system freezes the inventory balances at the beginning of the physical inventory process. Eventually, after the counts have been validated and approved, the system adjusts for the difference between the counted quantity and the frozen quantity. This contrasts with a cycle count type of adjustment that simply overwrites the current inventory quantity with the new cycle-counted quantity.

The system preprints inventory tags that become the basis for recording the actual counts. The tags are sequentially numbered, which assists in identifying lost or incomplete counts.

HI/MIS % Capable:

Many

Evaluation Notes:

1. Examine the mechanics of how the system processes a tag-oriented inventory. Can the tags be printed in order by location? Is there an approval function for the tag count? Is there a missing tag report?

Section: *Manufacturing & Distribution*

Module: *Job Costing*

Capability: **Estimated versus Actual Costs**

How Utilized:

Job-oriented manufacturers constantly need to evaluate the validity of their job estimating function and their ability to actually manufacture within the limits defined by original cost estimates.

Ways Supported:

The system allows the user to specify an original estimated amount of resources and associated costs that should be incurred to complete a job. It also tracks the actual expenditures of resources and the costs that accrue during the performance of a job.

***HI/MIS* % Capable:**

Many

Evaluation Notes:

1. Examine how the system reports the variance between estimated and actual costs for the job. Does the system assist in determining the cause of the variance?

Section: *Manufacturing & Distribution*

Module: *Job Costing*

Capability: **Application of Overhead Costs**

How Utilized: A significant portion of the overall costs in processing a job will relate to overhead resources. The job could not be completed if floorspace in the plant, supporting management personnel, and specialized equipment and tools were not present. The common method used to recognize the value of these resources is to apply a fair share of these overhead costs to each job that is processed. This can provide a more realistic view of the actual profitability of operations.

Ways Supported: The system allocates some of the overhead costs to each job by placing a burden amount on one of the direct job costs, such as labor time, machine time, or perhaps material dollars. The system adds this burden amount to the specified direct cost that accumulates during the completion of the job.

***HI/MIS %* Capable:** **Almost All**

Evaluation Notes: 1. Ensure that the specific methods supported by the software in allocating overhead costs make sense for your company's situation.

Section: *Manufacturing & Distribution*

Module: *Job Costing*

Capability: **Purchasing and Accounts Payable Interface**

How Utilized:	Job-oriented manufacturing often involves purchasing specialized materials to be used on specific jobs. Companies need to keep track of open purchase orders and expected receipts of material that are earmarked for these jobs. The actual costs of the procured materials, along with associated shipping and handling charges, need to be applied to the job. This is especially necessary if the job has been set up on a cost-plus basis, in which the customer pays the actual costs of the required materials, plus an agreed-upon markup.
Ways Supported:	The system ties purchase orders to specific jobs. The processing of vendor billings in accounts payable directly charges the actual material costs to the job.
***HI/MIS %* Capable:**	**Many**
Evaluation Notes:	1. If jobs are processed on a cost-plus basis, ensure that the reporting available from the system contains sufficient detail to support customer billing.

Section: *Manufacturing & Distribution*

Module: *Job Costing*

Capability: **Payroll Interface**

How Utilized:	Because reporting actual costs is often important in job-oriented manufacturing, direct production labor is often tracked. This enables companies to analyze not just the material costs associated with a job, but also the labor costs that have been incurred during the job's processing.
Ways Supported:	The system allows the entry of labor time tied to a specific job. The system then automatically charges the costs associated with this labor time to the job. Two modules in the system require labor time: the payroll module and the job-costing module. Most systems link the two so that the user needs to enter the labor time only once. If the labor time is first entered in the job costing module, the system automatically transfers the total actual hours worked for each employee to the payroll module. If the labor time is first entered into the payroll module, the system also accepts the data necessary to tie it to specific jobs and then automatically transfers this information to the job-costing module.
***HI/MIS %* Capable:**	**Many**
Evaluation Notes:	1. A workaround available for some of the systems that lack a payroll module is the provision of an interface to one of the common third-party payroll processing services.

Section: *Manufacturing & Distribution*

Module: *Lot Tracking*

Capability: **Single-Level Lot Tracking**

How Utilized:	Many companies find it useful to track incoming raw materials by lot. This can enable quality problems to be more easily isolated and traced to the vendor. Finished goods may also be organized by lot. Similarly, this can make it easier to isolate the extent of problems in shipped products and determine the involved customers. Some companies will be (for all practical purposes) mandated by regulatory agencies to keep track of their raw materials and finished goods by lot.
Ways Supported:	The system maintains not just one on-hand quantity, but an on-hand quantity for each lot. For example, a company may have a total of 10 finished units in stock, 6 in lot A and 4 in lot B. When the company ships one of these units to a customer, the user must specify which lot the unit came from. The system is then capable of later reporting the range of customers that received units from any particular lot.
***HI/MIS %* Capable:**	**Many**
Evaluation Notes:	1. Examine how restrictive the system's lot control is. Depending on your situation the system may be either too restrictive or too flexible for your needs. Can you ship a lot-controlled unit without specifying a lot number? Can you specify an incorrect number and force the system to drive the lot quantity negative? 2. Ensure that items can be individually specified as being under lot control. Lot control is burdensome to maintain; therefore a company will want to place only the most critical items under lot control. 3. Examine the types of additional information that can be associated with a lot. Your company may also have a need to keep track of the lot's creation date, a shelf life, certification numbers, or other parametric data.

Section: *Manufacturing & Distribution*

Module: *Lot Tracking*

Capability: **Multiple-Level Lot Tracking**

How Utilized:

Some companies in the food, drug, and electronics industries will need to track lots completely through the production process. This is sometimes referred to as *cradle to grave* lot tracking. To do it properly, the system must be able to track a lot through successive levels in the process. A raw material lot becomes part of a compound, the compound becomes part of an assembly, and the assembly becomes part of a higher level final-assembly that eventually becomes a finished unit in the hands of a customer.

If a problem is encountered by a customer, the user must determine the involved lot, trace it backwards through the successive levels of production, find the problem lot, and then trace back up the levels to determine the range of customers that may be affected. This can be a very difficult and time-consuming task to perform manually.

Ways Supported:

The system maintains a linked history of lot transactions. The usage of a lot in production is tied to the output of the lot being produced. This enables the system to report the ultimate source and destination of lots.

If lot splitting is properly supported, one input lot can be linked to multiple output lots or, in the reverse situation, multiple input lots can be linked to one output lot.

HI/MIS % Capable:

Very Few

Evaluation Notes:

1. Please also see the applicable notes under Single-Level Lot Tracking.
2. Ensure that the system properly maintains linkages. Are all lot issues to a work order tied to all output lots from the work order regardless of the sequence of transactions?

Section: *Manufacturing & Distribution*

Module: *Lot Tracking*

Capability: **Serial Number Tracking**

How Utilized:	Many companies find it useful to serialize their finished goods. For example, personal computers are most often given a serial number. This serial number can be used as the basis of tracking the particular configuration that was shipped, who it was shipped to, and whether it is still under warranty coverage.
Ways Supported:	The system maintains inventory on-hand balances of selected items by serial number. For example, a company may have two finished units in stock. The system keeps track of the fact that these two units are actually serial number 12345 and serial number 12346. When the company ships one of these units to a customer, the company must specify exactly which serial number is being shipped. The functionality is similar to single-level lot tracking, with the lot quantity always being equal to one.
HI/MIS % Capable:	**Many**
Evaluation Notes:	1. Examine how restrictive the system's serial number control is. Depending on your situation the system may be either too restrictive or too flexible for your needs. Can you ship a serial-controlled unit without specifying a serial number? Can you ship a serial number that is not in the system's records as being on hand? 2. Examine the types of additional information that can be associated with a serial number, such as a warranty expiration date.

Section: *Manufacturing & Distribution*

Module: *Lot Tracking*

Capability: **Lot Tracking Integrity with Backflush**

How Utilized:	The backflush transaction capability was described earlier in the Inventory Control module. Some companies need to utilize this type of transaction, which automatically relieves component material quantities, while at the same time maintaining the integrity of their lot traceability.
Ways Supported:	Upon the user specifying the quantity of the parent item produced, the system automatically creates individual issue transactions for all materials contained on the parent's standard bill of material. But before completing the issue transactions, the system prompts the user for the specific lots and quantities involved for all items under lot control. The user then informs the system of the specific lots that were actually used to fill the material issue.
***HI/MIS %* Capable:**	**Very Few**
Evaluation Notes:	1. Examine how the mechanics of this process works. Does the system provide any (or perhaps too much) help to the user in finding the appropriate lot numbers to use? Can the system suggest to the user the lots to be used based on a standard algorithm such as FIFO (first in first out)?

Section: *Manufacturing & Distribution*

Module: *Master Scheduling*

Capability: **Maximum Planning Horizon**

How Utilized:	For purposes of long-range planning, a company's Master Production Schedule may need to extend over several months, perhaps even a few years into the future. Certain events need to be anticipated well in advance, such as the need for a new assembly line.
Ways Supported:	Many systems support a bucketless planning method. Systems that utilize this method will typically have an unlimited horizon, or outside limit on how far into the future can be master scheduled. The bucketed systems will typically have a maximum number of time buckets. If the system uses weekly buckets, a limit of 100 buckets would yield a maximum horizon of just under two years. Regardless of the method used by the system, it is usually advantageous for the system to support a maximum planning horizon of at least 18 months.
***HI/MIS %* Capable:**	**Almost All**
Evaluation Notes:	1. Ensure that the system does not provide for the necessary horizon by simply making the buckets bigger. Some systems let the user define the time period represented by the system's buckets. For example, if a system is limited to only 10 buckets, and the company needs to plan two years into the future, the buckets could be defined as containing three months each. But this is an inferior solution since it will cause a loss of resolution that makes short-term scheduling less effective.

Section: *Manufacturing & Distribution*

Module: *Master Scheduling*

Capability: **Bucketless Scheduling with Bucketed Reporting**

How Utilized:

A bucketless system allows the entry of firm-planned orders, supplies, demands, forecasts, etc. tied to a specific date (e.g., January 16). A bucketed system allows entry of the same information but ties these inputs to predefined time ranges or buckets in the system (e.g., Week 3). Many master schedulers and production planners prefer bucketless systems since they provide the highest possible resolution; that is, if the planner knows the exact date that an order should be completed, the planner can input it into the system with that exact date.

At the same time, many master schedulers and production planners like to review the master schedule expressed in bucketed report format. This is commonly called the horizontal format, where each time bucket is a column on the report. This format facilitates quick review. The system will also have the capability to produce the more detailed vertical format report, which will list the specific order parameters and exact dates.

Ways Supported:

The system allows entry of master schedule data in bucketless fashion with subsequent reporting in both horizontal (bucketed) and vertical (detailed) formats.

HI/MIS % Capable:

Many

Evaluation Notes:

1. Examine how the bucketless systems produce the horizontal report format. Some systems will allow the user to change the specification for the time range of the reporting buckets each time the report is requested. The user then has the option to view the report expressed in weekly, monthly, quarterly, or even yearly buckets.
2. Also examine the horizontal report to ensure that the order and contents of the rows are reasonable. Typically, the last row will be an available-to-promise figure. Is this figure calculated and expressed in a manner that makes it meaningful and usable by your company?

Section: *Manufacturing & Distribution*

Module: *Master Scheduling*

Capability: **Scheduled Flag by Item**

How Utilized:	Typically, only top-level items, major stocked subassemblies, and planning items will appear on a master schedule. It is possible to include all items, all the way down to raw materials, but being selective in choosing which parts appear on the schedule will allow more focused and efficient analysis.
Ways Supported:	The system maintains a flag for each inventory item that controls whether or not the item will appear on the master schedule.
***HI/MIS* % Capable:**	**Almost All**
Evaluation Notes:	1. Ensure that setting the master schedule flag to *no* does not eliminate the generation of computer-planned orders for the item and its lower level components. This is a completely different function for which a separate flag should be used by the MRP module.

Section: *Manufacturing & Distribution*

Module: *Master Scheduling*

Capability: **Consumption of Forecast**

**How
Utilized:**

The master schedule, and in turn MRP, are most commonly driven by a combination of forecast and actual product demand. If the forecast is input as an addition to actual demand, the forecast amount must constantly be changed as new customer orders are booked. Obviously, this is a cumbersome method. The more common method is to input the forecast as the total projection of demand. As customer orders are booked, they consume, rather than add to, the forecast. If actual customer orders exceed the forecast, the higher customer order figure should then be used as the demand input to the master schedule and MRP.

**Ways
Supported:**

The system compares both the forecast and actual demand for an item and uses the greater of the two as the total demand figure on the master schedule.

**HI/MIS %
Capable:**

Almost All

**Evaluation
Notes:**

1. Some systems will let the user specify on an order-by-order basis if the forecast should be consumed by the order quantity. This is useful when unusual, unforecast orders occur, such as a one-time order from a new distributor to supply their initial stock.

Section: *Manufacturing & Distribution*

Module: *Master Scheduling*

Capability: **Planning Bills**

How Utilized: Planning bills are often used to forecast demand when forecasting at an item-by-item level is not feasible. For example, if a company produces computers with 4 memory options, 2 speed options, 3 display options, and 5 disk drive options, the total number of distinct items would be 4 x 2 x 3 x 5, or 120. Forecasting the weekly demand for each of these items for the next 12 weeks would require the input of 1,440 data points. Instead, a planning bill could be set up that includes the base unit and a forecast mix of the available options. Utilizing the planning bill, the input of the 12-week forecast now only takes 12 data points.

Ways Supported: The system supports the maintenance of planning bills of material. On the planning bill, the user specifies the forecast mix of options that can be expected to be demanded by the customers.

***HI/MIS %* Capable:** **Almost All**

Evaluation Notes: 1. Determine if the system can support effectivity dates used in conjunction with planning bills (see the Bill of Material module in this chapter for an explanation of effectivity dates). This can be a useful feature when the mix of options can be expected to change in the future due to special promotions, permanent price changes, or other factors.

Section: *Manufacturing & Distribution*

Module: *Master Scheduling*

Capability: **Family Product Groupings**

**How
Utilized:**

A problem arises for companies that utilize a combination of the two capabilities just discussed, Consumption of Forecast and Planning Bills. When the actual customer orders are booked, they are not for the planning item (planning bill parent), but for a very specific item. How can the system consume the forecast, which has been input for the planning item, with the actual demand that is tied to a completely different item?

One method that has been devised is the concept of product families. If all of the specific items that are encompassed by the planning bill can be considered as members of the same product planning family, their actual demand can be accumulated and applied against the forecast for the entire family.

**Ways
Supported:**

The system enables the user to specify individual end items as belonging to a product family. The system then consumes the forecast for the product family (equivalent to the planning bill) with the demand as it is actually booked for the specific end items.

**HI/MIS %
Capable:**

Very Few

**Evaluation
Notes:**

1. Some of the systems that do not specifically support product family forecast consumption support another concept called *product configuration* (please see the Sales Order Processing Module in this chapter). This can often be an acceptable workaround.

Section: *Manufacturing & Distribution*

Module: *Material Requirements Planning*

Capability: **Bucketless Planning with Bucketed Reporting**

How Utilized:
A bucketless MRP system utilizes the specific dates tied to firm-planned orders, supplies, demands, forecasts, etc., and generates computer-planned orders that are also tied to a specific date (e.g., January 16). A bucketed system utilizes the same information but ties it to predefined time ranges or buckets in the system (e.g., Week 3). Many production planners prefer bucketless systems since they provide the highest possible resolution, that is, if MRP generates a computer-planned order that is due at the very beginning of Week 3, a bucketless system makes this more visible by using the exact due date of January 16.

At the same time, many production planners, materials managers, and buyers like to analyze MRP in a bucketed report format. This is commonly called the *horizontal format,* where each time bucket is a column on the report. This format facilitates quick review. The system will also have the capability to produce the more detailed vertical format report, which lists the specific order parameters and exact dates.

Ways Supported:
The system processes MRP and generates computer-planned orders in bucketless fashion with subsequent reporting in both horizontal (bucketed) and vertical (detailed) formats.

HI/MIS % Capable:
Many

Evaluation Notes:
1. Examine how the bucketless systems produce the horizontal report format. Some systems allow the user to change the specification for the time range of the reporting buckets each time the report is requested (without having to rerun MRP). The user then has the option to view the report expressed in weekly, monthly, quarterly, or even yearly buckets.
2. Also examine the horizontal report to ensure that the order and the contents of the rows are reasonable. Typically, the last row will be a projected on-hand inventory figure, which does not include the effect of computer-planned orders. A quick scan of the figures on this last row, looking for the point in time that it goes negative, provides the user with an easy indication of how soon action must be taken.

Section: *Manufacturing & Distribution*

Module: *Material Requirements Planning*

Capability: **Outside Time Fence**

How Utilized: For long-range planning purposes, the Master Production Schedule may extend over a few years, but very few companies will actually want to plan and release shop orders and purchase orders that far in advance. An outside time fence is used to indicate to MRP that it need not continue calculating net requirements and generating planned orders beyond a certain number of days into the future.

For example, a company may have a 24-month Master Production Schedule but set their MRP outside time fence at 3 months. This can eliminate the generation of huge amounts of meaningless computer planned orders. If the standard order period for an item is one week's supply at a time, MRP would generate an extra 21 months worth (that would be 91 separate orders) for each required item. Even if the user chooses to ignore these superfluous orders, it will cause the system to take much longer to complete the execution of the MRP process.

Ways Supported: The system enables the user to specify an outside time fence, beyond which MRP will not calculate net requirements or generate planned orders.

HI/MIS % Capable: **Almost All**

Evaluation Notes: 1. Some systems will also enable the user to specify the outside time fence on an item-by-item basis. This can be useful in the situation where certain items have exceedingly long lead times.

Section: *Manufacturing & Distribution*

Module: *Material Requirements Planning*

Capability: **Inside Time Fence**

How Utilized:

Within a certain period of time, there is not enough reaction time to act effectively on any suggestion that MRP might give the user. For example, if a shipment of material from a vendor has been sitting in a truck making its way across country for the last week and is expected to arrive tomorrow, a suggestion from the MRP system to change the order due date to Thursday of next week is not of much practical value. An inside time fence indicates to MRP that it need not attempt to replan, cancel, or suggest other planner actions within a certain number of days into the future.

It is very important that the system enables the user to specify the inside time fence (as opposed to the outside time fence) on an item-by-item basis. The minimum reaction time can vary widely between items. For an item that is readily available from off-the-shelf local sources, the inside time fence may be set at 0. For an item that is being purchased from a single vendor who has been given a firm shipment schedule, the inside time fence may be set at 60 days or greater.

Ways Supported:

The system enables the user to specify an inside time fence on an item-by-item basis, within which MRP will not attempt to replan orders or suggest specific planner actions.

HI/MIS % Capable:

Many

Evaluation Notes:

1. Examine how the system handles the situation where an entire order, due to be received within the inside time fence, should be canceled. If, in the example given above, we suddenly no longer have a need for any of the incoming material, is there any way that the system still indicates this to the user? While it may be too late to cancel the order, it would be useful to avoid the cost of unpacking and possibly inspecting the material and then having to repack and ship the material back a few days later.

Section: *Manufacturing & Distribution*

Module: *Material Requirements Planning*

Capability: **Non-nettable Locations**

How Utilized:

Many companies need to keep track of inventory that is not available for use in the production process. For example, a company may use a certain microprocessor chip in the production of a computer product. In total, the company has 200 of the chips on hand. But not all 200 are available for use in production. 25 chips are held in a special location (called "SPARES") to be used as replacement chips in the repair of customers' computers that are returned for service. Fifty chips have failed initial performance testing and are being held in a special location (called "MR" for Material Review) awaiting further diagnostic testing and final disposition. Therefore, only 125 chips are actually available for immediate use in the production of new computers. If we need 200 chips to build our next batch of computers, the system, through MRP calculations, should inform us that another 75 chips need to be acquired.

Ways Supported:

The system enables the user to specify locations as being nettable or non-nettable for MRP purposes. Non-nettable locations indicate to MRP that the inventory quantities held within those locations should not be considered as available for production. In calculating net requirements, MRP includes as available supply only the inventory held in nettable locations and ignores any inventory held in non-nettable locations.

HI/MIS % Capable:

Many

Evaluation Notes:

1. Ensure that the maximum number of non-nettable (and the total number of nettable plus non-nettable) locations supported by the system is adequate.

Section: *Manufacturing & Distribution*

Module: *Material Requirements Planning*

Capability: **Net Change MRP Processing**

How Utilized:	There are two basic methods used in MRP processing, referred to as <u>*net change*</u> and <u>*regeneration.*</u>

The regeneration process, which is often called *re-gen,* always starts from scratch. All items on the inventory file are evaluated against all forecast demand, actual demand, on-hand balances, and planned supplies. The re-gen process encompasses all levels of all involved bills of material for any manufactured items that have a net requirement. The re-gen process makes extensive use of computer resources. It is typically run over a weekend, and may take many hours to complete processing.

The net change process only performs calculations against items that have had a *change* in forecast demand, actual demand, on-hand balance, or planned supply since the last time that MRP was processed. The resulting net requirements, reports, computer-planned orders, and planner exception messages should be the same as would occur with the regen method. The advantage of the net change method is that it can use significantly less computer resources. For example, if changes have occurred to only 50 out of a total of 5,000 items on a company's master file, the net change method will almost certainly be much faster to process than the re-gen method. Net change can make it feasible to run MRP on a daily basis.

Ways Supported: The system supports the net change method of processing MRP. The system automatically keeps track of items that have had a change occur in actual or projected supply or demand and performs MRP recalculation for only these items and their lower level components.

***HI/MIS* % Capable:** **Almost All**

Evaluation Notes: 1. It is advantageous that the system actually supports both net change and re-gen methods. Experience has shown that net change systems will sometimes (although very rarely) lose track of which items need to be replanned or will otherwise develop small glitches. When this occurs a re-gen-based run of the MRP process can be used to get the system back in synch. Failing this option, ensure that the system will allow the planner to manually specify items that need to be replanned and included in the net change MRP run.

2. There is nothing wrong with the re-gen method of processing MRP. The only drawback is the drain on computer resources and associated time required. If a company's files are relatively small and their computer equipment is fast enough to enable MRP to be run as frequently as needed, a re-gen-only system will be acceptable.

Section: *Manufacturing & Distribution*

Module: *Material Requirements Planning*

Capability: **Pegging of MRP Demands**

stabilize (prices)

How Utilized:

After MRP has completed processing, new net requirements figures will be available for all items. Production planners, materials managers, and buyers need to understand how MRP arrived at these figures.

For example, a planner receives a message from the system, after a new run of MRP, that 25,000 reverse-threaded 2-inch brass hex-bolts are required. This seems like an unusual quantity. The planner performs an inquiry in the system to see what is causing the demand for these bolts. The system is able to peg, or show the cause of, the demand for the 25,000 bolts. The system informs the planner that the entire demand for 25,000 is pegged to a single customer order for 5 red wagons. The planner becomes more suspicious, since this would indicate that 5,000 bolts are used in the production of 1 wagon. After further investigation, the planner discovers that there is a mistake on the bill of material for the red wagons. The bill of material correctly specifies the use of *five* reverse-threaded 2-inch brass hex-bolts, but the unit of measure is incorrectly listed as 1,000 count. The demand for the 25,000 bolts is therefore incorrect; only 25 are actually required.

The example given above was very simple. In another example, MRP may be correct. In fact, MRP turns out to be correct the majority of times. The important capability is that pegging of demand is available to allow the planner to easily investigate and validate MRP-calculated requirements figures.

Ways Supported:

The system is able to peg MRP-calculated demands to the customer order, forecast, shop order, or other origin that is causing the demand. A system inquiry or report will list for the user all of the pegged higher level requirements.

HI/MIS % Capable:

Almost All

Evaluation Notes:

1. Most systems will peg demand only one level up. In other words, the system will show the immediate parent of the component in question, but will not automatically show what is causing the demand for the parent. Other systems can peg demand through multiple levels and will show the full chain of parent parts that are causing the demand.

Section: *Manufacturing & Distribution*

Module: *Operations Routings*

Capability: **Standard Operations**

How Utilized:

Many parts may utilize the same operation in their manufacture. For example, a company may employ a standard procedure for the initial inspection of all cast parts before they are allowed to continue further in the production process. The description of this operation on the routing contains or references the detailed steps to be performed in the inspection process. By making this a standard operation and giving it a name, such as "S101", the data input requirement is reduced when adding a new part to the system.

Ways Supported:

When entering a new routing, the user can simply reference the standard operation. This eliminates the need to repeatedly enter all of the detailed steps involved in the standard operation.

HI/MIS % **Capable:**

Many

Evaluation Notes:

1. Does the system allow the user to modify a standard operation that has been copied into a specific routing?
2. If a change is made to the master copy of a standard operation, is that change automatically reflected in all routings that reference that standard operation?

Section: *Manufacturing & Distribution*

Module: *Product Costing*

Capability: **Cost Simulation**

How Utilized:	Manufacturing companies are frequently faced with decisions that will impact the costs of their products. An estimate of this cost impact will influence the decision. For example, a company is considering the purchase of a $75,000 machine that will reduce run times for certain types of operations. The company's management believes the machine should be purchased only if there is an economic payback through a reduction in total manufacturing costs. To estimate this total reduction, the company must consider many factors—the difference in run time, the variable cost applied to the run time, the number of components that will utilize the new machine in their manufacture, the number of final assemblies that contain those components, and the number of these final assemblies that can be expected to be produced in the foreseeable future.
Ways Supported:	The system utilizes the operation routings, bills of material, and master production schedule to automatically provide an estimate or simulation of the projected manufacturing costs. This estimate can then be compared to current figures to determine the impact on product costs and gross margin.
HI/MIS % Capable:	**Very Few**
Evaluation Notes:	1. Examine how the system handles the combination of several changes to cost factors. Can it simulate the combined effect of changing material prices, run times, labor costs, and production volumes on total product costs?

Section: *Manufacturing & Distribution*

Module: *Purchasing*

Capability: **Approved Vendor Maintenance**

How Utilized: A critical component used in production may have very demanding specifications. Only a certain number of vendors may be able to provide these components within the acceptable range of tolerances. The company may require prospective vendors of these components to complete a qualification process, in which their products are tested by the company's engineering or quality group before purchases from this vendor are authorized.

Ways Supported: The system maintains a list of approved vendors on an item-by-item basis. This information can be referenced by users in determining acceptable sources for the placement of purchase orders.

HI/MIS % **Capable:** **Many**

Evaluation Notes: 1. Some systems maintain additional useful information tied to the item/vendor combination. This information may include the vendor's part number, standard unit of measure, prices, lead times, and the original manufacturer (if the vendor is an intermediary supplier).

Section: *Manufacturing & Distribution*

Module: *Purchasing*

Capability: **Blanket Purchase Orders**

**How
Utilized:**
When the demand for certain materials can be confidently projected into the future, it often makes sense to make a long-term arrangement for their supply. In a typical situation, a purchasing manager might arrange with a vendor to provide a six-month supply of the material at an agreed-upon price and terms. But the company does not want the vendor to ship the large quantity of material to cover the full six months immediately. Instead, it is agreed that "releases" will be issued, perhaps weekly, for smaller quantities.

**Ways
Supported:**
The system maintains a blanket purchase order that contains the price and terms that will apply to all releases (shipments) on the order. The user can generate specific releases against the blanket at appropriate times, or an initial schedule of shipments can be specified on the blanket.

**HI/MIS %
Capable:**
Many

**Evaluation
Notes:**
1. Examine if the system maintains a cumulative receipt quantity for the blanket order. This figure may be important for reporting purposes if the arrangement with the vendor commits the company to receive the full quantity within a specified time period.
2. Examine how easy or difficult it is to specify an initial schedule of releases (shipments) and to later change the schedule.

Section: *Manufacturing & Distribution*

Module: *Shop Floor Control*

Capability: **Variance Analysis**

How Utilized:
Variance is the difference between the standard costs to manufacture a product and the costs that were actually incurred. Measurement and analysis of this variance can be important tools for companies to use in controlling and improving their manufacturing operations. Causes of variance include scrap, yield, resource usage rates, resource prices, substitution of alternate materials or methods, and changes in the volume of production.

Ways Supported:
The system accumulates actual costs and can compare those against standards to provide variance figures.

HI/MIS % Capable:
Many

Evaluation Notes:
1. Examine the variance reporting provided by the system. Is the variance expressed as just one total figure or is it broken out by type (cause)? Does the reporting facilitate further analysis to isolate the cause of the variance?

Section: *Manufacturing & Distribution*

Module: *Shop Floor Control*

Capability: **Unplanned Receipts**

How Utilized:	Production processes often yield coproducts and byproducts. (See the discussion of negative quantities in the Bills of Material module.)
	Standard work order processing begins by stipulating a specific quantity of one specific item to be produced. When other items are also produced, they need to be recognized by the system and their value should be reflected in the cost and variance history associated with the work order.
Ways Supported:	The system recognizes the coproduct or byproduct as an unplanned receipt of materials. This receipt is tied to the work order and its value is properly factored into variance computations.
***HI/MIS %* Capable:**	**Many**
Evaluation Notes:	1. A possible workaround to direct support of this capability is for the system to allow the recording of a material issue transaction with a negative quantity.

Section: *Manufacturing & Distribution*

Module: *Yield Reporting and Analysis*

Capability: **Reporting by Cause Code**

How Utilized: When downtime or scrap occurs, it is useful to immediately identify the cause. This enables more effective analysis. For example, knowing that a certain number of rejects were caused by "wrong parts" and another amount was caused by "out-of-tolerance" may be important. And knowing that an unusually large amount of downtime in an operating department was the result of "preventive maintenance," as opposed to "breakdown and repair," may also be helpful information. Through time, this type of information can be used to spot developing trends and thereby take corrective action more quickly.

Ways Supported: In recording certain types of transactions, such as scrap and downtime, the system enables the user to specify a cause code. This information is then available for subsequent reporting and analysis.

HI/MIS % Capable: **Many**

Evaluation Notes:

1. It is also useful for the system to associate downtime and scrap with individual operating departments, machines, standard operations, dates, work shifts, etc. Examine how the system can provide reporting that will help in analyzing the causes of production problems.

Section: *Marketing*

Module: *Sales Order Processing*

Capability: **Time Phased Available to Promise**

How Utilized:

When customers place orders, they specify what they need and confirm a price. Many times, the next question they ask is, "When can you ship them?" If the customer is promised a date that is too late, they may cancel the order and use a different supplier. If they are promised an earlier date, they will be dissatisfied if it is not met.

An accurate answer to the customer's question must be based on a knowledge of the on-hand quantities, preexisting demands, and future supplies due to be received. In many environments, the capability to accurately quote a promised shipping date (and maintain customer satisfaction) is dependent on this knowledge.

This is different than simply knowing the current-available quantity (the quantity on hand less what has already been allocated to other customers). When there is insufficient currently available inventory, available to promise (ATP) information, which takes future incoming supplies into account, allows the order processor to accurately state, "I don't have 300 in stock right now, but I can promise you 200 next week and the remaining 100 in the following week."

Ways Supported:

The system provides an ATP figure for use in promising ship dates to customers.

HI/MIS % Capable:

Many

Evaluation Notes:

1. Is ATP information quickly available to the order processor in the midst of taking an order, or must they suspend the process and run a separate reporting function?
2. ATP should be time phased. The horizontal, bucketed format is probably the best method of presenting the time-phased nature of this information. (See the discussion of bucketed scheduling/reporting in the Master Scheduling module.)
3. Also examine exactly how the system calculates ATP to ensure that it will be usable for order promising purposes.

Section: *Marketing*

Module: *Sales Order Processing*

Capability: **Product Configuration**

How Utilized: Certain types of products can be configured-to-order with different options. For example, a company may offer a personal computer (PC) system for sale that may optionally have five different main memory sizes, three choices of display monitors, four choices of hard disks, three choices of modems, two possible keyboards, and can be shipped with or without an operating system.

The company feels that they have a competitive advantage in being able to offer the customer the ability to configure their PC exactly as they need it. But without specialized support of this configuration activity, the company would need to set up separate part numbers and bills of material for each combination of options that are ordered.

This can grow into a huge amount of part numbers. In the example given above, 720 possible combinations of options can be ordered. A lot of work will be required to maintain part numbers and associated bills of material for each of these 720 configurations. And if the company decides that a network interface card would be another good option to make available with the system, another 720 parts and bills would have to be set up. This would raise the total number of parts on file to 1,440, just to support the sale of one basic PC model.

Automated support of product configuration can eliminate this burdensome requirement. When the customer places an order, individual options from each category can be chosen. There is no need to maintain separate part numbers and bills of material for each possible combination of options.

Ways Supported: The system maintains a base model along with tables of options that can be used to configure units to specific customer orders.

HI/MIS % Capable: **Many**

Evaluation Notes:
1. Some "options" may be mandatory. In the above example, a minimum of one megabyte of memory might be a requirement. Additional memory would be optional. If a similar situation exists at your company, determine if the system can support mandatory options.
2. Some options may influence the choice of other options. In the above example, it might be known that one of the modem choices will not

work properly when used in the same system with the network interface card. Obviously, a customer should not be allowed to order this combination. In another situation the choice of one option may require (as opposed to preclude) the choice of another option. If a similar situation exists at your company, determine if the system can support this interaction of options.

Section: *Marketing*

Module: *Sales Quotations*

Capability: **Quotation Maintenance**

How Utilized: Before customers place an actual order, they may request a quotation from the company. The quotation may specify the pricing, shipping schedule, and other terms that would be available to the customer. In a simple scenario the customer would subsequently approve the quotation. A regular sales order would then be created to mirror the quotation.

Ways Supported: The system allows the entry of a quotation, using the same time-saving tools available during the entry of a regular sales order. The quotation is treated separately by the system. It is visible, but it is not confused with the population of actual orders (e.g., it is not included in backlog). Upon approval, the quotation can automatically be turned into a regular sales order, without forcing the user to reenter information.

***HI/MIS* % Capable:**   **Many**

Evaluation Notes: 1. Look for additional helpful reports, such as a summary of new quotation activity, a listing of quotations older than a specified date, and lost quotation cause code analysis.

Section: *Marketing*

Module: *Sales Analysis*

Capability: **Bookings versus Sales**

How Utilized:	Bookings and sales are two distinctly different concepts. Bookings are orders that are taken (put on the books). Sales are orders that are shipped. There is often confusion over the term *sales*. In some companies, sales refers to bookings and shipments may be given a different name. It is important for a company to be able to analyze both bookings and sales. Current sales activity will have a relatively immediate impact on profitability and liquidity. Bookings activity will have a more distant impact on these factors. Backlog is the result of new bookings less new sales.
Ways Supported:	The software maintains bookings and sales transactions separately and can provide analysis reports of both activities.
HI/MIS % **Capable:**	**Almost All**
Evaluation Notes:	1. A very common question that is frequently asked is, "Based on current bookings, what sales can be expected this month and next month?" Examine the capability of the system to provide the backlog analysis necessary to answer this question.

Section: *Financial*

Module: *Accounts Payable*

Capability: **Receipt and Purchase Order Matching**

How Utilized:	Standard accounts payable procedures will prescribe that all incoming invoices must be matched to receipt documents before the invoices are paid. This can be a laborious, but necessary, control check. After receipt of the invoiced goods has been verified, the invoice is then examined to ensure that it is in agreement with the terms stated in the original purchase order.
Ways Supported:	The system alleviates some of this difficult task by automating the receipt matching process. As incoming materials are processed, electronic "receivers" are maintained in the system for future invoices to be matched against. The receiver may contain a variety of information, but at a minimum it will record the related purchase order, identification of the received material, and the quantity that has been received.
	The system also maintains a record of the details of the original purchase order, and is therefore able to notify the user if the terms of the invoice differ from the purchase order.
HI/MIS % Capable:	**Almost All**
Evaluation Notes:	1. There are a few situations where the invoiced price can be expected to vary somewhat from the price specified in the original purchase order. Examine how the system handles this situation.
	2. There is not always a one-to-one correspondence between invoices and receivers. Examine how the system handles multiple receivers tied to one invoice and vice-versa.

Section: *Financial*

Module: *Accounts Receivable*

Capability: **Application of Interest Charges**

**How
Utilized:**
Applying interest charges to overdue accounts is not only a method of generating additional revenue. Another, and perhaps even more important, benefit can be the effect on accelerating customer payments.

While many companies might like to employ this technique, most decide not to. The clerical overhead is too high. First, there is the calculation of the charge itself. Second, it seems to be a common business practice for customers to pay somewhat late and ignore the interest charge. The company must then either follow up with the customer to collect the small interest charge or enter an adjustment to their account for the amount of the charge.

**Ways
Supported:**
At each statement cycle, the system automatically calculates and applies interest charges to overdue customer accounts.

***HI/MIS* %
Capable:**
Almost All

**Evaluation
Notes:**
1. Since interest charges may vary by customer and perhaps even by order, ensure that the system has the flexibility to handle this.
2. Examine the ease or difficulty in forgiving interest charges. Some systems will require the user to enter a separate credit memo and then apply it against the interest charge. Others will allow the user to cancel the charge with one simple transaction.

Section: *Financial*

Module: *General Ledger*

Capability: **Multiple Company Consolidations**

**How
Utilized:**
For companies that are comprised of several subsidiaries, the monthly task of consolidating each unit's operating results is substantial. This consolidation is necessary for internal management purposes and will almost certainly be required for external reporting purposes.

Manual approaches to this task are time-consuming. Many companies use electronic spreadsheet software to somewhat automate the process. This method is prone to errors and poor controls.

**Ways
Supported:**
The system maintains separate ledgers for each subsidiary entity. Day-to-day transactions are posted directly to the subsidiary ledgers. At the end of a period, the system then automatically combines the financial results from the subsidiaries into a consolidated entity.

***HI/MIS %
Capable:***
Many

**Evaluation
Notes:**
1. If it is possible that the chart of accounts may vary by subsidiary, ensure that the system has the capability to map specific subsidiary accounts to parent accounts. This will eliminate the need for each subsidiary chart of accounts to be identical to the parent chart of accounts.

Section: *Financial*

Module: *International Operations*

Capability: **Multiple Currency Transactions**

How Utilized:	Buying from foreign vendors and selling to foreign customers often involves numerous transactions in foreign currencies. The proper accounting, risk management (hedging), and gain/loss recognition associated with these transactions is time consuming and difficult. If the volume of these transactions is significant, the system must be able to provide automated support.
Ways Supported:	The system can support purchasing, customer order processing, accounts payable, and accounts receivable transactions denominated in foreign currencies. Currency translation tables maintained within the system enable consolidated reporting of outstanding balances and transaction history valued in the company's local currency.
***HI/MIS %* Capable:**	**Very Few**
Evaluation Notes:	1. Ensure that the system has adequate field sizes to support the extremely large numbers that occur with currencies such as lira and yen.
	2. Examine the capability of the system to properly recognize gains and losses.

Section: *Financial*

Module: *International Operations*

Capability: **Foreign Entity Consolidations**

How Utilized: Due to certain legal and tax factors, companies often find it advantageous to set up subsidiaries in foreign countries in which they conduct business. The accounting for each of these foreign subsidiaries will almost certainly need to be conducted in the host country's local currency. Additionally, some countries will require the use of an unconventional chart of accounts.

In order to comply with GAAP (United States generally accepted accounting principles), U.S.-based companies must regularly collect each and every subsidiary's data, perform a complex semihistorical translation of currencies, and consolidate the financial results for final reporting in U.S. dollars.

Manual approaches to this task are very time-consuming. As with regular domestic consolidations, many companies use electronic spreadsheet software to somewhat automate the process. Again, this method is prone to errors and poor controls.

Ways Supported: The system maintains separate ledgers, denominated in the host country's local currency, for each subsidiary entity. Currency translation tables and account-specific translation method designators are maintained within the system. This enables the system to automatically combine the financial results from the subsidiaries into a consolidated entity. The entity's financial statements can then be expressed in the appropriate single reporting currency.

HI/MIS % Capable: **Very Few**

Evaluation Notes:
1. See notes under Multiple Currency Transactions above and under Multiple Company Consolidations in the General Ledger module.
2. The correct translation method to use will vary for different types of accounts. Ensure that the system supports each of the required methods and that the use of these methods can be designated on an account-by-account basis.

Section: *Financial*

Module: *Payroll*

Capability: **Automatic Hour Accruals**

How Utilized:	Many companies allocate certain benefits to employees based on the number of hours worked or on a period-by-period basis. An example would be a company policy in which employees accrue (earn) 2 hours of vacation time for each weekly period in which they work at least 35 hours.
Ways Supported:	The system maintains the rules for accrual of benefits and applies them automatically during each period's processing.
HI/MIS % **Capable:**	**Very Few**
Evaluation Notes:	1. Some systems may be capable of applying ceilings or limits on the accruals. Examine if the system can automatically discontinue accruals after a specified ceiling amount has been reached.

Section: *Other*

Module: *Field Service*

Capability: **Support Call Tracking**

How Utilized:	Companies with extensive field service (or internal customer support) operations will often have a well-developed system to ensure that customer service and support calls are handled quickly and competently. Incoming customer calls may be initially given a control number and assigned to a problem manager. Basic customer site, product, installation details, and warranty status may be made available to the problem manager. If the problem cannot be resolved in a certain period of time, the call may be escalated to the next level in the company's support hierarchy. Reports are generated on a regular basis to ensure that open calls do not remain unresolved and that service response times are at acceptable levels.
Ways Supported:	The system provides automated support of the above-described functions. Calls are automatically assigned a control number. The appropriate problem manager is electronically notified of the call and is sent the necessary background data. Call escalation may occur automatically. Reports can be generated automatically from system-maintained service records.
***HI/MIS %* Capable:**	**Very Few**
Evaluation Notes:	1. If your company charges for service and support, ensure that the system can support the mechanics necessary to capture (and bill) for time and material charges.

Section: *Other*

Module: *Process Control / Data Acquisition Interface*

Capability: **Direct Support of Bar Coding**

How Utilized: Bar coding is a type of automatic identification. It has proven very effective in streamlining and improving the accuracy of data acquisition.

The following example illustrates a simple application of bar coding. A picklist is printed and delivered to the stockroom. Directly next to each of the part numbers printed on the picklist is a barcode representation of the same number. There is also a preprinted, barcoded label affixed to each container in the stockroom. As the stockroom personnel locate each of the specified parts, they utilize a hand-held barcode scanner to scan both the picklist and the container to verify that they are picking the correct part.

Ways Supported: The system can print barcode representations of key data on shop paperwork for subsequent scanning.

Indirect support of bar coding is inherent in almost all systems. The capability to enter bar-coded information is usually entirely independent of the software application and can be easily accomplished.

***HI/MIS* % Capable:** **Many**

Evaluation Notes:
1. Some systems directly support the printing of barcodes. Others will support calls to external programs that perform the barcode printing. Depending on the application, the latter method may be superior since it is more flexible, allowing more logic and customized features to be included in the called external program.

Section: *Other*

Module: *Process Control / Data Acquisition Interface*

Capability: **Batch Input of External Data**

**How
Utilized:**
The unique nature of some processes may lead certain companies to use other, more specialized systems for portions of their operations. These ancillary systems are used as adjuncts to the main system. As an example, consider a semiconductor company that needs to measure several parameters at many process points. As a wafer progresses through the manufacturing process, measurements of oxide thickness, oven time, and temperature readings are fed automatically into a specialized monitoring system. The monitoring system produces histograms and real-time process control charts for immediate analysis.

To avoid the duplication of effort, this specialized system should be able to transfer certain information to the main system. In the example above, an interface between the ancillary system and the main system would record the issue of raw wafers into work-in-process and the receipt of completed wafers into stock.

**Ways
Supported:**
Probably the best way of supporting this type of interface is for the main system to have the capability to accept batches of input from an external data file. The contents of the external data file are treated like keystrokes being input by a user. By processing the incoming data through the normal input programs, all of the standard edits are employed and the proper update of related files is ensured.

**HI/MIS %
Capable:**
Very Few

**Evaluation
Notes:**
1. Given enough time, even the most stable, proven interface will eventually err and attempt to pass improperly formatted data to the main system. Examine how the system handles this situation.

Section: *Other*

Module: *Report Writing*

Capability: **Concurrent Access of Multiple Files**

How Utilized:
In creating new reports, the needed information will sometimes be located in different files. For example, consider a company that buys from and sells to the same outside entity. The entity is both a vendor and a customer of the company. If this entity is overdue making its payments to the company, the company may want to hold their payments going to the entity until the situation is resolved.

To create a report to check for the existence of the above-described situation, the system would need to access both the customer and vendor files. The report would list all entities that were shown to be both overdue by accounts receivable and at the same time due to be paid by accounts payable.

Ways Supported:
The system allows the user, within one report, to select fields from multiple files for inclusion on the customized report.

HI/MIS % Capable
Almost All

Evaluation Notes:
1. Examine if the system will allow the user to specify new relationships between files. In the example above, specifying a relationship between vendor name and customer name would have eased the process of creating the described report.

Section: *Other*

Module: *EDI (Electronic Data Interchange)*

Capability: **Import/Export of Transactional Data**

How Utilized:	Transactional data, such as shipping advice and new orders, can be electronically interchanged between the company and its customers and suppliers. Besides the inherent efficiencies built into this capability, it has the additional benefit of forging closer ties, improved communications, and increased service levels to the company's customers.
Ways Supported	The system allows the automatic input and export of transaction-oriented data. On the input side, this can consist of new customer orders, shipping advice from suppliers, and updated supplier schedules. On the output side, this can consist of new purchase orders to suppliers and order acknowledgments, shipping advice, and invoices to customers.
***HI/MIS %* Capable:**	**Many**
Evaluation Notes:	1. No system can guarantee that it will be immediately able to match up with the unique data formats that may be used by a company's suppliers and customers. But, it is helpful if the system can at least deal with the basic standards, such as ANSI X12 domestically and ISO 9735 (EDIFACT) for international communications.
	2. There are many third-party software products and established service bureaus available to help companies implement EDI and perform some of the difficult technical challenges on an ongoing basis. If the company plans on using one of these products or services, check to see if the *HI/MIS* product under study is already known and supported. If not, it would be prudent to determine the cost required for the third party to add this support.

SUMMARY

This chapter explored some of the capabilities that exist in current *HI/MIS* software products. The capabilities selected for discussion were some of the most advanced, complex, problematic, difficult to find, or otherwise notable capabilities.

Implicit in the approach used in this chapter is the premise that the vast majority of the basic capabilities are fully supported. But to state it explicitly, *HI/MIS* software products do have the capability to serve the critical needs of companies in complex, sophisticated environments. They are capable enough to be given serious consideration as solutions to the information system needs of a wide range of businesses.

6

HI/MIS and World Class Manufacturing

This chapter examines the relationship between *HI/MIS* and World Class Manufacturing (WCM). Companies implementing WCM exhibit a number of specialized needs since the term WCM (as used in this chapter) covers a variety of activities. Unfortunately, no single, dominant acronym describes the collection of techniques, approaches, methodologies, and philosophies that are currently being employed by companies to improve their operations. *World Class Manufacturing* is used here as an "umbrella" to cover this collection of techniques.

The adoption of WCM techniques is becoming a competitive requirement for businesses of all sizes. This is due to strategic changes taking place in the market— the customer is demanding new things of the manufacturer and the manufacturer is facing competition on a global scale.

Manufacturers are finding that customers are increasingly demanding higher quality in the product and are less motivated by brand loyalty in making their buying decisions. High quality, in its most comprehensive definition, means that the product must work right, look right, serve the customer reliably, and be available at a price that is perceived as valuable by the customer.

Also, customers want their products to be available precisely when they need them. Many commercial customers are adopting just-in-time (JIT) processes that require their suppliers to provide quick, accurate, and consistent delivery performance.

The advancement of global markets has increased the level of competition faced by manufacturers. Domestic manufacturers are finding that foreign companies with global manufacturing and distribution capabilities are entering their home markets and meeting their customers' demand for high-quality products. This trend has been accelerated by the increased use of partnering arrangements to achieve this global scale of manufacturing, distribution, and support capabilities.

The need to continuously improve operations in the quest to attain WCM status is clear. However, there are two different schools of thought regarding the role of information systems in this quest.

- The first contends that effective information systems provide a company with a competitive advantage and must be included as an integral part of the attainment of WCM status.
- The second school, focusing on the principles of JIT, believes that sophisticated, complex information systems divert resources away from adding value to the product, are the antithesis of simplification, and are a wasteful activity.

The first school offers several reasons to justify investing in information technology. First, an increasing number of companies have achieved a competitive advantage with information systems. On the marketing side of the business, there are dramatic cases of increased market share being attained by the innovative use of information systems to create new or improved channels. In the production area, there are also impressive cases of companies that have been able to bring new products to market in record time due to the use of advanced computer technology.

Less celebrated, but equally significant, are the competitive advantages that have been achieved by companies of all sizes by implementing manufacturing information systems. Used internally, these systems yield improvements in customer service, reductions in lead times, fewer stock-outs and missed deliveries, reduced inventory levels, reduced costs, and overall better management effectiveness due to an improved ability to rapidly identify developing problems and perform corrective actions. Used externally, these information systems can be used to establish proprietary automated links with customers and vendors.

The second school believes that manufacturers must focus on adding value to the product. Any process or resource that does not add value is waste and should be eliminated. According to this dictum, since complex information systems do not directly add value to the product, they represent a waste of resources and should be eliminated or at least minimized to the greatest extent possible.

This approach is a useful reminder to maintain a clear focus on the business mission. However, running a business requires some minimal level of administrative activity that is not directly a part of production, but is critical to the success and even survival of the business. For example, customers must be billed, vendors and employees paid, and resources for production planned and made available. Moreover, management must understand the financial results of business operations.

Practically all companies will use information systems for much more than just these basic needs. Unfortunately, these information systems are too often used (or misused) to automate wasteful activities or to artificially compensate for real problems. An example of this situation is a sophisticated information system function that utilizes a complex set of meticulously maintained rules and tables to automatically suggest alternate parts to use in production when a primary part is unavailable. This masks the real problem. The company should strive to have the right part, at the right time, available in the right quantity.

Information systems can also be misused by automating needless administrative tasks. Managers who are focused on adding value to their products should examine administrative procedures and completely eliminate those that are superfluous. The essential procedures are then good candidates to be automated if doing so will serve to minimize their cost and complexity.

HI/MIS is consistent with this objective to minimize costs. The costs to acquire and operate an *HI/MIS* are significantly less than those for traditional information systems. An *HI/MIS* solution, then, can support the essential administrative and manufacturing activities with a minimized level of resources.

It is the author's view that *both* schools are correct. It is unarguable that information systems have been used to attain competitive advantages. It is also unarguable that information systems have been misused to automate wasteful activities and institutionalize poor business practices. Reconciling these two schools and developing methodologies for companies to optimize the balance between them could be the subject of an entire book. Hopefully, "thought leaders" will soon address this important area.

The three WCM techniques that have the most direct impact on information system requirements are:

- Just-in-Time (JIT)
- Total Quality Management (TQM)
- Flexible Manufacturing Systems (FMS)

This chapter describes the software functions required to support these key WCM techniques and how *HI/MIS* provides that support.

JIT

Just-in-time (JIT) is most commonly defined as an overall philosophy. One of the cornerstones of the philosophy is the continuing elimination of waste. *Waste* is defined as anything that does not add value to the product. Inventory is viewed as waste and every attempt is made to drive it to its lowest possible level. Material is not produced, or pushed, to downstream processes until called for. The material is pulled through the process, arriving just-in-time.

An important software function that supports this JIT type of material flow is the backflush transaction. This capability allows the user to simply state the quantity of what was actually produced. The volume of transactions necessary to be reported in the information system is significantly reduced since there is no need to open a work order or kit materials.

When the user specifies the quantity of the parent item produced, the system automatically creates individual issue transactions for all of the materials that are contained on the parent's standard bill of material. Almost all current *HI/MIS* products directly support this capability. (Chapter 5 discusses this capability in greater detail and presents notes for evaluating whether this function works appropriately for specific situations.)

Another function, repetitive scheduling, is supported by specialized software functions that eliminate the need of using discrete work orders. There are two possible methods for the planner to utilize in repetitive scheduling. The first is for the planner to specify a *run-rate,* which is the production quantity per day or week, along with an indication of the time period the run-rate is in effect. The second method is to enter the daily or weekly production quantities directly into a table that is maintained by the information system. Many *HI/MIS* products support either one or the other of these two methods for repetitive scheduling.

The support of paperless receipts is another specialized function sometimes involved with JIT. It is becoming more common for paperless receipts to be used, especially when regular shipments of a raw material or subassembly are received daily from one vendor. The materials enter the assembly line in midstream, perhaps through a side bay off the plant floor. Through an agreement with the vendor, the administrative overhead necessary to handle the incoming materials is simplified by eliminating the receipt paperwork. If the end-items are eventually produced properly, then the company must have received the materials from the vendor in the right quantity and quality. The company then pays the vendor based on a count of the end-items that were produced.

Currently, almost no *HI/MIS* products provide direct support for paperless receipts. However, it is often possible to indirectly support this function when there is adequate flexibility in the system's standard functions plus good support of customized reporting.

Another important consideration is that a company implementing JIT will frequently find itself in a mixed-mode manufacturing situation. In this situation, both JIT/backflush flow and traditional work order flow are used concurrently in different parts of the company's operations. Some material currently in inventory will be used in both modes of production.

Typically, the company transfers a portion of this common material from the main stockroom to a separate location that is used to feed the JIT line. As the material is used in production, the backflush transaction in the information system should record its issue from this separate location, not from the main stockroom.

Another challenge related to mixed-mode manufacturing is that the system needs to be able to keep schedules straight when there is a mixture of repetitive scheduling and traditional (firm order) master scheduling. Many *HI/MIS* products currently provide adequate support of these mixed-mode situations.

TQM

Total Quality Management (TQM) is most commonly defined as a comprehensive approach, covering all aspects of a manufacturing organization. One of the fundamental elements of this approach is the methodology referred to as *Statistical Process Control* (SPC). One concept of SPC is that processes are continuously monitored, as opposed to the traditional after-the-fact inspection of completed goods. Among the various elements of TQM, it is SPC that requires the most specialized support from the information system.

One area of support is capturing the parameters of the manufacturing process. These parameters are measurements of the environment at the time the product was being processed. An example from the semiconductor industry is the measurement of parameters such as the temperature of an oven or the thickness of a deposited layer of oxide. Capturing this information enables the data to be correlated with other production metrics in a later quantitative analysis of the factors that affect manufacturing quality.

Current technology enables the information to be acquired in real time through electronic data-acquisition devices. Transferring that information to the manufacturing information system is possible, but doing it requires a customized software application. At this time, there is little actual field experience in automatically updating *HI/MIS* products with information from these data-acquisition devices. Even if an interface can be provided, only a few *HI/MIS* products would have the necessary fields available to record the captured information.

A somewhat related activity associated with SPC is the quick capture of the results of the manufacturing process. While SPC does not focus on inspection of finished goods, there is a focus on monitoring intermediate steps in the process to determine problems as quickly and early in the process as possible. Measurements will often be taken at intermediate steps in the process to record the number of units completed, rejected, and reworked. In addition, it is also viewed as important to record the reason for a less than perfect manufacturing result. For example, for each rejected item, the system might allow the entry of a "reason" code that indicates which of the different types of defects compromised the produced good. Many *HI/MIS* products directly support this type of data-gathering activity.

Once the necessary information has been recorded in the information system, additional SPC techniques can then be employed to isolate the factors at work that are undermining quality. One common technique is to search for trends in the data. This analysis might consist of simply plotting key measurements against time and then visually inspecting the plots. A few *HI/MIS* products directly support this.

A host of more sophisticated SPC techniques are also used to perform statistical analysis on the information. *HI/MIS* products currently support these techniques only through the interfacing of the recorded information to separate third-party statistical analysis products.

The use of control charts has become more and more common. These charts plot real-time measurements of key factors, such as the process parameters or the process results, against upper and lower boundaries. The control chart will then give a clear visual indication of whether a process is in control or whether it is trending towards one of the control boundaries. Heading towards a boundary is a sign that an abnormal influence is affecting the process. This trend triggers activity to identify and fix the problem. Control charts are not directly supported by *HI/MIS* products. Again, the best support for this technique is the timely transfer of the relevant data to a third-party product.

FMS

易感应的

Flexible Manufacturing Systems (FMS) is most commonly defined as an approach to the design of the manufacturing process that enables the responsive and economic production of a wide range of items. It involves standardized equipment cells, quick setups, and operators trained with multiple skills. Each cell is designed to be capable to perform as much of the total process as possible. This serves to dramatically reduce the interprocess transportation time and cost that would otherwise occur. While the cells (sometimes referred to as *machine centers*) are also intended to produce as many different parts as possible, some grouping of similar products and processes will still be necessary to make this cellular configuration feasible.

Product grouping is used to categorize similar products based on certain common product or process parameters. This enables the products in a group to be assigned to a specific workcell or line for efficient production. The workcell is designed to be able to produce any product in the assigned group with a minimal of setup effort and time and with very little manual intervention, such as finding and loading the right tool. Many *HI/MIS* products provide a sufficient number of fields in the item master record to enable the grouping of products to the necessary degree.

Another important FMS-related function is to support alternate routings through the manufacturing process. This means being able to assign a product to one of several possible routes. For example, several workcells or production methods that are in place might be able to manufacture a needed product acceptably. If the primary workcell is busy, the use of an alternate production route may be both expedient and prudent. Only a few *HI/MIS* products allow alternate routings for a product, but many support standard operations and frozen routings, which may be an acceptable work-around.

Tools used in the production process often must be tracked for an FMS to be fully effective. The right tools need to be present for the workcell assigned to the product, and they must be available as the workcell turns to manufacturing the product.

Only a few *HI/MIS* products provide direct support for tracking tools. A common work-around is to include the tool as an item on the bill of material. This somewhat meets the needs of the human operators and schedulers, but many workcells are automated. Automated workcells, working under CNC (Computer Numerical Control), need to be updated on the part to be produced and the tools to be used. Although it is possible to build a software interface between the *HI/MIS* product and the CNC workcell to automate this communication, none is yet on the market.

Providing optimized scheduling can be important with an FMS. Scheduling determines what gets worked on first and assigns the workcell that produces the item. In one sense, scheduling becomes simpler with FMS because of its inherent flexibility. But the increase in the number of alternatives makes optimizing the schedule to maximize throughput and to minimize cost more complex. Also, a technique usually referred to as *mixed-model* scheduling may become necessary to provide adequate line balancing. Planning at the aggregate level is challenging.

At this time, no *HI/MIS* products directly support optimized scheduling for FMS. Again, the best support for this is the timely transfer of the necessary information to a third-party product that is designed specifically for this purpose.

SUMMARY

This chapter examined the software functions required to support the three WCM techniques that have the most direct impact on information system requirements:

- Just-in-Time (JIT)
- Total Quality Management (TQM)
- Flexible Manufacturing Systems (FMS)

The degree of support for these key techniques found in *HI/MIS* products was also examined. *HI/MIS* products either directly or indirectly supported the majority of these WCM techniques.

For companies that aspire to advance even further into the realm of Computer Integrated Manufacturing (CIM), *HI/MIS* can provide support. The open nature of *HI/MIS* products and their operating environments allow them to be integrated with relative ease. *HI/MIS* products can perform competently as the planning and execution components of a comprehensive CIM system.

part 3

WHY UTILIZE *HI/MIS?*

7

HI/MIS Costs

This chapter examines the typical costs incurred with acquiring and operating *HI/MIS* and traditional, non-*HI/MIS* systems. Several of the factors affecting the cost of an information system are presented in the three cases for which costs are estimated. These factors include the size of the company, number of users, number of locations, and the existence of international as well as domestic operations.

The cases increase in order of complexity. The first shows the cost for a relatively small company (around five million dollars in annual revenue) with a small number of users located in one site. In the second case, the costs are presented for a larger company (about 20 million dollars in annual revenue) that operates in a more complex situation. There are several users located at two sites. Finally, the costs for a large organization (approximately 100 million dollars in annual revenue) that has a fairly large number of users are presented. This case also presents the costs stemming from international operations.

The analysis presents *HI/MIS* costs that would be incurred in both the local area network (LAN) and shared processor architectures. For the *HI/MIS* systems, the hardware costs are based on microcomputers or small minicomputers running nonproprietary operating systems.

In all cases, it is assumed that there is no existing equipment already in place. This can distort some of the cost estimates and has a particularly significant effect on the LAN alternatives. For example, a company that has many microcomputers already in place would probably not have to purchase entirely new ones to implement an *HI/MIS* LAN-based alternative. Therefore, the company's required capital investment would be less than the estimates given in this chapter.

For the traditional, non-*HI/MIS* systems, the hardware costs are for a midrange minicomputer in the first case, a large minicomputer in the second case, and both a large minicomputer and a mainframe computer in the third case. It is assumed that all hardware is running proprietary operating systems.

One of the major requirements that affects the cost of the system is the number of users—the greater the number of users, the greater the required performance level and associated hardware costs. The number of users is further classified into concurrent users and active users. For the purposes of this chapter, *concurrent* users will refer to the number of people who are expected to be online or logged-in to the software system at a particular time. *Active* users will refer to the number of people who are actively processing on the system (e.g., entering data, running a report, making a screen inquiry). The number of concurrent users has little effect on system performance. The number of active users is the critical factor. Usually, not all concurrent users are active at the same time. These cases assume that the average number of active users is one-half the number of concurrent users, which is a reasonable rule-of-thumb.

Another factor influencing costs is the level of functionality required in the system. Each of the three cases assume that the companies need integrated manufacturing, financial accounting, and marketing systems support. The estimated costs reflect providing for all of these capabilities.

Estimates are provided for both the initial capital investment and the ongoing expenses incurred to operate the system. The initial capital investment includes the following hardware, operating system software, and related items.

Hardware and Operating System

- Central processor
- File/database server
- Disk storage
- Operating system
- Terminals
- Workstations
- Printers
- Telecommunications equipment
- Site preparation

Other items that are purchased initially are the primary applications software product and a moderate amount of software coding that is assumed to be necessary to customize the product for the special needs of the company. The applications software is divided into two categories, domestic and international. The international category captures the cost of additional software licenses that would need to be purchased to run on the separate hardware systems physically located at the international sites.

Applications Software and Custom Coding

- Domestic applications

- International applications
- Custom coding

A company incurs other costs in purchasing an information system. The estimates include costs for bringing in a moderate amount of outside assistance to help in implementing the system. Also, the estimates include the costs for product training and for taxes that would apply on the acquisition.

Additional Resources

- External implementation assistance
- Product training
- Taxes

The estimates for operating the information system include the ongoing depreciation and amortization charges for the items that the company capitalizes. These estimates assume that the acquired products and services will be written off over a five-year period.

Depreciation/Amortization

- Hardware and operating system software
- Applications software and custom coding
- Additional resources (if capitalized)

Hardware needs to be maintained—from time to time, pieces of equipment need to be repaired or replaced. Software needs to be supported by the vendor— from time to time questions will arise, bugs will occur, and new upgraded releases of the software may become available. The estimates assume that maintenance/support contracts are utilized and their costs are based on a percentage of the initial hardware and software purchase prices.

Maintenance/Support

- Hardware and operating system software
- Applications software and custom coding

Companies that have users in multiple sites can be expected to incur telecommunications costs for transmitting data to and from the remote sites and the central system. The estimates for the companies having multinational operations also include a separate "international" category to illustrate these additional costs.

Telecommunications

- Domestic
- International

The information systems need at least a minimal level of staff to support them. The people supporting general system operations (such as the hardware, operating systems, and telecommunications) are listed as "technical systems support." Those providing support at the application level (such as systems analysts, internal trainers, and applications level programmers) are listed as "applications support."

Personnel Resources

- Technical systems support
- Applications support

The figures used in the estimates are based on the actual costs, at the time this book is being written, for representative software and hardware solutions. The representative software products chosen for both the *HI/MIS* and non-*HI/MIS* solutions were limited to the high-end industry leaders. This should provide the most fair and realistic comparison.

CASE 1: FOUR CONCURRENT/TWO ACTIVE USERS

Case 1 is a manufacturing company with annual revenue of around five million dollars that operates from one site. Four concurrent users, with an average of two actively using the system at any one time, should be sufficient to support the volume of transactions typically occurring in a company of this size, although this number can certainly vary from company to company.

The cost estimates in Tables 7-1, 7-2, and 7-3 apply to Case 1. Table 7-1 presents the estimates for the initial capital investment in the information system. The estimates for the *HI/MIS* alternatives in both the LAN and shared processor architectures are about the same. However, the estimated costs for the non-*HI/MIS* alternative are significantly higher.

Hardware and operating system costs are estimated at less than half of the total investment for each of the three alternatives. The cost of the applications software and the services to implement the system are estimated at 70 percent of the total investment for the *HI/MIS* LAN alternative, 77 percent for the *HI/MIS* shared processor alternative, and 60 percent of the non-*HI/MIS* minicomputer alternative.

External implementation assistance and product training costs are estimated to be substantially lower for the *HI/MIS* alternatives. This is due to the superior user interface and ease-of-use features that make these products significantly easier to train on and also somewhat less difficult to implement.

All three components of initial investment have higher estimated costs for the non-*HI/MIS* alternative. The total estimated cost for the non-*HI/MIS* alternative is about three times as high as the *HI/MIS* alternatives. The *HI/MIS* alternatives produce an initial savings of approximately $80,000.

The expenses estimated for operating the system are presented in Table 7-2. Because the initial estimated capital investment in the non-*HI/MIS* alternative is greater than for either *HI/MIS* alternative, the depreciation expense for the non-*HI/MIS* alternative is correspondingly greater as well.

TABLE 7-1 ESTIMATED CAPITAL INVESTMENT

CASE 1
FIVE-MILLION-DOLLAR COMPANY WITH
FOUR CONCURRENT/TWO ACTIVE USERS

	HI/MIS LAN	*HI/MIS* Sh-Proc.	Non-*HI/MIS* Minicomputer
A. Hardware and Operating System			
1. Central processor		$ 2,000	$ 40,000
2. File/database server	$ 3,000		
3. Disk storage	2,250	2,250	4,500
4. Operating system	1,500	1,000	5,000
5. Terminals		2,000	2,000
6. Workstations	4,000		
7. Printers	1,000	1,000	1,000
8. Communications equipment			
9. Network equipment	1,000		
10. Site preparation	1,500	1,500	2,000
Subtotal	14,250	9,750	54,500
B. Applications Software and Custom Coding			
1. Domestic applications	15,000	15,000	40,000
2. International applications			
3. Custom coding			
Subtotal	15,000	15,000	40,000
C. Additional Resources			
1. External implementation assistance	15,000	15,000	30,000
2. Product training	4,000	4,000	8,000
3. Taxes	1,463	1,238	4,725
Subtotal	20,463	20,238	42,725
TOTAL	$49,713	$44,988	$137,225

Similarly, due to the level of the initial cost, the total annual maintenance expense estimated for the non-*HI/MIS* alternative ($11,595) is more than three times greater than for the *HI/MIS* LAN ($3,668) or for the *HI/MIS* shared processor alternative ($3,173).

The largest component of ongoing costs is the additional personnel required to support the information system. All three alternatives require both technical and application support, but the estimated additional expense for either of the *HI/MIS* alternatives ($30,000) is only 57 percent of that for the non-*HI/MIS* alternative ($52,500).

The amount of ongoing system support resources should be substantially less for the *HI/MIS* alternatives. The Technical Systems Support position should be easier and require less time since the operating environment will be less complex. The cost for less than half of one headcount is estimated for this function. This is consistent with actual experience in the field, where typically an average of one day per week is adequate to provide the technical and administrative support for *HI/MIS* implementations of this size. The Applications Support job should also be somewhat easier due to the superior user interface, ease-of-use, and report-writing features that will enable end users to be more self-sufficient.

The total estimated annual operating expenses for the non-*HI/MIS* alternative is a little over twice as high as the *HI/MIS* alternatives. The *HI/MIS* alternatives produce a savings of approximately $50,000 per year.

If we assume that the system will have a useful life of five years, a total life-cycle system cost can be developed. Certain expenditures occur immediately, while others are paid throughout the useful life of the system. By discounting those future cash flows at 10 percent, over the five-year period, a total five-year system cost can be calculated and expressed in today's dollars. This figure will be referred to as the Total DCF (Discounted Cash Flow) System Cost. It is a combi-

TABLE 7-2 ESTIMATED ANNUAL OPERATING EXPENSES

CASE 1
FIVE-MILLION-DOLLAR COMPANY WITH
FOUR CONCURRENT/TWO ACTIVE USERS

	HI/MIS LAN	*HI/MIS* Sh-Proc.	Non-*HI/MIS* Minicomputer
A. Depreciation/Amortization			
1. Hardware and operating system	$ 2,850	$ 1,950	$10,900
2. Applications software and custom coding	3,000	3,000	8,000
3. Additional resources (if capitalized)	4,093	4,048	8,545
B. Maintenance			
1. Hardware and operating system	1,568	1,073	5,995
2. Applications software and custom coding	2,100	2,100	5,600
C. Telecommunications			
1. Domestic			
2. International			
D. Personnel Resources			
1. Technical systems support	15,000	15,000	30,000
2. Applications support	15,000	15,000	22,500
TOTAL	$43,611	$42,171	$91,540
Percent of Sales	0.9%	0.8%	1.8%

TABLE 7-3 TOTAL SYSTEM LIFE-CYCLE COSTS—DISCOUNTED CASH FLOW
(Five Years @ 10% Discount Rate)

CASE 1
FIVE-MILLION-DOLLAR COMPANY WITH
FOUR CONCURRENT/TWO ACTIVE USERS

	HI/MIS **LAN**	*HI/MIS* **Sh-Proc.**	**Non-***HI/MIS* **Minicomputer**
A. Depreciation/amortization	$ 49,713	$ 44,988	$137,225
B. Maintenance	14,384	12,443	45,477
C. Telecommunications			
D. Personnel resources	117,663	117,663	205,911
TOTAL	$181,760	$175,094	$388,613

nation of the initial purchase costs plus five years of operating expenses, expressed in today's dollars.

Table 7-3 shows the estimated Total DCF System Costs. It is interesting to note that the cost of the additional personnel needed to provide ongoing support to the system is the largest single cost component. This additional personnel resource is more costly than the hardware and operating system software.

The total estimated DCF cost for the non-*HI/MIS* alternative ($388,613) is about twice that for the *HI/MIS* alternatives in either the LAN ($181,750) or the shared processor ($175,094) environments. The *HI/MIS* alternatives produce a total five-year savings of approximately $200,000.

CASE 2: 16 CONCURRENT/8 ACTIVE USERS

Case 2 is a manufacturing company generating around $20 million in revenue annually and operating from two sites. The volume of transactions at this company will require 16 concurrent users, about 8 of whom are typically active at a particular time.

The cost estimates in Tables 7-4, 7-5, and 7-6 apply to Case 2. Table 7-4 presents the estimates for the initial capital investment in the information system.

Hardware and operating system estimated costs are a relatively small component of the total costs for each of the three alternatives. For the *HI/MIS* alternatives, these costs are 38 percent in the LAN environment and 23 percent in the shared processor environment. For the non-*HI/MIS* alternative, these costs are still only 31 percent of the total. The largest component of the estimated total cost for all three alternatives is for the applications software and the services to implement the system.

Again, all three components of estimated initial investment are more expensive for the non-*HI/MIS* alternative. The total estimated cost for the non-*HI/MIS* alternative is about two times as high as the *HI/MIS* alternatives. The *HI/MIS* alternatives produce an initial savings of approximately $130,000.

The expenses estimated for operating the system are presented in Table 7-5. Because the initial estimated capital investment in the non-*HI/MIS* alternative is greater than for either *HI/MIS* alternative, the depreciation expense for the non-*HI/MIS* alternative is correspondingly greater as well. Also, the higher ini-

TABLE 7-4 ESTIMATED CAPITAL INVESTMENT

CASE 2
20-MILLION-DOLLAR COMPANY WITH
16 CONCURRENT/8 ACTIVE USERS

	HI/MIS LAN	*HI/MIS* Sh-Proc.	Non-*HI/MIS* Minicomputer
A. Hardware and Operating System			
1. Central processor		$ 4,000	$ 50,000
2. File/database server	$ 4,000		
3. Disk storage	4,500	4,500	9,000
4. Operating system	4,000	1,000	5,000
5. Terminals		8,000	8,000
6. Workstations	26,000		
7. Printers	4,000	4,000	4,000
8. Communications equipment	2,000	2,000	2,000
9. Network equipment	4,000		
10. Site preparation	4,500	4,500	5,000
Subtotal	53,000	28,000	83,000
B. Applications Software and Custom Coding			
1. Domestic applications	30,000	30,000	85,000
2. International applications			
3. Custom coding	5,000	5,000	10,000
Subtotal	35,000	35,000	95,000
C. Additional Resources			
1. External implementation assistance	30,000	30,000	45,000
2. Product training	16,000	16,000	32,000
3. Taxes	4,400	3,150	8,900
Subtotal	50,400	49,150	85,900
TOTAL	$138,400	$112,150	$263,900

tial cost for the non-*HI/MIS* alternative means that its total annual maintenance expense ($22,430) is considerably higher than either the *HI/MIS* LAN alternative ($10,730) or the *HI/MIS* shared processor alternative ($7,980).

The additional personnel resources needed to support the system is the largest annual operating expense. Providing the technical and application support for either of the two *HI/MIS* alternatives is estimated to be only 38 percent of the cost for the non-*HI/MIS* alternative. The reasons for this lesser amount of required personnel resources were discussed earlier in Case 1.

The total estimated annual operating expenses for the non-*HI/MIS* alternative is a little over twice as high as the *HI/MIS* alternatives. The *HI/MIS* alternatives produce a savings of approximately $110,000 per year.

If we again assume that the system will have a useful life of five years, the total life-cycle system cost can be developed. Table 7-6 shows the estimated Total DCF System Costs.

The total estimated DCF cost for the non-*HI/MIS* alternative ($846,060) is

TABLE 7-5 ESTIMATED ANNUAL OPERATING EXPENSES

CASE 2
20-MILLION-DOLLAR COMPANY WITH
16 CONCURRENT/8 ACTIVE USERS

	HI/MIS LAN	*HI/MIS* Sh-Proc.	Non-*HI/MIS* Minicomputer
A. Depreciation/Amortization			
1. Hardware and operating system	$10,600	$ 5,600	$ 16,600
2. Applications software and custom coding	7,000	7,000	19,000
3. Additional resources (if capitalized)	10,080	9,830	17,180
B. Maintenance			
1. Hardware and operating system	5,830	3,080	9,130
2. Applications software and custom coding	4,900	4,900	13,300
C. Telecommunications			
1. Domestic	6,000	6,000	6,000
2. International			
D. Personnel Resources			
1. Technical systems support	15,000	15,000	60,000
2. Applications support	30,000	30,000	60,000
TOTAL	$89,410	$81,410	$201,210
Percent of Sales	0.4%	0.4%	1.0%

TABLE 7-6 TOTAL SYSTEM LIFE-CYCLE COSTS—DISCOUNTED CASH FLOW
(Five Years @ 10% Discount Rate)

CASE 2
20-MILLION-DOLLAR COMPANY WITH
16 CONCURRENT/8 ACTIVE USERS

	HI/MIS LAN	*HI/MIS* Sh-Proc.	Non-*HI/MIS* Minicomputer
A. Depreciation/amortization	$138,400	$112,150	$263,900
B. Maintenance	42,084	31,298	87,973
C. Telecommunications	23,533	23,533	23,533
D. Personnel resources	176,495	176,495	470,654
TOTAL	$380,512	$343,476	$846,060

about twice that for the *HI/MIS* alternatives in either the LAN ($380,512) or the shared processor ($343,476) environments. The *HI/MIS* alternatives produce a total five-year savings of approximately $500,000.

CASE 3: 64 CONCURRENT/32 ACTIVE USERS

Case 3 is a manufacturing company that produces an annual revenue of about 100 million dollars. The company operates from several sites. To illustrate the impact of international operations on costs, this case also assumes that a number of the sites are in foreign countries. Let us further assume that the volume of transactions at this company will require a total of 64 concurrent users, about 32 of whom are typically active at a particular time. Approximately half of the users are located at a single domestic site.

The cost estimates in Tables 7-7, 7-8, and 7-9 apply to Case 3. Because of the scale of this company's operations, a fourth alternative has been added—a non-*HI/MIS* software product running in a mainframe environment.

The estimates for the initial capital investment in the information system are presented in Table 7-7. Again, the estimated total acquisition costs for the non-*HI/MIS* alternatives are higher than for the *HI/MIS* alternatives. It is interesting to note the wide difference between the two non-*HI/MIS* alternatives. The non-*HI/MIS* alternative in the minicomputer environment is estimated to cost $699,450, as compared to the non-*HI/MIS* alternative in the mainframe environment, which is estimated to weigh in at a hefty $1,748,400.

It is also interesting to note that the hardware expense for both of the *HI/MIS*

TABLE 7-7 ESTIMATED CAPITAL INVESTMENT

CASE 3
100-MILLION-DOLLAR COMPANY WITH
64 CONCURRENT/32 ACTIVE USERS

	HI/MIS **LAN**	*HI/MIS* **Sh-Proc.**	**Non-*HI/MIS*** **Minicomputer**	**Non-*HI/MIS*** **Mainframe**
A. Hardware & Operating System				
1. Central processor		$ 12,000	$125,000	$ 500,000
2. File/database server	$ 8,000			
3. Disk storage	18,000	18,000	36,000	36,000
4. Operating system	8,000	5,000	10,000	50,000
5. Terminals		32,000	32,000	32,000
6. Workstations	119,000			
7. Printers	16,000	16,000	16,000	16,000
8. Communications equipment	6,000	6,000	7,000	14,000
9. Network equipment	14,500			
10. Site preparation	18,500	6,000	18,000	50,000
Subtotal	208,000	95,000	244,000	698,000
B. Applications Software & Custom Coding				
1. Domestic applications	45,000	45,000	120,000	750,000
2. International applications	90,000	90,000	85,000	
3. Custom coding	20,000	20,000	40,000	40,000
Subtotal	155,000	155,000	245,000	790,000
C. Additional Resources				
1. External implementation assistance	60,000	60,000	90,000	90,000
2. Product training	64,000	64,000	96,000	96,000
3. Taxes	18,150	12,500	24,450	74,400
Subtotal	142,150	136,500	210,450	260,400
TOTAL	$505,150	$386,500	$699,450	$1,748,400

alternatives approaches the cost of the non-*HI/MIS* minicomputer alternative. This is because the *HI/MIS* hardware would need to be physically resident in all of the individual sites. The non-*HI/MIS* minicomputer hardware cost estimate is based on only two machines. The assumption is that the total system would be configured with a midrange minicomputer residing at the primary domestic site and another smaller minicomputer at one primary foreign site. Only inexpensive terminals would therefore be required at each of the individual remote locations. However, the downside is telecommunication costs. Notice in Table 7-8 the increased telecommunication costs that are estimated to occur when this configuration is used.

All three components of estimated initial investment are more expensive for the non-*HI/MIS* alternatives. The least expensive alternative, the *HI/MIS* shared processor, is estimated at only 55 percent of the total estimated cost for the non-*HI/MIS* minicomputer alternative and at only 22 percent of the cost for the non-*HI/MIS* mainframe alternative. Even when compared to the lower of the two non-*HI/MIS* alternatives, the *HI/MIS* alternatives will still produce an initial savings in the range of $200,000 to $300,000.

The operating expenses for the systems are presented in Table 7-8. Again, due to the correspondingly higher initial investment costs, the non-*HI/MIS* alternatives show higher depreciation expenses and ongoing maintenance expenses.

The largest component of ongoing costs continues to be the additional personnel required to support the information system (with the exception of the non-*HI/MIS* mainframe alternative, where it is approximately equal to the annual depreciation/amortization costs). All four alternatives require both technical and application support, but the estimated additional expense for either of the *HI/MIS* alternatives ($120,000) is only 50 percent of that for the non-*HI/MIS* minicomputer alternative ($240,000) and only 40 percent of that for the non-*HI/MIS* mainframe alternative ($300,000).

TABLE 7-8 ESTIMATED ANNUAL OPERATING EXPENSES

CASE 3
100-MILLION-DOLLAR COMPANY WITH
64 CONCURRENT/32 ACTIVE USERS

	HI/MIS LAN	*HI/MIS* Sh-Proc.	Non-*HI/MIS* Minicomputer	Non-*HI/MIS* Mainframe
A. Depreciation/Amortization				
1. Hardware and operating system	$ 41,600	$ 19,000	$ 48,800	$139,600
2. Applications software and custom coding	31,000	31,000	49,000	158,000
3. Additional resources (if capitalized)	28,430	27,300	42,090	52,080
B. Maintenance				
1. Hardware and operating system	22,880	10,450	26,840	76,780
2. Applications software and custom coding	21,700	21,700	34,300	110,600
C. Telecommunications				
1. Domestic				
2 International	12,000	12,000	60,000	150,000
D. Personnel resources				
1. Technical systems support	60,000	60,000	120,000	180,000
2. Applications support	60,000	60,000	120,000	120,000
TOTAL	$277,610	$241,450	$501,030	$987,060
	=======	=======	=======	=======
Percent of Sales	0.3%	0.2%	0.5%	1.0%

Even the least expensive of the non-*HI/MIS* alternatives involves estimated annual operating expenses that are about two times as high as the *HI/MIS* alternatives. The *HI/MIS* alternatives produce a savings of approximately $250,000 per year compared to the non-*HI/MIS* minicomputer alternative and about $700,000 per year compared to the non-*HI/MIS* mainframe alternative.

By again assuming that the system will have a useful life of five years, the total life-cycle system cost can be developed. Table 7-9 shows the estimated Total DCF System Costs for the four alternatives.

The total DCF estimated costs for the *HI/MIS* alternatives are far less than those for the non-*HI/MIS* alternatives. The total DCF estimated costs for the *HI/MIS* LAN ($1,197,717) and the *HI/MIS* shared processor ($1,030,315) are only a fraction of the estimated costs for the non-*HI/MIS* minicomputer ($2,115,882) and the non-*HI/MIS* mainframe ($4,248,277).

The *HI/MIS* alternatives produce a total five-year savings of approximately one million dollars compared to the non-*HI/MIS* minicomputer alternative and approximately three million dollars compared to the non-*HI/MIS* mainframe alternative.

SUMMARY

The three cases presented in this chapter illustrated the costs associated with *HI/MIS* and non-*HI/MIS* alternatives. It was demonstrated that for small, medium, and large companies, the *HI/MIS* alternative cost significantly less to purchase and operate. Figures 7-1, 7-2, and 7-3 summarize these findings.

TABLE 7-9 TOTAL SYSTEM LIFE-CYCLE COSTS—DISCOUNTED CASH FLOW
(Five Years @ 10% Discount Rate)

CASE 3
100-MILLION-DOLLAR COMPANY WITH
64 CONCURRENT/32 ACTIVE USERS

	HI/MIS LAN	*HI/MIS* Sh-Proc.	Non-*HI/MIS* Minicomputer	Non-*HI/MIS* Mainframe
A. Depreciation/amortization	$ 505,150	$ 386,500	$ 699,450	$1,748,400
B. Maintenance	174,848	126,096	239,798	734,926
C. Telecommunications	47,065	47,065	235,327	588,317
D. Personnel resources	470,654	470,654	941,307	1,176,634
TOTAL	$1,197,717	$1,030,315	$2,115,882	$4,248,277

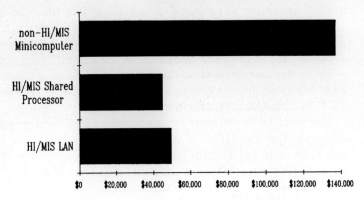

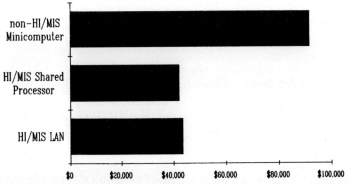

Figure 7-1. Case 1—Five Million Dollar Company With Four Concurrent/Two Active Users.

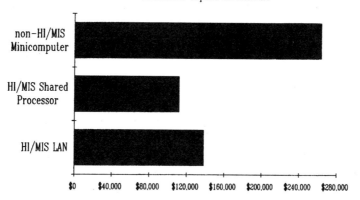

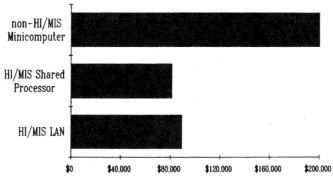

Figure 7-2. Case 2—Twenty Million Dollar Company With Sixteen Concurrent/Eight Active Users.

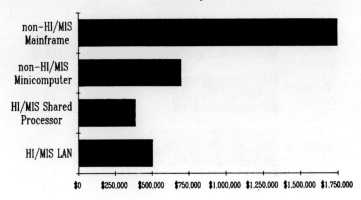

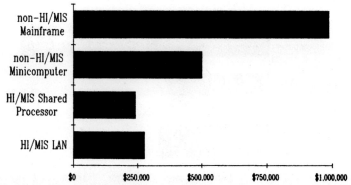

Figure 7-3. Case 3—One Hundred Million Dollar Company With Sixty-Four Concurrent/Thirty-two Active Users.

8

HI/MIS Benefits

This chapter examines the benefits that can be derived from implementing an *HI/MIS*. The first part of the chapter discusses the benefits inherent in all information systems. It makes sense to consider these, since *HI/MIS* is the key to making the implementation of *any* fully functional system a possibility for many companies. Finally, the advantages specific to *HI/MIS* are examined.

Some of the most important benefits that can be derived from any fully functional information system are in the area of customer service. Improvements in customer service can result from:

- More accurate order promising
- Improved order status tracking
- Reduced lead times
- Higher customer satisfaction through better performance

Accurate order promising is often a key to keeping customers satisfied. Just after the customer confirms the product desired and its price, they want to know when the company will ship it. Customers want an accurate, dependable answer to this question.

The system's ability to accurately keep track of current inventory levels is, of course, the starting point in correctly answering this question. Additionally, the system's support of a Master Production Schedule and MRP enable the company to see beyond just its current inventory. By looking at work-in-process, open purchase orders, and firm production plans, the system projects available-to-promise (ATP) quantities of the needed product. With this information, the company can see how many units of the product will be available to ship in the future and precisely when they can be promised to the customer.

The system keeps track of the promised shipping date. This date becomes the key parameter in planning shipments, allocating available inventory, and measuring the company's on-time delivery performance. The system is also able to keep track of the date the customer would like the products (their requested ship date). If the inventory becomes available earlier than the promised date, the customer's requested ship date can be used to determine if an early shipment of the product is advantageous.

All orders in backlog are made visible to the company's responsible personnel. They can therefore manage and optimize shipments to provide the best level of overall customer satisfaction. There are times when partial shipments may be necessary. The system can keep track of whether this is acceptable to the customer and, when a partial shipment is made, the system will keep track of the remaining products and quantities (backorders) that are still owed to the customer.

Order status tracking can be greatly improved with the help of an information system. The quotation, order approval, allocation, and shipping cycle can be streamlined. But the biggest advantage is that orders simply do not get lost as they flow through this cycle. When the customer makes an inquiry about the status of an order, the system can accurately find the order, report on its current status, and determine where it is in the cycle.

No matter how well the company complies with its promised shipping dates, customers may still be dissatisfied if these dates are too far out in the future. The system can help reduce this lead time between customer request and actual ship dates in at least two ways. The first is through better planning and management of forecast. The system can't guarantee that the forecast is accurate, but it can automate some of the important mechanics necessary to keep it updated and can integrate it with the rest of the planning processes. Secondly, the improved visibility and management of actual backlog can yield an overall reduction in average lead time.

The last factor that affects an improvement in customer service is simply better performance. Performance can be measured in several ways. For companies that typically ship immediately from stock, the number of stock-outs may be an important performance measure. For companies that pride themselves on meeting their promised ship dates, the number of missed ship dates or number of days late will be an important measure. For practically all companies, the number of partial order and partial line-item shipments will be important. A well implemented, fully functional information system can help improve all of these performance measures.

In addition to improvements in customer service, a second general area of benefit that can be derived from a fully functional information system is its support of World Class Manufacturing (WCM) activities. The implementation of WCM philosophies, techniques, and tools (see the discussion in Chapter 6) have their own implicit benefits. Effective information systems help, and in some cases are integral, to achieving these benefits. An example of this can be seen in the way information systems can be used to support Total Quality Management (TQM) activities.

TQM measurement and control activities can be significantly enhanced by the effective use of an information system. The ability to measure, monitor, improve, and control quality is improved through:

- The availability of reliable process information, measurements of what happened during the production process, and the conditions that were in effect at the time of production
- The availability of field information, field failure analysis, and the correlation of this information back to the original production data
- The ability to monitor and control processes in real time, enabling corrective action to be taken before scrap or poor quality parts are produced
- The ability to statistically analyze all of this acquired data

Providing better information more quickly is another important advantage of an information system. Management response time is improved due to an enhanced ability to rapidly identify developing problems. Corrective actions can be taken before developing problems result in scrap, obsolescence, rework, or field failures.

Cost analysis can also be greatly facilitated by an information system. Opportunities for cost reductions and process improvements can be identified through the availability of reliable costing information. This information can vary in its format. Some companies attempt to capture and analyze actual costs on an ongoing basis. Other companies periodically set up standard costs that serve as benchmarks for the generation and analysis of variances. Others use a combination of these methods. An effective information system is also a practical requirement for companies that wish to utilize certain costing methodologies, such as product life cycle or activity-based costing.

No discussion of benefits to be derived from a manufacturing-oriented information system would be complete without mentioning potential inventory reductions. Well implemented systems have been shown to produce dramatic reductions in inventory levels. With this comes an increase in the availability of capital, improvements to ROI (return on investment), and reductions in inventory carrying costs and floor space requirements.

The resulting reduction in inventory carrying costs may have the most direct and immediate impact on the company's bottom line. It is quite easy, in most industries, to show that it costs in excess of 20 percent annually to carry inventory. In other words, it costs a company $2 million on their bottom line to carry a $10 million inventory for a year. While this figure may initially seem high, consider the following average costs for carrying inventory:

Interest Expense	10 %
Operational Costs	
obsolescence	
stock movement	
periodic counting	
shrinkage	6 %

Floor Space Costs
    depreciation/rent
    utilities
    maintenance   3 %

Taxes/Insurance
    property taxes
    liability insurance
    casualty insurance   1 %

Total Annual Carrying Costs   20 %

This is a fairly conservative estimate of annual costs associated with carrying inventory. A case could be made that the actual costs are in excess of this. This is especially true in high-technology industries where short product life cycles and high engineering change activity can cause rapid obsolescence.

The final benefit that can be derived from any fully functional information system is the more efficient use of personnel. An entire range of activities are streamlined and facilitated by an effective information system. This can have a pervasive effect on a company, making personnel from all functional areas more efficient in performing their work. This can allow a company to meet its growth requirements with minimal increase in headcount. It also enables existing personnel to refocus their energies away from tedious, inefficient tasks and begin to concentrate on more valuable improvement activities.

HI/MIS Added Benefits

Like the other fully functional systems, *HI/MIS* can also yield the benefits detailed above. But there are additional benefits that are specific to *HI/MIS*. One very obvious benefit is simply the cost. *HI/MIS* have significantly lower initial costs for both the software and the hardware. (Chapter 7 examines costs in greater detail.) In addition to these lower up-front costs, there are significant reductions in ongoing operational costs. This lower level of ongoing expense is a result of:

- Lower amortization due to lower initial software costs
- Lower depreciation due to lower initial hardware costs
- Lower monthly or annual maintenance and support charges
- Potentially lower telecommunications costs, since processors can affordably be located at multiple sites
- Lower technical support costs, since the technical environment is usually less complex
- Lower functional support costs, since the user interfaces, modifiability, and report-writing capabilities are typically superior

Recent surveys indicate that many companies are still spending 2 percent or more of their annual revenues on MIS. *HI/MIS* can yield the same benefits, but often at a fraction of one percent of annual revenues. This percent-of-revenue savings can be considered additional margin. The company can then decide to use this margin to immediately increase bottom-line profitability or to invest it back into the business to obtain competitive advantage.

Another area of benefit specific to *HI/MIS* is its relative ease of use. *HI/MIS* software is typically easier to learn and implement, which can be critical when limited time and personnel resources are available.

HI/MIS products also tend to be easier to use on an ongoing basis, which leads to more efficient use of personnel time. This relates to an important benefit identified earlier. The more efficient use of personnel can have a pervasive effect on a company, by enabling it to grow with minimal increase in headcount and by allowing its people to concentrate on valuable improvement activities. *HI/MIS* products support this concept to an even greater degree, since the information system itself is significantly easier and more efficient to use.

The final area of benefit specific to *HI/MIS* relates to the underlying technology. One major benefit of this technology is that it is typically easy and relatively inexpensive for companies to improve system performance. This is made possible by the multiplatform, nonproprietary nature of the hardware and operating systems that support *HI/MIS* products. It is a great benefit to rapidly growing companies to know that their migration path is both ensured and affordable.

Technologies such as fourth-generation languages (4GL) and relational database management systems (RDBMS) have also proven themselves to be of significant benefit to companies. Besides facilitating report writing, they enable a company to more easily and efficiently make necessary modifications and add functionality to the product.

SUMMARY

This chapter examined the benefits that can be derived from implementing both information systems in general and, more specifically, *HI/MIS*. Information systems in general provide important benefits that range from improvements in customer service to the potential for significant reductions in inventory levels. These benefits were discussed since the lower cost of *HI/MIS* products is often the key to making the acquisition and implementation of *any* fully functional system feasible.

HI/MIS also provides this same full range of benefits. However, *HI/MIS* provide additional benefits based on their significantly lower up-front costs, lower operational costs, relative ease of use, and underlying technologies.

9

Caveats Associated with *HI/MIS*

This chapter examines some of the unique challenges, potential problem areas, and valid reasons to *not* attempt the implementation of an *HI/MIS*. The first part of the chapter discusses the caveats inherent in all information systems. It makes sense to consider these, since they also apply to *HI/MIS*. Next, the caveats specific to *HI/MIS* are examined.

The first and perhaps the most important caveat is the company's ability to implement *any* fully functional system. An honest assessment is that most systems, including *HI/MIS*, fail to achieve all of their originally intended benefits for this reason alone. Implementing a fully functional, integrated system that encompasses manufacturing, finance, and marketing is a big job (see Chapter 12).

It is especially difficult for small companies to make the necessary level of implementation resources available. A company would be well advised to make a candid appraisal of their capabilities. If it is not clear that the time, money, and skill base is present to do the job right, it may be better not to attempt a full implementation.

One important element of the necessary skill base is the company's internal system support capabilities. Again, this is an especially challenging problem for small companies. Inexpensive hardware, especially microcomputers, and very easy-to-use products like spreadsheet programs can create a false sense of security.

This leads some companies to view their new, fully functional information system like any other microcomputer system. But the new system is not just a nice-to-have productivity tool such as a word processor or spreadsheet. It is an essential part of the company, responsible for billing customers, controlling inventory, and performing other vital functions. Therefore, the new information system should be supported with the same degree of competence and completeness as would be appropriate for any critical system.

Technical support requirements encompass the following broad categories:

- Security, which includes the physical security of the equipment and the logical security of system data to protect against unauthorized access
- Procedures that cover the routine operations of the system and ensure that adequate backup processes are in place
- Management, which provides control for the day-to-day operation of the system and maintains plans for its future development

The amount of effort that must be expended in each of these areas can vary widely, based on the complexity of the company's environment and the technical nature of its chosen information system. While these technical support requirements are reduced with *HI/MIS*, at least a minimal amount must be provided and available on an ongoing basis.

Application support is also required, which is often provided by a systems analyst. In this context, a systems analyst is an individual extremely familiar with the functionality of the system who works with users to optimize and coordinate their use of the system. If a modification to the system is required, the analyst helps define the user's needs and communicates this information to the programming staff or outside contractor.

The amount of effort that should go into application support can also vary widely, based on the skills and experience of the company's user base and the complexity of its chosen information system. While this application support requirement is also often reduced with *HI/MIS*, at least a minimal amount must be provided and must be available on an ongoing basis.

HI/MIS Concerns

The concerns detailed above apply to *all* systems, including *HI/MIS*. The following caveats apply to all systems but are particularly characteristic of the current *HI/MIS* environment.

Vendor Size and Support

The first concern relates to the product vendor's size. The typical *HI/MIS* vendor is small. Some of the vendors have well under 100 employees. This has implications on the vendor's ability to provide adequate support. Too often support is centered in just a few individuals. When they are not available, support services suffer. Should these individuals for some reason become permanently unavailable, vendor support could be dramatically impaired.

Another significant caveat associated with size is the vendor's ability to finance its own growth and the advancement of its product. Does the vendor have the resources available to enable its company to grow and compete successfully?

Will it be able to continue to put resources into the enhancement of its product to keep up with changing technologies and business demands?

This leads into the most basic caveat of all. Since the vendor is small, its stability or staying power may be in question. Will the vendor be in business next year? In five years from now? This is a critical concern. An orphaned product will need to be replaced quickly, a difficult and expensive process.

There are a few other, less obvious concerns related to vendor size. First, a small vendor may be overly influenced by a single large customer. Unless you are that single large customer, this can be a disadvantage. The concern is that the vendor will allocate a disproportionate amount of its development resources to the esoteric needs of this one customer. Second, a small vendor probably also has a small installed base of its product in the field. This may make it more difficult to locate personnel with previous product experience in the job pool.

Smaller vendors have additional challenges in the support area. Without a large staff, the primary method of support may be limited to over-the-phone problem solving. (See Chapter 3 for additional types of support services.) If on-site support is available, it may be limited geographically. For vendors providing support from just one facility, the hours of operation may also prove to be a limitation. This could be true especially when the vendor is located on the opposite coast from the company or is several time-zones distant.

The consistency of response times may also vary based on vendor size. Statistically, a small support staff has more difficulty with peaks in demand. During one of these peak demand periods, the responsiveness of support services can be expected to deteriorate.

Software Modification

Aside from vendor support, the availability of modifications is another important area to consider. Not all *HI/MIS* software vendors provide for this. In a few cases, modifications are entirely unavailable. In other cases, modifications are available only from the vendor itself or from a very limited number of sources.

Modifying software can be an expensive process that involves a certain amount of risk. Even if the modification goes well, the company is left with the task of continually having to reimplement its modification as new updates and versions of the core system are released. Many companies have painted themselves into a corner by allowing modification activity to proceed unchecked. They find themselves completely unable to move to new versions of the software and expending a lot of effort and expense to keep their modifications up and running on an on-going basis.

Products should be selected that most closely meet the needs of the company without requiring any modification. But future business changes may absolutely necessitate a modification. For this reason, a company should ensure that at least the *capability* to make modifications is available. If this capability is not available, the company might be forced, sometime in the future, to discard the existing system, then acquire and implement an entirely new one.

When modifications are available only from the vendor or from a very limited number of sources, the result is a noncompetitive environment. Consider a company that absolutely must have a modification and the vendor is the only source. Both the company and the vendor know that changing to an entirely different product would seriously disrupt operations and take enormous resources. Obviously, the company is in a poor position to negotiate on price for its needed modification.

Source Code

The availability of source code is another area of concern. As discussed above, it makes sense to avoid modifications whenever possible. A company making its own modifications to a product's source code can find itself in a difficult, expensive, and risky situation. With each new release of the base product, the company will need to examine and possibly recode all of the previous modifications.

Despite these concerns, the company may someday find itself in a situation where a modification to the source code becomes an absolute necessity. If modifications are not available, the company may then be forced to either obtain the source code and perform its own modifications, or abandon the system.

Another concern is the risk that the vendor may cease operations. The company would then be forced to provide its own support. Support is not just an option, it is a requirement. Software can bomb or develop serious glitches even after being in the field for a long time. The right combination of transactions can cause a new bug to manifest itself at any time.

Beware the situation where source code appears to be available but really is not. If the source code is priced out of a reasonable range, the answer may technically be that yes, the source code is available, but in a practical sense, it is not. It's best to determine the source code price up front (even if it is not being purchased initially) and to ensure that it will remain available at a reasonable price in the future.

Escrow arrangements are often offered by vendors to alleviate concerns regarding the control of source code should the vendor terminate operations. In these arrangements, the source code, usually in both electronic and printed form, is held by a third party. A common practice is to simply use a bank safety deposit box. In the event the vendor goes under, the agreement governing access to the box then allows the other appropriate parties to access (obtain a copy) of the source code.

This escrow arrangement is of some, but actually very limited value. The biggest problem is that vendors don't go officially belly-up quickly. There is a long period of time while they flounder, providing little or very poor support for their product. At that time, the vendor organization may consist of nothing more than the two original founders, their kitchen table, and the revenue from the installed base that continues to pay annual maintenance fees. But they are not technically dead (insolvent, filed Chapter 11, etc.).

Some escrow agreements trigger the transfer of source code rights on this lack of support, as opposed to a legal dissolution of the vendor's business. But even this method provides only marginal additional assurance. Unfortunately, the definition and determination of when the vendor becomes "incapable of providing adequate support" becomes problematic and arguable.

One last concern related to the appearance of source code availability is that the source code may not be usable in a practical sense. It may be poorly documented, poorly constructed, or coded in a low-level language. The specialized compilers, tools, and libraries of associated programs that may be necessary to make adjustments to the source code feasible may not be made available under the escrow arrangement.

Specialized User Needs

The presence of very specialized needs is also an area of concern. A company must be careful to determine if there is any specialized functionality, unique to the company or industry, that requires a specialized product. Extremely large companies need specialized systems (assuming they want a single system to cover all operations). Chapter 3 discussed the specialized functional needs within the purchasing area of such a company.

Companies in certain industries need specialized support. Chapter 3 gave the example of a semiconductor company with extensive foundry operations. How do you know if your company is better off with a specialized package? One good method to determine this is to ask the vendors of the specialized software products to enumerate what makes their product different from the standard manufacturing software products. Then determine the value of these differences to the company. It may also be prudent to contact the vendors of the standard products and ask them to suggest their best available workarounds to compensate for these differences.

One last caveat to consider: In Chapter 5, the general capabilities of the current crop of *HI/MIS* products were discussed. Beware of the situation where a company has many requirements that fall into the "Very Few" support category. The odds are slim that any one product can be found that will meet all these requirements.

SUMMARY

There are caveats to consider before leaping into an *HI/MIS* implementation. Some of the factors discussed above represent risk, which means that the company should evaluate these risks, take steps to minimize them and proceed if the risk level is deemed acceptable. The factors in this category are:

- The size of the vendor
- The vendor's support capabilities
- The availability of modifications (a complete absence of this probably represents an unacceptable risk)
- The availability of source code

Some of the other factors discussed above may represent absolute reasons to *not* attempt the implementation of an *HI/MIS*. The factors in this category are:

- The company's own ability to implement *any* fully functional system
- The company's internal systems support capabilities
- The presence of very specialized needs unique to the company or its industry

part 4

HOW DO COMPANIES ACHIEVE *HI/MIS*?

10

Evaluating and Selecting *HI/MIS* Products

This chapter presents proven methodologies to use in the process of defining a company's information system requirements and selecting the best available solution. In keeping with the overall theme of *HI/MIS*, these methodologies can be utilized relatively quickly and make efficient use of limited resources.

The evaluation and selection process can be broken down into the following nine steps:

1. Formation of the project team
2. High-level systems planning
3. Definition of requirements
4. Initial product screening
5. Structured product demonstrations
6. Site checking
7. Hardware configuration
8. Vendor contract evaluation
9. Final vendor negotiations

Each of these steps are discussed in the following sections.

STEP 1: FORMATION OF THE PROJECT TEAM

A team approach is the best method to use. It helps to ensure that the team members will accept, adopt, and fully support the ultimate decision. This "buy-in" by the members is critically important because *any* system will fail if it is not supported by the users.

The team members should support the new system and, in some cases, may even become cheerleaders for it back in their home departments. Also, buy-in by the full user base will be more likely to occur if it is clear that each user's functional area was represented and involved in the decision-making.

The team approach also leverages the company's resources. With more people involved, less time is needed on the part of an individual member to explore the issues and sort through options. The resulting decision is a better one because it reflects the entire group's combined knowledge of the company's business and each individual's detailed understanding of his/her functional area.

Cross-Functional Representation

The members of the team should be selected from each of the functional areas that are affected by the new system. For a typical manufacturing company, the team might be comprised of representatives from the following areas:

- Manufacturing
- Engineering
- Finance
- Marketing/sales
- MIS
- Each separate plant or operating unit

The reason for this broad representation base is that the members bring their specialized expertise and knowledge of key issues in each of their areas to the process. Each is best positioned to identify, prioritize, and evaluate the features of the software that pertain to their functional area and is best able to evaluate whether a suggested workaround will prove to be acceptable.

It is unlikely that personnel from any one area will have all the knowledge that is necessary to fully identify the needs and interests for all areas of the company. For example, manufacturing may not spot a potential problem with the inventory valuation support within a particular package. If finance participates, they would most likely be able to spot this problem, judge its importance and evaluate any workaround solutions. In addition, broad functional representation enables the company to examine the interfunctional communication and integration issues that should be handled by the software products.

In all cases, there should be representation from MIS. This is necessary to ensure that all technical, support, and operational issues are properly factored into the analysis. Also, many MIS personnel will possess significant systems analysis and project management skills that can be used to great advantage in the course of the process.

Project Team Size

Although cross-representation is important, the team should not include so many functional areas that it becomes too large to be effective. A large team often is unwieldy. It will be difficult to schedule meetings and coordinate project activities. Also, the more members, the greater the possibility of encountering personality conflicts that inhibit progress.

The objective should be to ensure buy-in, leverage, and adequate cross-functional representation with the minimum number of team members. It is best to keep the total group size under 10. If there is an ideal number, it is probably in the range of five or six members.

One approach for involving more people in the process while keeping the team to a manageable size is to create subsidiary teams within the functional areas. A primary team member representing a functional area assumes the role of coordinating with their subsidiary team. In this role, each primary team member takes relevant issues to their subsidiary team, and, in turn, communicates their concerns and views back to the primary team. In this way, the user base within the functional areas can be further assured that their needs are being reflected in the decision-making process.

Selection Criteria for Project Team Members

Having the right mix of people on the team can be critically important to its success. There are several factors to consider when choosing team members. First, the selected people should want to see the project succeed. A lot of energy, work, and creativity will be asked of them, so only properly motivated people should be chosen.

Second, interpersonal components and group dynamics should be considered. For example, having a contentious member who typically argues with everybody over everything would seriously disrupt the group. It also would not be prudent to select a combination of particular people who have a history of battling each other.

It is desirable to select people who cooperate in a group environment. Cooperative people are willing to compromise their views or the interests of their functional area in order to attain the greater good for the whole company.

However, good team members should not be passive or submissive. They should speak their mind and champion the needs of their functional area. They should also be good communicators so that they can clearly convey their opinions to the team.

One aspect of group dynamics—dominance—can present a problem. If not managed, the team will in reality become just one person, and that person will effectively be making all of the important decisions. Some degree of dominance seems to arise naturally in group dynamics. This is due to the different traits and problem-solving methods inherent in individuals. However, one important source of dominance, rank in the corporate structure, can be controlled in the selection process. A wide disparity in the rank of team members can lead to dominance problems.

For example, if marketing is represented by a senior vice president while the other team members are much lower in rank, the needs of marketing might receive greater attention than those of the other functional areas. If possible, team members should be selected from about the same level within the corporate hierarchy.

Time Availability

Prospective team members who meet the other criteria (and, perhaps because they have those desired qualities) will quite often be people of key importance to the company. Their available time will probably be very limited and it will be difficult to find substitutes to competently perform their regular duties for an interim period. Since many of the team's activities are performed as a group, a scheduling problem with one or two members can affect the productivity of the entire team. A very important criterion, therefore, is having the time available to devote to the project team.

Structure of the Team

The two key positions on the team are the team leader and the facilitator. The designated team leader should not have an apparent bias on the major issues facing the team; all team members should view the leader as being open to their views and, therefore, fair in the decisions made.

It is especially important that the team leader not dominate the group. Accordingly, the leader should not be an overly assertive member, but at the same time should be able to speak up when necessary to keep the group on track. Picking a higher-ranking individual as team leader might help keep the group motivated, but this person should be careful to not allow his or her rank to cause dominance problems.

The other key position within the team is the facilitator (often called the coordinator). This person is responsible for scheduling the project resources, such as the meeting times, meeting places, work materials, and coordination of members' schedules. In addition, the facilitator summarizes (and hopefully documents) the progress made at team meetings, the decisions reached, and the open items yet to be resolved. Most importantly, the facilitator provides a degree of guidance to the team by preparing the agendas, facilitating the discussions, and otherwise doing whatever is necessary to keep the group moving and on track.

Reporting the Team's Progress

The project team should report its progress regularly to the executive group (or steering committee) that set up the project. The team leader, perhaps accompanied by the facilitator, will most often make the routine reports. Usually, when the project team is at a key milestone for the project, the entire team will present the results to the executives. The executive group should evaluate the quality as well as the timeliness of the team's progress and ensure that the direction the team is taking is consistent with the company's strategic objectives.

STEP 2: HIGH-LEVEL SYSTEMS PLANNING

Strategic Company Plans

High-level systems planning involves consideration of the long-term strategic factors that will have an impact on the company's information system needs. A system that is acquired to address only the company's current situation might not meet the company's needs in a few years. Although the project team cannot be expected to predict the future, it should be expected to select a system that is consistent with the company's current plans for the future.

Important parts of the company's view of the future include the expected growth rate over at least a five-year horizon and the degree to which the company will be expanding into new markets. Also, new products in development, new directions in research, changes in distribution channels, and the potential for acquisition or divestiture of business units will shape the decision on information systems.

The project team should also consider the company's information technology strategy. The direction that MIS has formulated for software systems, systems architecture, data communications, hardware platforms and operating environments are important factors for the team to consider. The project team should ensure that its decisions are consistent with and can be integrated into the company's overall long-range information systems plan.

Limiting the Range of Alternatives

Factoring in the strategic company plans will save the project team unnecessary work. For example, there is no reason to consider $500,000 solutions if only a $50,000 expenditure is economically feasible and justifiable for the company. Certainly, the system cost should not be the first consideration, but it is a waste of time to worry about products that are an order of magnitude above feasible expenditure levels.

The results of the high-level planning can be used to direct the team's efforts. There is no need to consider products that conflict with the high-level plans. For example, since the system must be able to accommodate the projected growth profile of the company, the project team need not consider products that do not provide an acceptable migration path. In this manner, the range of alternative solutions to be considered is reduced and the project team can proceed more efficiently through the remaining steps.

Estimating Resource Requirements

A part of the high-level systems planning effort should be a realistic estimation of the total resources necessary to successfully implement the system. These total resources include the costs paid to external parties for the software, hardware, training, consulting, and other professional service fees incurred in implementing the system.

Internal costs to implement the system should also be included in the estimate of total resources. Primarily the internal costs will consist of the time expended by the project team, MIS staff, and the entire user base in training on and implementing the system. Similarly, the estimate for the ongoing costs involved in maintaining and supporting the system, including the expense for any additional staff that might be required, should be included.

Estimating the total resources required for the successful implementation and ongoing operation of the system is a major milestone. At this point, it is probably appropriate that the project team presents this information to the company's executive group.

If this level of resource expenditure is deemed not feasible or prudent for the company, the project should not be continued. The project team may then be asked to developed alternative action plans. If the executive group does decide to make a commitment of the required resources, the project team can then begin to focus its efforts on the remaining steps.

STEP 3: DEFINITION OF REQUIREMENTS

Defining the requirements for the information system is a critical early step in the selection process. Obviously, you must first decide what it is you want to accomplish (where you are going) before you can decide what can best help you get there. The requirements definition process is also valuable since it provides a *consistent* basis for evaluating the alternative products.

In simple terms, the requirements definition is the project team's shopping list. Everyone knows that you shouldn't go to the grocery store until you've made your shopping list. You tend to wind up with a shopping cart full of cookies, relishes, candy bars, and the super-colossal-giant-size jar of peanut butter (enough to last a family of four approximately a decade) that the store was having a special on that day. Unfortunately, you also sometimes forget to get the meat and potatoes, the original object of going to the store. Like a shopping list, the requirements definition can help to keep attention focused on the essential issues.

Interviewing Techniques

Defining the requirements for the system should involve interviewing the people who will be using it. They will have useful ideas about what should be included in the system and will raise issues that need to be considered in evaluating the products. In addition, talking with the end users includes them in the decision-making process and helps ensure their acceptance of the new system.

Effective interviewing is a challenging process. Careful listening is a key skill. It usually takes just a few simple questions to get the discussion started. Following are some general questions that can be used within interviews to help facilitate the flow of information:

- What does the current system do that you like?
- What does it not do, or do inadequately?
- What information do you use in performing your job?
- Where does that information come from?
- How do you use it? (This is a key question for understanding the requirement and its priority.)
- Who uses the information that you produce?

An effective interview allows time for open discussion during which the user has the opportunity to raise issues that might not have occurred to the project team. Also, this open discussion time allows the user to express any concerns that may exist about the new system and enables the project team to gauge the level of support that will exist for its implementation.

Checklists of Requirements and Software Features

Predeveloped checklists of requirements can be useful. They facilitate the interviews by providing the user with something specific to comment on or react to. The checklists stimulate discussion and ensure that certain issues are not overlooked.

One negative aspect of using checklists in the requirements definition process is that the lists may shape the users' responses. Users seem to have a natural tendency to designate everything on a given checklist as being an absolute requirement. This sets up the users for disappointment since it is unlikely that any selected product will satisfy every item on everyone's checklist.

This phenomena can also reduce the value of the interviews since there will be little data from which to set priorities on the requirements. Also, the identification of too many requirements will impair the ability to explore the qualitative aspects of how alternative products meet the company's more essential needs.

STEP 4: INITIAL PRODUCT SCREENING

Automated Software Selection Products

Software tools that facilitate selecting information systems products are available. These tools contain extensive automated lists of functions and features. The user chooses from among the items on these lists to specify the company's requirements.

Some of these tools also provide a database that records the features found in existing products. Once the required features have been identified, the software automatically correlates these requirements with the capabilities of the products in the database.

The usefulness of these tools depends upon the accuracy of the information in the database. Some vendors test the systems or otherwise validate the information contained in the database. Others use unfiltered information directly supplied by the system vendors.

Regardless of the source, the freshness of the data should be examined. Information systems products (especially *HI/MIS* products) change rapidly, with new features added and deficiencies rectified on a regular basis. The information in the database may be dated and not reflect the current capabilities of the products.

There are other important limitations that should be considered in using an automated software selection product. It is virtually impossible to word the requirements or questions so that there is no room for ambiguity. Related to this issue is the problem that the database cannot contain qualitative information. An answer might technically be yes, the product performs the required function, but the database does not say how well the product does it, or whether it will even be practical to use this function given the specific manner in which it is supported.

Given these inherent limitations, it is inappropriate to use these tools for product *selection*. They should not be used to arrive at the final conclusion that one particular information system product will definitely work and that it is the best alternative.

However, used with care, these tools can help streamline a portion of the process. It is appropriate to use these tools for initial product *screening*. They can help narrow the range of alternatives down to a smaller number of prime candidates for further hands-on review. The evaluation of only a small number of key requirements should be necessary to accomplish this task. Again, the above-mentioned limitations must be carefully taken into account when using these tools.

Requests for Proposals

The use of formalized, printed Requests for Proposals (RFPs) has been the traditional method of gathering product information for evaluation. This method begins with the project team interviewing the users and preparing extensive lists of detailed requirements for each functional area within the company. These lists are combined with general company information and vendor proposal submission rules into one document (the RFP), which is often several hundred pages in size.

Copies of the RFP are then sent to a large number of vendors, often using a shotgun approach to ensure that a wide range of solutions are considered. Time passes while each vendor decides whether to respond. Some good vendors will decide not to respond to the RFP because of time constraints or the cost involved. After several weeks, the responding vendors submit their answers to the questions posed in the RFP along with the other requested information, such as product literature and documentation.

The flood of incoming responses to the RFP pools into a small ocean of material. At an appropriate time, the project team wades into the ocean, and, using some sort of evaluation matrix, emerges some weeks later with the winning fish. The team contacts that vendor and, together, they engage in further evaluation tasks to confirm the selection.

There are several problems with this traditional RFP-based method for selecting a system. The biggest is also found with the automated screening tools — the accuracy of the information about the product. It is unavoidable that the RFP will have contained ambiguous questions, which resulted in nonuseful answers. It can also be expected that the vendor will have answered some percentage of the questions inaccurately. Also, the answers will not contain the qualitative data that is necessary to truly evaluate a system.

Another problem is that the RFP method can produce too much information. The project team feels itself drowning in the ocean of material and, in desperation, will grab any old fish, just to get the process over with and get back on dry land. This natural human response can make the entire exercise a waste of effort.

For many companies, the RFP process simply takes too long. If everything goes smoothly, it will still take several months for the RFP to be prepared, distributed, and the responses evaluated.

A Modified Approach

The following discussion explains a modified approach that yields better results. The project team defines the key requirements by interviewing the essential users in each functional area and identifying their critical information requirements. After the interviews, the team, using criteria derived from the high-level system planning step, assigns priorities to the requirements and assembles a list. The list contains the key requirements for the system, which should number well less than 100.

From the key requirements list, the project team selects a *few items* that serve as the cut criteria. The team uses these criteria to eliminate products from more intensive review. Accordingly, the selected criteria should be those that tend to differentiate products quickly.

Important functional requirements that are not commonly supported by software serve this purpose, as do important high-level factors such as the business profile of the vendor or technology-related issues. The cut criteria should also be relatively unambiguous so that the project team can easily assess whether a product passes the cut.

The project team applies the cut criteria against a reasonable number of candidates, rather than trying to cover every conceivable long-shot possibility. Information about the candidate products is gathered by:

- Communicating directly with the prospective vendors
- Using automated software selection products or published databases
- Retaining an experienced consultant
- Discussing possibilities with industry contacts

If a software product fails any of the cut criteria, the project team drops it from the list and does not consider it further. By the end of the cut process, only a very few products remain in contention for additional evaluation. This short list of prime candidates should contain perhaps three or four products.

The project team subjects the remaining candidate products to an online RFP process. It contacts each software vendor and asks for a live, full-day demonstration of the product. During the demonstration, the team evaluates the product against the specific items on the list of key information system requirements — hence the term, *online RFP*.

Live product demonstrations allow the users to see first-hand whether a product meets their key requirements. This is a superior method for gathering accurate, understandable product information. Moreover, the users gain a feel for the qualitative issues pertaining to the product, can ask follow-up questions, and can observe how suggested workarounds actually function.

This modified approach does have one drawback. The perceived quality of the candidate products will be affected by the quality of the vendor's personnel conducting the demonstration. A good product that is poorly demonstrated may appear to be inferior to a lesser product that is demonstrated masterfully. The evaluators should keep this fact in mind and also not allow the personality traits or sales styles of the vendor personnel to overly influence their perception of the products.

It is helpful for the project team to document the results of the demonstrations for later review. A way to facilitate this is for each of the attendees to have a list of the key requirements in a format that simplifies note-taking. As the demonstration proceeds, the attendees can note on their lists which requirements were and were not met along with qualitative comments about the product. The notes from all of the attendees can later be compiled into a matrix form to provide a side-by-side comparison among candidate products. This method leads to a consistent basis for evaluating the candidate products.

STEP 5: STRUCTURED PRODUCT DEMONSTRATIONS

An unstructured product demonstration invites the vendor to control the session. To the vendor, the demonstration is a sales opportunity. In an unstructured environment, the vendor is able to show the product's strong points and either gloss over or totally avoid the weaker ones. Sales talk, rather than actual system time, can consume several precious hours of a full-day session.

Another problem sometimes develops when one team member takes too much of the group's time focusing on one particular issue or on relatively unimportant points. In this situation, the demonstration will not fulfill its purpose. At the end of the day, the project team still has not completed the evaluation of how the product performs the key requirements.

Providing a structure to the product demonstration can avoid these problems that are inherent in an unstructured setting. The structured product demonstration offers the most effective way to spend the time available to evaluate products. The project team is able to examine the functionality that is really important to the company and to compare the actual performance of contending products systematically.

A one-day demonstration cannot reasonably cover everything the users would like to see. Consequently, the team should concentrate on verifying that a product performs the important functions and delve into the qualitative aspects of how it does so. This will typically provide more value than attempting to review many functions in a cursory fashion.

The framework for the structure is a script that lays out the activities to be completed during the demonstration. The team includes only critical areas of functionality in the script.

Demonstration Script

The project team would normally prepare the script in advance and agree to stick to it through the course of the day. The team leader assumes the role of directing both the vendor and the team through the script to ensure that the vendor demonstrates all key functions. The team facilitator prepares and distributes copies of the script to the team members so that they can write their assessments on the script.

An outline for a typical demonstration might look like the following:

1. Introducing the vendor personnel and the project team
2. Vendor background (30 minutes)
   - Business history
   - Technology
   - Support services
   - Future product development plans
3. Key requirements
   - Functional Group 1 (90 minutes)
   - Functional Group 2 (120 minutes)
   - Remaining Functional Groups (. . . minutes)
4. Wrap-up (30 minutes)

As an example of what might be contained in the script for the key requirements section, consider the following hypothetical situation. The company processes hundreds of orders each day, most of which are for relatively inexpensive items. The company feels that one of its most important competitive advantages is the high quality of its customer service and on-time delivery. As a consequence, Functional Group 1 (Marketing) listed *the efficient processing of customer orders* as its first key requirement.

To test the software's ability to satisfy this key requirement, the script calls for the following actions:

1. Add a new customer.
   - Were look-ups available in many areas to reduce the data entry requirements?
   - To facilitate order taking, can the order-processing personnel be allowed to use this function, while restricting access to credit fields to finance personnel?
2. Enter an order.
   - Were the necessary types of look-ups available to quickly find the specific part the customer needed?
   - Is ATP (available to promise) information immediately accessible during the order entry process to enable the accurate quoting of promised delivery dates?

The script would, of course, continue through each of the tasks that the software must perform to meet the company's definition of its key requirement—the efficient processing of customer orders.

It works particularly well to script the overall demonstration to simulate a complete business cycle. The actions proceed in a logical flow covering key criteria in their natural order of occurrence, such as:

- Introduce a new product
  - Add item master information
  - Add bill of material information
  - etc.
- Enter forecast demand for the product
- Master schedule production
- Run the MRP (Material Requirements Planning) function
- Examine raw material requirements
- Create purchase orders
- Receive materials
- Build the product
  - Open work order
  - Kit and issue materials
  - etc.
- Ship the product
- Bill the customer
- Report financial results

The sections on adding a new customer and entering an order would be slotted into the appropriate place in the overall script. This arrangement of the steps into a natural order helps to conceptualize the workings of the system and understand how it supports the interrelationships between functional areas.

Coordinating with the Vendor

For an effective product demonstration, the project team should communicate in advance with the vendor. This communication might include the meeting agenda and the demonstration script. By being informed about what needs to be demonstrated in detail, the vendor can have the right people present to explain and demonstrate the product.

The vendor can prepare carefully to show how the product meets the key requirements. They also have the time to develop their best available workarounds for those specific instances where the product does not perfectly match the requirements. The vendor can load up sample data in advance to save time during the demonstration. However, the project team should still spend some time examining how the system handles adding information in those areas where the efficiency of the data entry process is important.

Product Documentation

It is an unfortunate fact that product documentation is almost universally poor and is not a good tool for accurately judging a product's functionality. However, the team should examine the quality of the available documentation in order to assess the amount of training and support services that will be necessary to implement the system.

STEP 6: SITE CHECKING

After identifying a leading candidate, the project team should arrange to review selected sites using the product. Most companies want to select a *proven* winner, not just one that looks good on paper or in a demonstration. This essential step validates the information gained so far in the selection process. Another benefit is that the process often uncovers additional important issues.

How to Select Reference Sites

A list of references should be requested from the vendor. It is important that the selected sites be as similar as possible to the company doing the evaluation. Site references should be requested that are similar in size, operate in the same industry, and are located in the same geographic region.

There will be a natural tendency for the vendor to bias the reference list with cream of the crop sites. There are several techniques that can be used to counter this bias and obtain a more accurate picture of the capabilities of the product and the vendor.

One technique is to simply ask for the vendor's entire customer list. The majority of vendors are unwilling to do this, so more imaginative techniques are usually called for. (If there is an active user group, lists of companies using the product may be more easily obtainable.)

To avoid bias, the vendor can be requested to provide sites based on a random selection. The vendor's customer number scheme is one possible basis for devising a random selection. Another method to find additional sites is to ask each initially contacted site to provide the name of another company that is also using the same product.

In picking sites to review, it is advantageous to select at least one older site that has been running the system for more than two years. This site should have the system fully implemented, and the users should have had time to run into the majority of the system's problems. It is also good to select at least one relatively new site that has been working with the system for less than six months. This site will be able to give information about how the vendor has been providing support recently.

Visiting Sites

If possible, it is advantageous to visit some of the selected sites. The system can be examined in action. Users have very different perceptions about what is fast and what is slow. A site visit provides the opportunity to examine the system running under load and directly evaluate its performance.

A site visit will also usually provide the opportunity to talk with more people. It is particularly important to talk with the functional people who really know and use the software on a daily basis. There is a natural tendency for the original decision makers who selected the product to not admit either weaknesses in the system they chose or that they may have made a bad decision. The functional users will likely be less reserved in pointing out any shortcomings.

Questions to Ask

Because the personnel at the site have their own jobs to do, they will probably be able to spend only a limited amount of time discussing their experience with the system. Therefore, it is a good idea to prepare a short list of concise questions to ask, including:

- How long since the system was purchased?
- Which modules have been implemented?
- How did you decide on this product?
- Were any modifications made to the system?
  - What were the types and extent of the modifications?
  - Who performed them and were they of high quality?
- What hardware equipment currently supports the system?
- What is the system's current level of performance?
  - What is the number of concurrently active users?
  - What is the system's average response time?
  - How frequently is MRP run and how long does it take?
- What support services does the vendor supply?
  - What is the quality of these services?
  - What is the timeliness of these services?
- How often are bugs encountered?
  - How timely were the vendor's fixes?
  - How adequate were the vendor's fixes?
- How useful was the vendor's training?
- What were your three biggest disappointments?
- If you could do it over, would you choose this system again?

In assessing the information obtained from the sites, it is important to keep in mind that many less-than-perfect implementations are not the fault of the products. Factors relating to people issues and the site company's business environment can, and often do, have more of an impact than the quality of the software products themselves.

STEP 7: HARDWARE CONFIGURATION

Estimating Performance Requirements

The first step in this process is an estimation of the factors that affect the required level of hardware performance. One useful method to initiate this estimation is to survey the company's current systems. Current numbers of users, types of usage, file sizes, and existing equipment performance can serve as a baseline for estimating the requirements for the new system.

The number of users who will be active on the new system must be projected. Further, the nature of their activities must be characterized, since different types of activity will place widely varying demands on the system. A heavy user might be a person in order processing, who uses the system constantly and intensively throughout the day. A light user might be one of the company's executives, who will use the system a few times a day to check the status of a handful of major orders.

The projected file sizes must be estimated to arrive at the total amount of system storage required. Also, if the product uses a singular database, ensure that the size of this database can be supported by the hardware and operating system. Some systems will have a problem if the database (which may appear to the operating system as one large file) exceeds a certain size or must span across multiple disk drives. File sizes can be derived from a knowledge of parameters such as the number of parts the company will be working with, the number of bills of material, the average number of component parts on each bill, the number of customers, the number of open orders, etc. Many vendors will provide worksheets that will detail these factors, along with simple formulas to project the resulting file storage requirements.

The volume of transactions that will be processed through the system should also be estimated. The number of customer orders taken, purchase orders released, inventory movements recorded, journal entries booked, and a host of other transactions will impact the required performance. The rate at which these transactions accumulate in the system will also impact the data storage requirements.

Large batch processes, such as MRP, should be estimated separately. It is also important to consider how the company plans on using these batch processes. For example, a five-hour MRP run that requires exclusive use of the system is not a problem for a company that plans on running this batch process weekly. It can be set up to run on the weekend, when no one else is on the system. However, if the company operates on three shifts and plans on running MRP daily, there would be a problem.

Because systems are most often intended to last several years, all of the parameters discussed above should be estimated for both now and into the future. A common—and conservative—rule of thumb is to increase the estimate for the current performance requirement by 50 percent. Since the future is uncertain, an even wider performance cushion is often specified, typically a factor of two times the estimate of future required performance.

This does not mean that the company must purchase this performance level initially. However, the vendor must be able to provide assurance, *today*, that the future expansion is both technically and economically feasible. If it is apparent that an upgrade in the hardware will be required at some point, it is prudent to estimate when this will occur. Depending on the timing, it may be advantageous to delay the purchase of expanded performance. The factors influencing this decision include:

- The time-value of money
- The industry history of providing increased hardware performance at lower prices
- The interim savings in lower hardware maintenance costs

Finally, it is important to validate the estimates of these performance factors. This can be done by checking with the reference sites that are using the same product and are similar to the company in both size and business profile.

Choice of Architecture

Another decision needs to be made regarding the choice of architecture for the system. The optimal configuration for the system may be based on either a local area network (LAN) or a shared processor architecture. There are important advantages and limitations to each. (Chapter 4 contains a discussion of these architectures.) This decision involves complex issues, and the company may need to seek competent advice that is *independent* of the vendors. Because there is a natural tendency for hardware vendors to be biased toward their supported architecture, independent advice is of particular importance.

Expressing Performance Requirements

Performance specifications can be expressed in several ways. One approach is to use technical terms. Technical measures are useful in projecting system performance. Some of the basic indicators that measure system performance include:

- MIPS—"Millions of Instructions Per Second." This measure can be used to determine if CPU performance is within a reasonable range; a requirement for 50 MIPS is not likely to be satisfied with a system rated at 5 MIPS, regardless of other technical considerations.
- I/O channel speed. This measure is especially important with data-intensive applications; a difference between 1 Megabyte/second or 10 Megabyte/second channel speed will make a big difference in system performance.
- Maximum internal main memory. The capacity should be sufficiently large to cache enough data to keep the hit ratio high and, even more importantly, to avoid swapping of applications to disk storage.

On the other hand, technical specifications can be misleading. For example, there is a lot of controversy about the validity of the MIPS performance measurement, which can be somewhat manipulated by vendors to produce the desired benchmark results. This has led some to offer a new definition of MIPS: "Meaningless Indication of Performance."

Hardware vendors like to boast about their technology—RISC, CISC, CMOS, Bipolar, BiCMOS, internal cache, external cache, cache controllers, etc. The complex interplay of all of these technologies and the inability to compare apples to apples means that a sole reliance on technical specifications is inappropriate.

Another approach is to express the requirements in terms of class-of-machine specifications. This approach has the advantage of being easier to understand. As an example, assume that a very similar company is operating successfully on a certain brand and model of hardware. The solution for the company can therefore be expected to be in the same class of machine.

A common mistake in following this approach is to use price as the definition of machine class. If the similar company is using a $75,000 machine, it would *not* be appropriate to simply assume that the best solution can be obtained by purchasing a machine at about that price. In the realm of computer equipment, price and performance correlate poorly.

It is important to find sites that are running the same software product being considered. A particular brand and model of hardware equipment may give perfectly adequate performance for another similar company, but their application software may have very different performance requirements. It would therefore be a mistake to assume that the same hardware would preform optimally in running the selected software.

After the performance requirements have been developed, prospective vendors can then be requested to provide quotations on their specific recommended models and configurations.

Sources for Hardware Equipment

There are two basic types of hardware sources. The first is a *turn-key* vendor, which supplies both the software and the hardware. This offers the advantage of dealing with only one vendor whenever a problem arises. It is also possible, because the vendor receives volume pricing on the hardware, that a lower total cost for the system may be obtainable. On the other hand, the turn-key solution may be more expensive because the choice of hardware alternatives will be limited.

A concern to keep in mind is that there may be a tendency to undersell the hardware in this situation. The vendor may want to keep the total cost of the initial purchase low to help ensure the sale. The danger is that the costs of upgrading the undersized system to meet the necessary performance level might actually make this a more costly choice. The company will also be in less of a position to negotiate the price of the upgrade after the original purchase has been made and few, if any, alternatives exist.

Another type of source is a different vendor that separately provides the needed hardware. One advantage of using this source is that it may provide a wider range of hardware alternatives from which to choose. This greater choice may enable the company to find better price-performance alternatives than the turn-key vendor can offer.

The downside is that when two vendors are involved, the responsibility for problems may become the subject of debate. As with the turn-key vendor, the hardware-only vendor may tend to undersell, making the equipment appear to be less expensive, but in reality setting the company up for an expensive up-grade. It is also quite possible that the vendor will attempt to oversell, if there are indications that the company is willing to purchase unnecessary capacity.

The software vendor can be consulted on the appropriateness of equipment configurations being proposed by the hardware-only vendor. But the software vendor may also have a natural bias. They may want the company to purchase more capacity than should be required. Software just looks and feels better when it runs extremely quickly. Raw speed can even compensate for certain elements of poor software design.

The best information to use in correctly deciding on the brand, model, and exact configuration of the necessary hardware will come from knowledgeable, unbiased sources. These sources may be the company's internal experts, inde-pendent consultants, or the first-hand experiences of personnel at sites that are running the same product.

STEP 8: VENDOR CONTRACT EVALUATION

When evaluating vendor contracts, *the company's legal counsel should always be consulted.* The company is about to make a significant transaction and enter into a contractual relationship with a third party that will continue to be of impor-tance for the next several years.

The following discussion is not intended to be a substitute for legal advice. Its purpose is to bring to the readers' attention certain issues that are somewhat unique to the type of equipment, license rights, and services being purchased. Many common terms, such as *force majeure, jurisdiction and venue, severability, arbitration,* and *attorney's fees* can be expected to be part of the contracts, but are not discussed here.

The value of written contracts is more than just forming a legal basis for trans-actions and the ensuing relationships. The process of documenting, in detail, what is expected from the parties on both sides of a transaction is of great bene-fit. This reduces misunderstandings, which are often the cause of failed relation-ships.

A company can expect these major documents to be a part of the acquisition of a full system:

- Hardware Purchase Agreement
- Software License Agreement
- Custom Software Development Agreement
- Maintenance/Support Agreement

These agreements should be looked at early in the process of evaluating prod-ucts. If a major problem is found and the vendor is unwilling to compromise or change its standard contract, it may be prudent to drop the product from further consideration. The earlier this determination is made, the better. Sample agree-ments can be requested from the vendors soon after initial contact.

If modifications to the contracts do need to be made, or if the vendor will be asked to use the company's version of a contract, expect this process to take a fairly long time. The vendor will need to have the changes reviewed by their executives and their legal counsel. This is another reason to examine the contracts early in the process.

Common Terms

A handful of common terms can be found in most or all of the four types of agreements listed above. These terms are discussed here to avoid the need to repeat them in each of the following sections.

The first common term to expect is a *disclaimer of implied warranties.* Vendors, justifiably, include this term since they often have little control on *how* their products are used. For example, consider another type of vendor that markets two products, squirrel guns and elephant guns. Both are very good products. But the fellow who goes out squirrel hunting with an elephant gun is probably going to come home hungry. And the fellow who goes out elephant hunting with a squirrel gun is probably not going to come home at all.

However, it is reasonable to expect the vendor to provide some level of expressed warranties. (If the instruction manual specifically states that the elephant gun will definitely kill an elephant, then it should be capable of doing exactly that.) The agreements should call for the products to perform according to the documentation and the written specifications that have been provided.

Another common term is a *limitation on damages.* Most often the limit is set at the original purchase price of the product, specifically disclaiming any "consequential damage" and "loss of profits" liability. Certainly the failure of a vendor's product or service can cause damage beyond just the original purchase price. But it is probably not feasible for a vendor to assume the massive, aggregate liability that would be incurred from its entire user base. Also, a vendor that did not use this limitation on damages could possibly be put out of business by a single failure.

Integration is a key term to look for. Consider the case of a company using separate software and hardware vendors. The company may have no need for the new hardware if the software vendor fails to deliver an acceptable product. Can the company ship the hardware back and obtain a refund? They can if the agreements with the vendors were integrated. Both agreements should have made reference to each other and specified that successful performance on both were required.

Indemnity is another common, important term to look for. Ensure that the hardware vendor and software vendor(s) agree to indemnify the company for any patent, copyright, or other claims that are asserted relative to the products they supply.

The following sections contain terms that can be found in each of the four types of agreements.

Hardware Purchase Agreement

System Description

This should be a detailed listing of all equipment, describing the brand, model, configuration, and quantities. This is an important term that serves as a final check that all necessary components are included and that there is agreement on exactly what will be provided.

Payment Terms

It is important for the company to stage, or schedule their payments to the vendor. This will allow the company to maintain leverage on the vendor to perform in compliance with the agreed-upon delivery schedule. It is also prudent to link the final payment to the final acceptance (see next term) of the delivered, installed, and tested system.

Acceptance

The agreement should define what the acceptance parameters are and how long the company will have to test the delivered hardware to determine its acceptability. This is another important term that allows the company to ensure that the hardware is installed and set up correctly and performs according to the agreed-upon specifications.

Ownership and Risk Transfer Point

Who pays for freight and where is the FOB point where the risk of damage to the hardware passes to the company? This should be specified in the agreement. Also, the company should make sure that adequate insurance coverage is in place starting at the time of risk transfer.

Site Preparation

Usually, very little site preparation is required for *HI/MIS* hardware. There are some exceptions, such as hazardous environments or when there is a need for exceptional security. However, the need for power conditioning, standby power systems, or an uninterruptable power supply (UPS) is common, and the agreement should specify which party is responsible for providing this equipment.

Equipment Installation and Set Up

The agreement should specify who is responsible for the physical installation and hook-up of the equipment. It should also specify who will be loading and configuring the operating system.

Warranty

The warranty should describe what equipment is covered and for what period the warranty is in effect. The timing for the start of service under the maintenance agreement should be coordinated with this warranty period.

Time Schedule

The agreement should spell out when the delivery of equipment should occur and when any installation services will be completed.

Backup Processing Arrangement

The company should have a Disaster Recovery Plan. If a casualty occurs to the equipment, the company will need to quickly find an alternate way to process their information system requirements. Depending on how difficult it would be to get replacement equipment, it may be advisable to arrange in advance for this situation. Some vendors can provide temporary processing on their equipment, provide an emergency loan of equipment, or expedite the immediate shipment and setup of replacement equipment.

Software License Agreement

System Description

This should be a detailed listing containing information on:

- Which modules are included
- Which release or version
- For use with what hardware and operating system
- The maximum number of allowed users

This is an important term that serves as a final check that there is agreement on exactly what will be provided. For example, it should be understood who will be responsible for providing any other necessary support software such as a database management system (DBMS), operating system, or compiler.

Source Code

If the agreement calls for the inclusion of source code, the company should also ensure that other useful materials, such as technical documentation, flowcharts, data dictionaries, variable cross-reference tables, and subroutine libraries are included. The agreement may also specify the vendor's responsibility for ongoing support after the company has made modifications to the product.

If source code is not included, the company should, at a minimum, ensure that an acceptable escrow arrangement is in place. If it is possible that source code will be purchased in the future, the purchase price should be agreed upon now.

License Term

In all probability, the company will not be purchasing a software product. Instead, it will be purchasing (licensing) the rights to use the software. There are technical, legal considerations for structuring the transaction this way, and it has become the accepted industry standard.

Vendors will typically not license their software for an indefinite (perpetual) period. This is because there have been instances where a perpetual, or a 99-year license, have been deemed to be de facto transfers of ownership of the product itself. The stated license terms for most products are fine, but do take time to examine this term. In a few cases, the license term is less than 20 years, which may be of concern to some companies.

Restrictions on Usage

This can be an extremely important term. Make sure that there is a clear understanding on the following:

- The number of the company's sites that can use the software.
- If a site is a subsidiary, will it be viewed as a separate entity and therefore necessitate the purchase of a separate license?
- Most agreements will contain a restriction on the company acting as a service bureau, where the software is made available on a time-sharing basis to outside parties.
- The license might be granted for only one specifically identified piece of computer equipment and the software may be encoded with the machine's identifying number to prevent it from being copied or transferred to other equipment.
  - Be careful if this is the case. Equipment upgrades and even certain maintenance activities will need to be coordinated with the vendor.
  - This may also cause difficulty if there needs to be an emergency equipment replacement or if the software needs to be temporarily run on loaned equipment.

Sale or Transfer of License Rights

Most standard license agreements provided by vendors do not allow the sale, transfer, or assignment of license rights to any other party. If the company's business needs change and they wish to move to another software product, it will not be able to resell or salvage any value by transferring its existing software to another party.

While this has also become an industry standard, the company should seek certain exceptions. The exceptional cases should include:

- Transfer to a parent or successor entity if the company is acquired or merged

- Transfer to a subsidiary or successor entity if the company or a portion of the company is spun-off

Payment Terms

Similar to the hardware purchase agreement, it is important for the company to also stage, or schedule, their payments to the software vendor. This will allow the company to maintain leverage on the vendor to perform in compliance with the agreed-upon delivery schedule for any custom modifications and in fixing any initial problems. It is also prudent to link the final payment to the final acceptance (see next term) of the system.

Sales and other taxes may apply to a portion of the software acquisition. The company's financial counsel should also review the agreement to ensure that the company is structuring the transaction in the best manner from a tax perspective. In some tax jurisdictions, there may be a possibility that electronic delivery of the software code can reduce the tax liability.

Acceptance

The agreement should define what the acceptance parameters are and how long the company will have to test the delivered software to determine its acceptability. This allows the company to ensure that the software (including any custom modifications) is functioning as expected and has been installed and set up correctly.

Time Schedule

The agreement should spell out when the delivery of the base software and the agreed-upon modifications should occur and when any installation or training services will be completed.

Warranty

The warranty should describe what software is covered and for what period it is in effect. The timing for the start of service under the software maintenance/support agreement should be coordinated with this warranty period.

Custom Software Development Agreement

Custom Software Description

This should be a detailed listing containing information on:

- The business purpose of the software
- The detailed design specifications (or a reference to the appropriate documents)

This is an important term that serves as a final check that there is agreement on exactly what will be provided. For example, it should be understood who will be responsible for providing:

- User and technical documentation
- User training
- Any necessary data conversion tasks
- Any other required software or hardware
- The source code for the base system (which would be required for a third-party vendor to perform the modifications)

Source Code

The vendor performing the custom software development or modification of the base system may deliver the software in compiled and/or source code formats. It is prudent for the company to obtain the source code. This ensures that the company can subsequently use another vendor to provide additional modifications, without being locked into a noncompetitive situation with just one vendor.

If the agreement does call for the inclusion of source code, the company should also ensure that other useful materials are included. If source code is not included, there are a few steps the company should consider to protect its interests. (See the discussion on page 175 under Software License Agreement.)

Ownership of Developed Software

The agreement should specify whether the developed software is the exclusive property of the company. Will the company allow the vendor to resell the software (or its design specifications) to other companies? The decision depends on cost, confidentiality, and competitive considerations.

It is possible that the vendor will deliver the software via a license arrangement. If this is the case, the company should evaluate the agreement in the same manner as outlined in the above Software License Agreement.

Restrictions on Usage

See the discussion under Software License Agreement.

Payment Terms

Similar to the other types of agreements discussed earlier, it is important for the company to stage, or schedule, their payments to the software development vendor. Actually, due to the nature of the software development process, this scheduling of payments is of particular importance.

It is best to keep the initial payment low to ensure that the vendor remains motivated to deliver quality development work according to the agreed-upon schedule. It is also advisable to have several checkpoints in the development process. At each of these checkpoints, the company can ensure that the development work that has been accomplished matches its needs. Payments can be tied to the successful passing of these checkpoints. Also, consistent with the previous agreements, it is prudent to link the final payment to the final acceptance of the system.

Sales and other taxes may apply to a portion of the software development work. (See the discussion under Software License Agreement.)

Acceptance

Consistent with the prior agreements, the software development agreement should define what the acceptance parameters are and how long the company will have to test the delivered software to determine its acceptability. This allows the company to ensure that the developed software performs as expected and has been installed and set up correctly.

Time Schedule

The agreement should spell out when the final delivery of the complete, developed software should occur along with dates for each of the previously specified checkpoints. It may be advisable to include "time is of the essence" wording as part of this term. If a vendor is demonstrating an inability to meet the specified checkpoints according to schedule, the company may want to change vendors early in the process. The agreement should cover the basis for terminating the relationship, the period the vendor has to remedy the situation, who owns the work completed to-date, and a set of agreed-upon procedures for executing the termination.

Warranty

See the discussion under Software License Agreement.

Maintenance/Support Agreement

This section lists factors to consider in evaluating agreements for the maintenance/support of both hardware equipment and software systems.

Description of Hardware/Software

This should be a detailed listing of all equipment or software modules that are covered under the agreement. This is an important term that serves as a final check that all necessary components are included and that there is agreement on exactly what will be supported.

For software agreements, it is also important to gain a clear understanding of what future product enhancements will be provided at no additional charge to the company. The wording and definitions can be critical. Will the company be entitled to new *upgrades, releases, versions,* and/or *modules*?

Payment Terms

It is usually advantageous to schedule maintenance/support payments on a monthly or quarterly basis, as opposed to an annual or longer term basis. This allows the company to more easily move to another provider if the service level begins to deteriorate.

Related to payment terms is a concern about future increases in maintenance/support costs. This is of particular concern for software support, especially when source code is not available. There may not be alternative sources for this service, which would leave the company in a noncompetitive situation. In this situation, it is prudent for the company to seek limits on the future increases that can occur in support service prices.

Time Schedule

It is useful for the agreement to provide guidelines on what the expected times should be for responses to service requests and for the resolution of problems. The company should expect "best efforts" wording to be a part of this term. Most vendors will not provide an absolute guarantee of response time. However, it is reasonable for the company to ask for certain "escalating" actions to take place in the event of a difficult problem. These actions might include the assignment of more senior vendor personnel to the problem or perhaps a stipulation that vendor personnel will visit and remain on site until the problem is resolved.

Backup Processing Arrangement

See the discussion under the Hardware Purchase Agreement. If a backup processing arrangement is not a part of that agreement, it could be included here.

Remote System Diagnosis

It is a common and very effective support method for the vendor to be able to dial in to the company's system. This allows the vendor to more quickly diagnose the cause of problems, determine the extent of any damage, and perform fixes. Many maintenance/support agreements specify that the company must maintain a modem for the vendor's remote access of their system.

The company should be careful, from an operational standpoint, that this dial-in access is properly controlled. The company should be fully in charge of their system's security. The vendor should be given a system password that gives it only a restricted set of rights or activities that they can perform on the system. If this access proves to be too restrictive in a particular situation, the vendor should coordinate a temporary expansion of access privileges with the company's appropriate personnel. Also, the company may choose that the modem will not operate in an automatic answer mode. This will reduce the likelihood of unauthorized access to the company's system by outsiders.

In all cases, this remote access diagnosis and problem-solving activity should be monitored and logged. Don't automatically assume that the vendor will accurately keep track of all fixes and changes made to the company's system. The company's internal personnel should maintain ultimate responsibility for managing and controlling this activity.

STEP 9: FINAL VENDOR NEGOTIATIONS

The Vendor as a Business Partner

In negotiating with the vendor, it is best to set the overall objective as a business deal that is fair to both parties. The company doesn't win by tricking or forcing the vendor into a bad deal. It is not a good situation to set the vendor up as an adversary. It is better to attempt to establish a relationship with them as a business partner. Since the system is intended to be a key part of the company's framework for many years to come, the company needs to establish a working relationship with the vendor that will last for the life of the system.

Negotiating Techniques

A few vendors discount prices significantly, most discount somewhat, and a few do not discount at all. Most companies will want to negotiate with the vendor(s) when the software and hardware purchase will represent a significant expenditure. Following are a few negotiating techniques that have proven to be useful:

• *Always keep more than one option open.* Keeping more than one option, or at least giving the appearance that there are other options, is critical to maintaining leverage in the negotiations.

It may be prudent to enter a "quiet" period after the selection of products has been made. During this period, there should be no communication between the general project team members and the vendor. This may help prevent the accidental communication to the vendor that their product is the only acceptable alternative and that the company is willing to pay any price necessary for it.

• *Don't rush the process.* The general rule is that the longer a company spends in the negotiation process, the better the result. But a quick ultimatum sometimes works. For example, the company says "I'm going to make a decision today and your product and the other one are identical in my evaluation. If you want the order, I'm willing to pay X amount." While this method can appear to be quite effective, it is likely that the company would have done even better by allowing the process to take a little longer.

Not rushing the process does *not* mean dragging it out for an extended period. The company should determine the point where further delay does not make sense. For example, even though another week of negotiation might yield a $2,000 savings, it may not be worth the additional effort involved, plus a delay in the implementation of a system that will produce $5,000 a week in benefits to the company.

• *Give the vendor a reason to justify a discount.* Vendors are often unwilling to give a straight discount from the list price. They are concerned that this information will become common knowledge and that all future purchasers will expect the same level of discount. Giving the vendor a "reason" for the discount reduces this concern. If the discount becomes known, the vendor can explain that it was a special case and cannot be granted to others.

One possible reason to give the vendor to justify the discount is an expectation that the company will implement the system at other sites in the future. So, in a way, this deal was part of a volume purchase and thus warranted a discount. Another possible reason might be that the company is the first to implement the system in a new industry segment for the vendor.

Another approach to avoid the straight price discount concern is to negotiate for other terms and services. For example, the company might ask for product training to be included free of charge or at a reduced rate. Or the company could request a grace period during which the vendor waives product maintenance fees.

Related to this approach is negotiation relative to any needed modifications. There is usually some latitude for determining whether or not the modifications are to become a standard part of the product and therefore should be provided free or at a reduced cost.

USING OUTSIDE CONSULTANTS

Evaluating the Consultants' Competence

Not all consultants possess the experience and skills necessary to truly be of benefit to the company. Before selecting consultants, a company should take the time to evaluate their level of competence.

Prior experience is one key element of competence. The prospective consultants will ideally have significant experience in:

- High-level systems planning
- Product evaluation and selection
- Hardware configuration
- The company's industry
- The relevant range of alternative products

In verifying the consultants' experience and capabilities in these areas, the company should talk with clients who have previously used their services. Consultants who have delivered quality service to clients willingly provide references.

When evaluating a consulting firm, a company should determine which specific individual(s) will be performing the services. The quality of the firm is less important than the quality of the individuals who will actually be assigned to do the work. These individuals should be met with directly and the company should seek assurance that these same people will be the ones who provide the services.

There are a few acid tests that can be used to verify that prospective consultants possess the necessary level of competence. Listen carefully to see whether the consultants can explain technical issues in language understandable to the layman. This is a good indication that the consultants actually do understand the issues well and do not resort to buzzwords to gloss over holes in their knowledge.

Similarly, see if the prospective consultants can explain their recommended approach to issues such as high-level systems planning, product selection, and hardware configuration without resorting to predeveloped slides or diagrams. This is a good indication that they actually do understand these processes and have experience in providing these types of services.

The Consultants' Role

The most appropriate role for the consultants is to serve as advisory, nonvoting members of the project team. They should be viewed as a resource or tool available to the team. The consultants should not cast votes in decision-making processes. The team members and the users are going to take ownership of the chosen system. Therefore, they should be the only ones to vote.

Some consultants prefer to work in a different role. They will interview the users, gather requirements, go away for awhile, and then come back after a few weeks and say "The answer is. . . ." This is not the best method. The project team members know more about the company, its operations, and its business needs than outside consultants could possibly learn during the life of the project. Consequently, the team can do a better job than the consultants in defining the company's requirements and selecting the best solutions. Moreover, allowing the consultants to furnish the answers undermines the principle that the users must buy into the process and the chosen solutions.

Where Consultants Can Be Useful

Qualified consultants can actually be useful in all of the steps involved in evaluating and selecting an *HI/MIS* product. The following discussion suggests how they could potentially be used in each step.

> In Step 1, *Formation of the Project Team*, consultants can advise on the appropriate size of the team and the right mix of people. Consultants can also help with setting up the coordinating/facilitating function to ensure that the chosen individual understands the nature of this role and its contribution to the team. Finally, based on experience with similar projects, the consultants can explain to the team the reason for its formation and its objectives, suggest methods for its operation, and provide a vision of the process that lies ahead.
>
> In Step 2, *High-Level Systems Planning*, the consultants can help ensure that all of the company's critical strategic factors have been considered. They can also suggest some of the key high-level issues that the team can use to quickly and efficiently narrow the range of solutions to be considered.

In Step 3, *Definition of Requirements*, consultants can spot requirements that might have been overlooked and help the team to differentiate between bells and whistles and key requirements. They can also help in interviewing users. A skilled and experienced interviewer can be more productive, and sometimes users are more open when talking with an outside party. The consultants can also provide an independent, unbiased view on the relative importance of requirements from different functional areas. In this manner, they can help the team find a proper and rational balance between the competing concerns of different areas.

In Step 4, *Initial Product Screening*, the project team could benefit from the consultants' experience in working with automated software selection products. The consultants could also assist in isolating key requirements and the cut criteria, based on their knowledge of what tends to differentiate currently available software products. In the online RFP demonstration, the consultants could help the project team stay focused on the key issues. They can also help to ensure that the vendor provides accurate and complete information without resorting to smoke and mirrors, or other tricks that might obscure, complicate, confuse, or distort the true picture of the product's functionality.

In Step 5, *Structured Product Demonstrations*, the consultants can help develop the script for the demonstrations. During the actual demonstrations, they can readily spot significant issues that arise during the activities. By asking the right questions at the right time, the consultants can help the project team evaluate the qualitative aspects of how the product performs key functions.

In Step 6, *Site Checking*, consultants can assist in developing the short list of important questions to use in communicating with the reference sites. The consultants' interviewing skills may also be of use in eliciting the most information from the sites. Some sites will be concerned that outsiders might be competitors and will be more comfortable talking with an independent third party (the consultants) about their business situation. The consultants can also help evaluate the results of the site checking and assist in analyzing the causes of a site's satisfaction or dissatisfaction with a product.

In Step 7, *Hardware Configuration*, the consultants may be able to supply the specialized technical knowledge that is required and is unavailable internally within the company. The consultants are also a source of independent advice to help the company avoid being undersold or oversold.

In Step 8, *Vendor Contract Evaluation*, the consultants can provide the benefit of their experience with similar situations. (They may even have prior experience with the chosen vendor's contracts.) The consultants, along with the company's legal counsel, can advise the company on what terms may be problematic and what may be missing in the contract.

In Step 9, *Final Vendor Negotiations*, the consultants may have some information on the current street price, or discounts that purchasers have been obtaining. They can also help the company in evaluating what constitutes a fair deal and in establishing the appropriate business relationship with the vendor.

SUMMARY

This chapter presented proven methodologies to use when defining a company's information system requirements and selecting the best available solution. A concise list of the primary steps in this process is presented below. Before taking the first step, the company should consider using outside consultants and, if appropriate, engage them for assistance as early as possible in the process.

- Form the project team.
- Develop a high-level systems plan.
- Define the key system requirements.
- Perform initial product screening via the online RFP or another acceptable method and narrow the list by applying cut criteria.
- Arrange for structured product demonstrations for the short list of remaining alternatives.
- Perform site checking on the primary selection(s).
- Configure the necessary hardware.
- Evaluate the vendor's contracts.
- Negotiate a fair deal with the vendor and make the acquisition.

11

Leading *HI/MIS* Products

The purpose of this chapter is to present some of the leading *HI/MIS* products available today. In several places within this book, it has been stated that *HI/MIS* products are highly functional and make use of advanced user interfaces. These assertions can be supported by enabling the reader to take a quick look at some of the leading products.

One way to enable the reader to get a feel for the products is to include reproduced images of actual product screens. If it is true that seeing is believing, perhaps these screen images will provide some evidence to the reader on the degree of functionality and ease-of-use of *HI/MIS* products.

The presentation of each product begins with one page of general information. The vendor's name and address, product release date, and other background information are listed. Please note that all of the information was provided by the vendors themselves. For example, the text contained in the section entitled *Product Summary* was crafted by each of the vendors. The vendors were requested to use this section to describe the primary market for their product and some of the product's more unique characteristics.

Following each of these introductory pages are several reproduced screen images of the products themselves. These images were obtained by using screen capture software to take an electronic snapshot of the computer screen while the actual products were running. The screen images included for each product were chosen by the vendors. It was suggested to the vendors that they include the product title screen, the main menu screen, screens for item master information, MRP analysis, MRP exception reporting, and other screens of their choice that would demonstrate some of the more unique characteristics of their products.

Reading the general product information and looking at the screen images will certainly *not* provide the reader with enough information to make a product decision. There will be little opportunity to ascertain what may be negative about a product. At best, there may be the opportunity to see some of the positive aspects of a product. It would be inappropriate for the reader to use this chapter as a tool in choosing between products. But it would be very appropriate for the reader to use this chapter to get a feel for some of the *HI/MIS* products and as a basis to decide whether the *HI/MIS* products, as a group, are deserving of further consideration and detailed evaluation.

In the interest of providing an impartial view of the *HI/MIS* products, only objective information is presented. This chapter is not intended to be a review of the products. No subjective information is offered. In keeping with this theme, there is no mention made of any of the products elsewhere in this book. The case studies presented earlier, while based on real company experiences, were composites intended to eliminate any possible tie to specific products. By restricting all specific product information to this chapter and ensuring an impartial presentation, the participating vendors could be assured that the book would not be slanted towards any particular products.

The only editing of the vendor-supplied information was to identify obvious inaccuracies or misleading statements. This identification was based on the author's previous experiences with the products. Any identified problems were discussed and resolved with the vendor. Additionally, it was stipulated that the screen images must be from a version of the product that is in current release. Images from future product versions still in development were not allowed.

New, enhanced versions of several of the *HI/MIS* products will have been released by the time the reader examines the contents of this chapter. The vendor and product information contained in this chapter changes on a continual basis. The reader should contact the vendors for updated information if there is any interest in learning more about their products.

All of the participating vendors have agreed to make additional product information available to *HI/MIS* readers. To request more information, see the Information Request Card at the end of this chapter.

At the very beginning of this book, *HI/MIS* was defined as:

Any of several fully functional, high performance, integrated information systems serving the needs of manufacturing, finance, and marketing that are based on advanced technologies and are available at a cost that is within the reach of small and medium-size companies.

To be consistent with this definition, a few simple criteria were used in qualifying products for inclusion in this chapter:

1. The product must be affordable.
   a. The software purchase price, with a minimum number of users, but containing full system functionality, must be under $50,000.
   b. The software must be able to run on a standard desktop micro-computer.

2. The product must be highly functional.
   a. The software must be capable of supporting the majority of manufacturing, finance, and marketing requirements that can be expected to be present in a company with moderately complex needs.
   b. A non-fully integrated product may be included if it is intended to be used in conjunction with the other *HI/MIS* products or combined with other products to form an *HI/MIS*.

The reader should be the ultimate judge on whether a product is an *HI/MIS*. Consider the products presented in this chapter to be candidates for *HI/MIS* status.

The products described in this chapter cover a rather broad range of capabilities and prices. They are intended for different market segments. Some companies will demand a very high level of sophisticated functionality and can afford a moderate investment in information systems. Other companies will need only a moderate level of functionality but will require the software to be extremely inexpensive.

Due to limited space, only a certain number of products can be presented. The products presented here are known to the author. But there are certainly other products currently available that should qualify for *HI/MIS* status. And in the future there will be even more.

The inclusion of a product in this chapter should not be viewed as an endorsement. And the exclusion of a product should not be viewed as a negative assessment. Again, the purpose of this chapter is not to evaluate specific products, but to "showcase" some of the *HI/MIS* capabilities and characteristics.

Important Points

1. All of the products presented in this chapter have succeeded in providing benefits to companies. And all of these products, given the wrong set of circumstances, can fail. The reader must take responsibility to carefully evaluate whether a particular product is appropriate for a particular situation.
2. Specific vendor and product information was provided by the vendors. While the information was reviewed, the author cannot guarantee the accuracy of all information.
3. The author assumes no liability for the reader's selection and implementation of any of the products that were made known to the reader by their inclusion in this chapter.

Product Name: SYMIX

Current Version: V2.6
Release Date: 05/91

Number of
Installed Sites: 1,100+

Product Summary:

SYMIX is a fully integrated system of 15 modules that may be purchased individually or as a complete system. SYMIX is designed for discrete manufacturers who operate in make-to-order, make-to-stock, and combination environments. Comprehensive scheduling, multidivision and multi-currency capabilities, detailed job costing, and flexible custom report writing are just a few of the strong features within SYMIX.

Vendor Name:	**Symix Computer Systems Inc.**
Address:	2800 Corporate Exchange Drive Columbus, Ohio 43231
Number of Employees:	214
Phone:	(614)523-7000 FAX: (614)895-2504
Support Services:	Installation and engineering, implementation and consulting, on-site training, regularly scheduled classroom training, telephone and modem support, electronic bulletin board, and systems integration.
Modifications:	Services available. Contact local account manager to coordinate quotation.
Source Code:	Included in midrange systems price.

Full System Product Pricing (in U.S. $)	under $20,000	$20,001 -40,000	$40,001 -60,000	$60,001 -100,000	over $100,000
4 users	x				
16 users		x			
64 users					x

(all figures are based on approximate U.S. sales price, and are subject to change at any time)

Product Distribution:

Direct full-service district offices located in Columbus, OH; Philadelphia, PA; Charlotte, NC; Dallas, TX; Chicago, IL; and Newport Beach, CA. Satellite offices are located in 21 cities across the United States. International sales are through direct offices and distributors.

Language/Database:

PROGRESS 4GL. Can import/export with ORACLE, RMS, and RDB.

Operating Platforms:

Available on over 400 hardware platforms under these operation systems: UNIX, SCO UNIX, AIX, HP-UX, XENIX, Ultrix, VMS, DOS, OS/2, and LANs.

11/04/91   SYMIX 2.6R2   15:56:26

```
(I) Inventory w/ Engineering Change Notices   (F) File Maintenance
(O) Order Entry w/ Product Configurator       (C) Codes and Parameters
(P) Purchasing                                (M) Menu of Outputs and Reports
                                              (U) Utilities
    Shop Floor Control Module
(E) Estimating                                (A) Advanced Manufacturing - MRP
(J) Job Definition                            (D) Data Collection
(W) Work Center Capacity and Dispatching
                                              (Q) Query Editor
(1) General Ledger                            (T) Progress FAST TRACK
(2) Accounts Receivable                       (S) Show Installed Modules
(3) Accounts Payable
(4) Payroll                                   (L) Log in
(5) Fixed Assets                              (R) Return to MSDOS

                         SELECTION: 
```

Choose a menu item.

F01. SYMIX is a fully integrated approach to manufacturing.

11/04/91   SYMIX JOB ORDERS   15:59:04

```
Job:        46-000      Revision:                Status: R (Released)
Item:       SP-11000                             Job Date: 04/05/91
            Model 30 Sprocket
Qty Ordered:    55.000                           Released:       55.000
                                                 Completed:      54.000
            Ref: 0 20      1                      Scrapped:        1.000
Order Date: 04/05/91                             Last Trx Date: 11/10/90
Due Date:   06/25/91
    Est Job: 43-000                              Sched Method: BM
    Customer: 5   Control Bicycle Inc.           Start: 03/27/91
                                                   End: 03/29/91
Parent Job: 45-000                               MRP End Date:
      Oper: 30    Seq: 3                          Priority:  5,672.727
Finish Job: 44-000                               Low Level Code: 2
WIP Total: 12200-   986.36   -                   Start Job Hrs:   0.00
                                                 Finish Job Hrs:  0.00
WIP Acct:                   WIP Inventory
```

(N)ext (P)rev (U)pdate (A)dd (F)ind (D)elete (O)utput (Q)uery (L)ist (R)eturn
(I)tem routing (S)chedule (J)ob Trx (M)atl Trx (X)ref Job (C)opy (T)ext: N
Enter data or press ESC to end.

F02. Material and labor are controlled with job routings and operations.

11/04/91   JOB ROUTE SCHEDULE BY OPERATION   17:07:55

```
Job:    55-002     Schedule: BM   Move Start:  0.00    Start: 11/04/91
Item: SP-11000     Freeze: No     Move End:    0.00    End: 11/14/91
Status: R          Job Type: J    Priority:    1.296
```

Oper	WC	Start	End	Frz	Move	Queue	Setup	Hours	Rem Hrs	Fix Hr	Offset
10	SMP-10	11/06/91	11/06/91	No	0.2	0.0	3.0	0.17			?
20	MC-300	11/06/91	11/07/91	No	0.1	0.0	3.1	4.95			?
30	HT-220	11/07/91	11/11/91	No	2.0	0.0	0.0	16.00	16.0		?
40	INS-10	11/11/91	11/11/91	No	0.2	0.0	0.0	0.23			?
50	PLT-10	11/12/91	11/14/91	No	2.0	0.0	0.0	16.00	16.0		?
60	INS-10	11/14/91	11/14/91	No	0.2	0.0	0.0	0.46			?

Page 1 of 1

(N)ext Line (P)rev Line (F)ind (U)pdate (S)chedule (C)alendar (R)eturn
(O)utput (1)Prev Pg (2)Next Pg (3)First Pg (4)Last Pg (5)Chg Disp (M)ove Oper:
Enter data or press ESC to end.

F03. You can use a variety of scheduling methods (forward, backward, finite, infinite).

11/04/91   VISUAL LOAD   16:02:13

Department: 100   Cap Hrs: 226

Manufacturing Processes   Start: 03/31/91

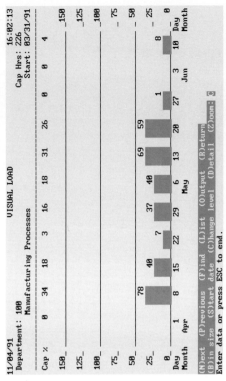

(N)ext (P)revious (F)ind (L)ist (O)utput (R)eturn
(B)in size (S)tart date (C)hange level (D)etail (Z)oom:
Enter data or press ESC to end.

F04. You can schedule machines, work centers, crews, and department capacities.

```
(A) Master Planning Display      (1) MRP Generation
(B) BOR Display                  (2) MRP Display
(C) RCCP Generation
                                 (3) Forecasts
(D) User Defined RCCP Resources  (4) Load Planned Orders
                                 (5) Horizon Calendar
(O) Outputs and Reports          (6) Exception Priority
(R) Return                       (7) MRP Parameters


                    SELECTION: [ ]
```

Enter data or press ESC to end.

F06. The MRP module synchronizes material receipts to operation start dates.

Planner: JAS
Suggested Action: Manufacturing Orders To Be Firmed

Order Number	Item	Description	Qty	Release Date	Due Date
PLN	431	BK-27000-0002 27" Customized Bicycle	100.000	05/03/91	05/25/91
PLN	432	BK-27000-0002 27" Customized Bicycle	100.000	05/31/91	06/23/91
PLN	433	BK-27000-0003 27" Customized Bicycle	50.000	05/20/91	06/05/91
PLN	434	BK-27000-0003 27" Customized Bicycle	50.000	06/04/91	06/19/91
PLN	447	FA-27000 Model 30 Frame Assembly	100.000	05/03/91	05/10/91
PLN	448	FA-27000 Model 30 Frame Assembly	50.000	05/22/91	05/28/91

Press space bar to continue.

F08. The Order Action report helps you react to changes in your business.

WC/Mach: DRL-10/1   Cap Hrs: 35
15" Bench Drill   Start: 05/19/91

LOAD DETAIL

Date	Item	Job	Hours Mach	Nxt WC
05/22/91	SA-50910	30.000	1.28	1 AC-440
05/23/91	SA-50910	30.000	8.00	1 AC-440
05/24/91	SA-50910	30.000	8.00	1 AC-440

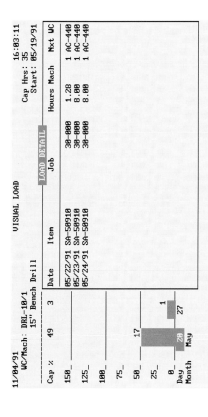

```
Cap %
150_
125_
100_
 75_
 50_
 25_     17       1
  0_         28  27
Day
Month    May
```

Press space bar to continue.

F05. The Visual Load report graphically depicts the available and actual capacity.

```
Planner: JAS              Page: 1       Order Mult:     10.000
  Item: MPS-10000                        Order Min:     10.000
  Desc: 70cm EuroCycle - Model 100      Days Supply:     1
On Hand: 0.000     Net Change: N       Safety Stock:    0.000
MPS Flag: Y    Dock-to-Stock: 0          Last MRP:  04/08/91
Prod Code: FG  Fixed Lead Time: 0    Var Lead Time:   0.35300
```

Date	Projected On Hand	O/S Reqmt	O/S Receipt	Original Qty	Reference
06/05/91	0.000			5.000	MPS 1
07/05/91	5.000			5.000	MPS 12
08/05/91	10.000			5.000	MPS 13
08/10/91	15.000		25.000	25.000	FCST 08/10/91
09/04/91	-10.000			5.000	MPS 14
10/05/91	-5.000			5.000	MPS 3
10/10/91	0.000		25.000	25.000	FCST 10/10/91
11/05/91	-25.000			5.000	MPS 15
	-20.000				

(N)ext (P)rev (F)ind (O)utput (R)eturn (1)Page Backward (2)Page Forward
(3)Summary (4)Shift (5)Inventory (6)Order Entry (7)Purchasing (8)Job (9)Firm [ ]
Enter data or press ESC to end.

F07. Available To Promise is calculated using dependent and independent demands.

Master Planning Display

```
11/04/91              MASTER PLANNING DISPLAY                16:10:26

Planner: JAS                        MASTER PRODUCTION SCHEDULE
Item: MPS-10000                     MPS #  Due Date    Quantity
Desc: 70cm EuroCycle - Model 100      1   05/05/91       5.000
                                     12   07/05/91       5.000
                  Past Due  11/04/91 13   08/05/91       5.000
     Forecast:      50.000    0.000  14   09/04/91       5.000
  Indep Demand:      0.000    0.000   3   10/05/91       5.000
    Dep Demand:      0.000    0.000  15   11/05/91       5.000
 Receipt (MPS):     25.000    5.000  17   12/05/91       5.000
    Proj Avail:    -25.000  -20.000  16   01/05/92       5.000
Avail to Promise:    0.000   30.000   5   02/04/92       5.000
                                     18   03/06/92       5.000
                  12/02/91  12/09/91 19   04/06/92       5.000
     Forecast:      0.000    25.000  20   05/05/92       5.000
  Indep Demand:     0.000     0.000   7   06/05/92       5.000
    Dep Demand:     0.000     0.000  21   07/05/92       5.000
 Receipt (MPS):     5.000     0.000  22   08/05/92       5.000
    Proj Avail:   -15.000   -40.000  23   09/04/92       5.000
Avail to Promise:   0.000     0.000   9   10/05/92       5.000

(N)ext (P)rev (U)pdate (A)dd (F)ind (D)elete (E)xceptions (R)eturn
(1)Page Backward (2)Page Forward (3)Firm (4)MPS Processor
Enter data or press ESC to end.
```

F09. MPS allows you to develop a valid manufacturing plan with due dates and quantities.

Standard BOM

```
11/04/91                    STANDARD BOM                     16:11:25

Item: FA-10000        26" Bicycle Model 30

  Oper: 10   WC: AC-400 Final Assembly Area

Move Hrs: 0.20    Man Hrs/Piece: 0.15    Fix Sched Hrs: ?
Queue Hrs: 0.30      Crew Size: 1.00       Offset Hrs: ?
Setup Hrs: 0.00       Mach Req: ?       Effective Date:
                                         Obsolete Date:

Item/Desc            Typ  Quantity Per   Cost Ref Scr Fct  Effective
SA-50910             M     1.00000 U    51.69000  J  0.0000  06/17/90
Model 30 Frame Assembly
SA-61500             M     2.00000 U    12.63000  I  0.0000  06/21/90
26" Wheel Assembly
PB-10000             M     1.00000 U     4.90000  I  0.0000  06/21/90
Seat Assembly
PK-44560             M     1.00000 U     0.00000  I  0.0000  06/21/90
Model 30 Shipping Box

(N)ext (P)rev (U)pd (A)dd (F)ind (D)elete (O)utput (L)ist (T)ext (E)CN (R)eturn
(I)tem change (C)opy (V)iew FROM Fields (1)Page Backward (2)Page Forward
Enter data or press ESC to end.
```

F10. Inventory Control maintains both standard routings and bills of material.

Customer Order Line/Releases

```
11/04/91            CUSTOMER ORDER LINE/RELEASES             16:12:09

  Order: 29              Status: O (Ordered)
Customer: 11          Order Date: 05/02/91
 Contact: Al Limerick    303-292-4288

 Bill To: Ray's Bike Shop        Misc Chgs:     0.00
          Steve Wolf             Sales Tax:     0.00
 Cust PO: AB-1002                  Freight:     0.00
Cust Type: B                   Total Price:

Line #: 1    Status: O (Ordered)  Qty Ordered:    0.000
Item: BK-27000                     Unit Price:    0.00000
      (No Description)
CI:                                 Ext Price:    0.00000

Due Date: 06/01/91 Ready To Ship:  0.000 I  0.0%/Net:   0.000
Last Ship:         Shipped:        0.000    Ref:
Prom Date:                                  Whse: MAIN
Config String:
```

Enter ? for Item Information

Enter the Item Master number

F11. SYMIX relates customer order information throughout all modules.

Product Configurator

```
11/04/91              PRODUCT CONFIGURATOR  SREFLECT         16:12:39
                     FEATURE GROUP: SREFLECT

Item Number  Item Description       Qty Per   Increm. Price
RF-10000     Rear Reflectors       1.00000    1.63000
RF-20000     Front Reflectors      1.00000    1.63000
RF-30000     Wheel Reflectors      1.00000    1.63000
SKIP CHOICE  (NO SELECTION)        0.00000    0.00000

                                                    Page  1 of  1
Prom Date:                         Whse: MAIN
Config String: CG-10-TS-,,-RWB-,,-BL-,,
```

Use Cursor keys to position, press ENTER to select

F12. Product Configurator allows you to simulate products with multiple product options.

```
                Multi Currency Enabled: Yes
                Global Currency Master: No
                      Domestic Currency: US$
                  Currency Gain Account: 40800  -
                                                    Currency Gains
              Currency Loss Account: 50600  -
                                                    Currency Losses

              Multi Div. Enabled: No
                          Division:        -       -
                     Division Name:
              Global Customer Master: No
              Global Vendor Master: No

          Report Header:              Symix Computer Systems Inc.
```

Choose a command.

F14. The Multi-Currency and Division module supports foreign trade and separate operations.

```
     ECN:        2   Status: R (Requested)    Requested Date: 05/02/91
                                               Approved Date:  05/03/91
          Item: FA-20000                       Effective Date: 05/03/91
                26" Model 50 Bicycle           Completed Date:

     Revision: REV-3
     Drawing Nbr: D-17484-3

     Originator: David Daniels

          Priority: 02  Change Within 24 Hours
          Reason: STD  Standard Product Enhancement
          Dist: UP  All Vice-presidents

          Notes: Delete packaging operation.
```

Enter data or press ESC to end.

F16. Engineering Change Notice maintains tight control of item changes.

```
   (P) PO Receiving            (A) Barcoded Reader Menu
   (S) Shipping                (B) Barcoded Item Labels
   (C) Cycle Counting          (D) User-Defined Label Layout
   (M) Misc Issue/Receipt      (E) User-Defined Label Report
   (J) Job Material            (F) Barcoded Intermec Utility Menu

   (1) Stock Movement          (H) Transfer Ship
   (2) Physical Inventory      (I) Transfer Receive
   (3) Job Labor
   (4) Time & Attendance
   (5) Time & Attendance Log   (U) User Menu (runs usrmenu.p)
   (6) Job Receipt             (R) Return
```

SELECTION:

Enter data or press ESC to end.

F13. Data Collection automates material, labor, and Time and Attendance transactions.

```
Cust: 7          Travel Time Bicycles    Credit Limit:   35,000.00
Cust Currency: US$ On Order Bal:  1,646.00  Posted Bal:    3,794.85
```

Type	Invoice	Order	Chk/Ref	Inv Date	Due/Pmt	Amount	Abbrev Descr
I	120	1	0	12/16/90	01/13/91	16,498.00	Invoice 120
P	120		3204		01/13/91	498.00CR	Payment 3204
P	120		3288		01/20/91	8,000.00CR	Payment 3288
P	120		3391		01/20/91	8,000.00CR	Payment 3391
I	129	9	0	02/20/91	03/22/91	3,794.85	Invoice 129

Page 1 of 1

Choose a command.

F15. SYMIX provides financial support with AR, AP, GL, Payroll, and Fixed Assets.

Product Name: THE JIT ENTERPRISE RESOURCE SYSTEM

Current Version:	V4.01	Number of	
Release Date:	07/15/91	Installed Sites:	70+

Product Summary:

JIT's enterprise-wide, fully integrated, turnkey solutions for manufacturing, distribution, and financial functions are client-server graphical user interface menu-driven packages. Based on Oracle Corporation's relational database technology, including structured query language (SQL) and fourth-generation language (4GL) software tools. This system provides management with "real-time" visibility into the operations of their entire enterprise so they are able to make tactical and strategic adjustments as world markets change.

Vendor Name: **Just in Time Resources International, Inc.**

Address: 1705 S. Capital of Texas Hwy.
Suite 400
Austin, TX 78746

Number of Employees: 70+

Phone: (800)433-2467 (512)328-1241

Support Services: 800 number telephone support, on-site consulting and regularly scheduled training classes are also available.

Modifications: Available directly from Just in Time.

Source Code: Source code is available.

Full System Product Pricing (in U.S. $)	under $20,000	$20,001 -40,000	$40,001 -60,000	$60,001 -100,000	over $100,000
4 users			x		
16 users				x	
64 users					x

(all figures are based on approximate U.S. sales price, and are subject to change at any time)

Product Distribution:
Direct sales through U.S. regional offices. International sales through distributors.

Language/Database:
ORACLE Relational Database, 4GL, SQL, ORACLE Forms, ORACLE Plus, ORACLE CASE

Operating Platforms:
Any platform and operating system that ORACLE supports. Examples: IBM-AIX, DEC-VMS & Ultrix, HP-MPE & UX, DG-AOS & Unix, Sun, Prime, MIPS, Bull, Tandem, NCR/AT&T, Motorola, Unisys, etc.

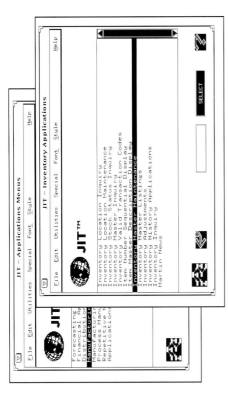

F01. JIT's Graphical User Interface brings Macintosh and Windows ease of use to multi-user manufacturing systems through the use of icons, menu bars, pop-up windows, and pull-down lists. Note the *help* and *system browser* icons.

F02. We have chosen Manufacturing from the main menu and then selected the Inventory submenu to be brought forward to show some of the JIT inventory functions. You can see how multiple windows stack. Also note the scroll bar.

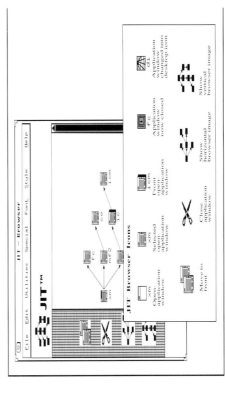

F03. We have selected an Inventory Maintenance window to overlay the Inventory submenu. Note the JIT inventory functionality.

F04. The JIT System Browser, with its browser icons, is dynamically built as you access parts of the system. The Browser lets you know where you are and gives you a fast path to anywhere you have already been.

(PSPS)   Planning Sheet   Page 1 of 3
MATERIAL REQUIREMENTS PLANNING INQUIRY

Planner Code : MRP   Planning Type: II
Item No : T-216   DATA COLLECTION TERMINAL   ECL : A
U/M : EA   On Hand: 122   Floorstock: 0   MRB: -8   Recv: 6

Date Required	DEMAND Forecast	Independent	Dependent	SUPPLY Released	Planned	Firmed
06/28/91	0	0	0	123	1	0
08/08/91	0	0	0	124	6	0
08/11/91	0	0	0	130	16	0
09/06/91	6	0	0	140	3	0
09/11/91	49	0	0	143	19	0
09/11/91	0	0	0	113	5	0
09/17/91	38	0	0	118	16	0
09/20/91	0	0	0	36	0	0
09/27/91	50	0	0	-14	0	0
10/04/91	47	0	0	61	0	0
10/11/91	50	0	0	-111	0	0
10/18/91	50	0	0	-111	0	50

Count: #1

F06. JIT Material Requirements Planning Inquiry displays by item number with planner code groups for the demand, projected on hand, and supply (released, planned, and confirmed) by required date buckets as generated by the MRP run.

(PSPS)   Planning Sheet   Page 3 of 3
MATERIAL REQUIREMENTS SUPPLY INQUIRY

Item No : T-216   DATA COLLECTION TERMINAL   Date : 06/28/91

Order No	Type	Firm	Started	Status	Ordered	Released	Complete	Scrapped
0111	10	Y	06/28/91		25		24	0

Count: #1

F08. JIT Material Requirements Supply Inquiry displays by item number the supply status that exists or has been planned by MRP.

F05. Here you can see the JIT Browser window and a series of windows that have taken you from a main menu to the submenu and to a detail entry window.

(PSPS)   Planning Sheet   Page 2 of 3
MATERIAL REQUIREMENTS DEMAND INQUIRY

Item No : T-216   DATA COLLECTION TERMINAL   Date : 06/28/91

Parent / Source	Project	WBS	Type	Quantity

FRM-40350: Query caused no records to be retrieved.
Count: #0

F07. Material Requirements Demand Inquiry displays by item number the parent-source demand pegging used by the MRP run.

```
(ICCM)    Inventory Cost Data Maintenance
          INVENTORY COST DATA MAINTENANCE                    Page 1 of 4
Item Number : T-216            Unit of Measure : EA
Descriptior: DATA COLLECTION TERMINAL

Cost Type    : S.  FIXED STANDARD COST

Routing Revision A   and ECL A     were used to calculate product costs.

Recalculate (Y/N) : Y              Date Last Recalculated : 09/05/91
Accounting Lot Size:      10       Date Last Roll-up      : 09/02/91

Incr. Material     :       124     Accum. Material     :  194.935
Incr. Labor        :     218.2     Accum. Labor        :  254.62
Incr. Service      :         0     Accum. Service      :      0
Incr. Variable O/H :     17.11     Accum. Variable O/H :   18.93
Incr. Fixed O/H    :    126.07     Accum. Fixed O/H    :   72.72

Average Purch Cost :               Unburdened Cost     :  449.575
Exchange Unit      :               Mfg. Unit Cost      :  463.505
Exchange Rate (Hist):              Mfg. Unit Cost      :  541.225

Count: *1                                              ⟨Replace⟩
```

F09. JIT Inventory Costs displays the incremental and accumulated cost by cost type for each part number.

```
(ICME)    Inventory Master Entry
          INVENTORY MAINTENANCE                              Page 1 of 4
Item Number : T-216            Plant : [
Description: DATA COLLECTION TERMINAL    Unit of Measure : EA

Current Revision      : A      Equipment Group
Cur Rtng Rev          : A      Stock Area                        AIS
Project Ctrl (Y/N)    : N      Bin Location                      20000
Lot Controlled        : N      Multi-Location        (Y/N)       Y
Serial Controlled     : N      Inv. Relief Method (M/A)          M
Warranty Days         : 360    Inspection Required (Y/N)         Y
Item Type             : B      Phantom Item (Y/N)                N
Material Type         : RESALE         Shelf Life
Product Code          : AAA100         Count Cycle (Days)        0
Product Group         : PRODUCT GROUP A   Status (A/I)           A
Account Class         :        Drop Ship Flag (Y/N)              N
ABC Class             : A      Tax Authority 1                   I
CAD Code              :        Tax Authority 2                   I
Drawing Reference     : IMAGE          Tax Authority 3           I
Vendor Number         :        Tax Authority 4                   -
Vendor Item No        : Test Vendor    Tax Authority 5           -
Manufactures No       : CID-2000       Tax Authority 6           -

Count: *1                                              ⟨Replace⟩
```

F10. JIT Inventory Maintenance (page 1 of 4) shows the depth of function-ality of this JIT module. This screen sets up the basic data elements relating to a part number; these default values are used for validation system wide.

```
(ICME)    Inventory Master Entry
          INVENTORY LOCATION MAINTENANCE                     Page 2 of 4
Item Number : T-216    Unit Meas: EA   Wt:     25  Cube:     1000
Description: DATA COLLECTION TERMINAL   Reorder: _  Disocnt: _  Replaced: _

Picking Stock Area: AIS          Safety Whse #3
Bin Location      : 2000         Bin Location
Zone              : 100          Zone
Reorder Point     :              Reorder Point
Minimum Order Qty :              Minimum Order Qty:

Safety Whse #1    : AIS          Substitute Item 1:
Bin Location      : 2000         Substitute Item 2:
Zone              : 3            Substitute Item 3:
Reorder Point     : 500          Replacement Date :
Minimum Order Qty : 1000         Replacement Qty on Hand:
                                 Primary Ship Method : 100 TEST
Safety Whse #2    :              Secondary Ship Method: 002 OUR TRUCK
Bin Location      :
Zone              :              Promotional Qty   : 2
Reorder Point     :              At Location       : 101
Minimum Order Qty :

Count: *1                                              ⟨Replace⟩
```

F11. Page 2 of JIT Inventory Maintenance by part number.

```
(ICME)    Inventory Master Entry
          WAREHOUSE MANAGEMENT DATA                          Page 3 of 4
Item Number : T-216            Unit of Meas: EA
Description: DATA COLLECTION TERMINAL

Units per Case    :     5
Cases Per Layer   :     4
Layers per Pallet :     3

Case Weight  :     28

Case Dimensions:          Height:    12
(in inches)               Width:     24
                          Depth:      9

Count: *1                                              ⟨Replace⟩
```

F12. Page 3 of JIT Inventory Maintenance by part number.

F14. The JIT Inventory Planning Maintenance Screen is used to set up the planning data elements for a part number, including values like make or buy, order policy code, order quantity amounts, and so forth.

F16. The JIT Purchase Order Buyer History screen displays by part number the preferred vendor by rank and actual PO transactions.

F13. Page 4 of JIT Inventory Maintenance by part number.

F15. On this JIT Bill of Material Inquiry screen, a bill of material is displayed in an indented multiple-level format.

Product Name: **MPS**_plus_

Current Version:	4.0	Number of	
Release Date:	10/18/91	Installed Sites:	45

Product Summary:

MPS_plus_ is a powerful, PC-based production scheduling, finite capacity planning, and what-if system that substantially enhances the planning capabilities of MRPII and other manufacturing systems. Versions address Repetitive, Process, and Discrete manufacturing plus combinations. Computer Aided Scheduling (CAS) module features both Auto and Interactive scheduling. Multi-Route, Multi-Level, Aggregate, Process Planning, and other modules available as well.

Vendor Name: **Bridgeware, Inc.**

Address: 3541 Investment Blvd., Suite 4
Hayward, CA 94545-3705

Number of Employees: 12

Phone: (510)784-0354 FAX: (510)784-0381

Support Services: A complete line of integration services including turn-key integration with MRPII or other host systems. Customer support program including technical support and system upgrades. Education, training, plus business and technical consulting.

Modifications: Three types of system modifications are available: (1) User-generated via Report Writer; (2) Bridgeware-generated via Report Writer; or (3) Bridgeware-developed modifications to the package (95 percent included in standard system to date).

Source Code: Generally not provided with license. Source code escrow option is available.

Full System Product Pricing (in U.S. $)	under $20,000	$20,001 -40,000	$40,001 -60,000	$60,001 -100,000	over $100,000
4 users		x			
16 users			x		
64 users				x	

(all figures are based on approximate U.S. sales price, and are subject to change at any time)

Product Distribution:

Direct sales through U.S. offices in Hayward (San Francisco) and Chicago. International sales through distributors in United Kingdom and Israel. Additional distributorships pending. Also complementary vendor relationships with ASK Computer Systems and Hewlett-Packard.

Language/Database:

Clipper (Nantucket 4GL) and C. dBASE data structures. Next release will support client/server architecture and variety of SQL servers.

Operating Platforms:

IBM or compatible microcomputers under MS-DOS, Version 3.1 or later. Multiuser systems run on any OS/2, Unix, or Novell-based server.

Schedule Balancing...
Schedule Change By Item...
Schedule Cut By Load Center...
Schedule Add By Load Center...
Schedule Tradeoff...
Schedule Demand (C/O DMND)...
Schedule Capacity...
Routing Tradeoff...
Schedule Disaggregation...
Auto Scheduling...

Esc=Cancel

F02. Main menu with Computer Aided Scheduling (CAS) submenu pulled down. Functions selected via light bar or trigger characters.

LOAD CENTER DATA   10/01/91

* Load Center ID: LABOR-1   Description: OPERATORS
  Load Center Type: C   Constraint: Y
  Unit of Measure: HRS   Text ID:

Effectivity Date	Rate Or Discrete	Capacity (Units/Day)
11/02/91	R	2700.0
11/04/91	R	2000.0

Ret/Beg/End/Next/Prev/Modi/Add/Copy/Del/Tally/Unzoom/Quit
Modify the current record

F04. Load Center Data. Time-phased capacity data for key resources such as machines, labor, or important materials.

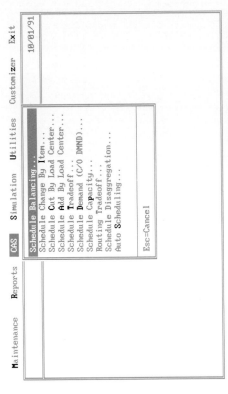

M P S p l u s - C

Copyright (c) 1988, 1989, 1990
Bridgeware, Inc. All Rights Reserved

Release: 4.0-00   Single-User

Password:

SN: MP9-6014 Licensed To: BWI-Marketing

Licensed Modules : ▶Basic   ▶Simulation   ▶Multi-Level
                   ▶CAS   ▶Co-Products   ▶Aggregate
                   ▶PBOM   ▶Multi-Route

F01. MPSplus Logon screen. Choice of system-level password or operator/function-specific security.

ITEM DATA - PAGE 1   10/01/91

* Item No: TR-100   Desc: 3-LINE OFFICE PHONE
  Unit of Measure: EA   Type: 1
  Inventory Balance: 2400   Primary PAB Code: F
  Planner: DS   Item Priority: 1
  Safety Stock Policy: D   Safety Stock (Days): 12
  Multiple Quantity: 1   Minimum Quantity: 0
  Time Fence: 15   Excess Filter: 9999999
  Forecast Retention: 0   C/O Dmnd Horizon: 0
  Group Number: Sub-Group Number:

Ret/Beg/End/Next/Prev/Skip/Modi/Add/Copy/Del/List/Filt/Tally/2ndpg/Quit
Go to the next record (same ↓)

F03. First page of the Item Data screen. Product data for master scheduled items. Lotus-style Command Line at bottom for inquiry/maintenance.

LOAD PROFILE DATA INQUIRY

Item No: AR-100   Desc: 3-LINE OFFICE PHONE   10/01/91

Load Profile ID	Load Center ID	U/M	Eff Date	Load Units	Load Ofst	Load Drtn
1	COST-1	DOL	01/02/91	32.000000	0	1
2	LABOR-1	HRS	01/02/91	1.000000	1	1
3	P100	HRS	01/02/91	1.500000	3	1
4	PACK	HRS	01/02/91	0.200000	1	1
5	MATERIAL-1	EA	01/02/91	1.000000	9	1

Page: PgDn/PgUp   Scroll: ↑↓   Top: ^PgUp   Bottom: ^PgDn   Quit: F3,/,Home

F05. Load Profile Data Inquiry. Describes resources used by this item during manufacture. Time-phased. Note usage rates and time offsets.

MASTER SCHEDULE INQUIRY

10/01/91

Planner: DS   Group Number:
                 Sub-Group Number:

Item No: AR-100   Desc: 3-LINE OFFICE PHONE

Type	Class	U/M	PaB Code	Fcst Retn	C/O Horz	Excess Filter	S/S Days	Tm Fnc	Multiple Supl Qty	Invntry Balance
M		EA	F	0	0	99999999	10	15	1	2400

Type	PASDUE	OCT-91	NOV-91	DEC-91	JAN-92	FEB-92
Demand Fcst		9500	10000	10000	14000	10000
C/O Demand	0	4532	10000	9000	6000	10000
MPS Supply	0	6398	12264	10570	13167	13966
PAB(F)	2400	-702	1562	2132	1299	1265
ATP	0	4266	2264	1570	7167	3966
SS Goal	5000	4348	5263	5833	7368	7000
PAB(F) $Cost						0
DOI(F)	4	-1	2	3	1	1

Page: PgDn/PgUp   Scroll: ↑↓   Top: ^PgUp   Bottom: ^PgDn   Quit: F3,/,Home

F06. Master Schedule Report. Supply/Demand data, calculations, and periods all customizable. Exception summary at end.

SUMMARY LOAD ANALYSIS INQUIRY

10/01/91

Load Center: LABOR-1   Type: C   Desc: OPERATORS
U/M: HRS   Constraint: Y

Period	Req Load	Capacity	Load%	O/S Cap	** Cumulative ** Load%	O/S Cap
OCT-91	20714.5	54000.0	38	33285.5	38	33285.5
NOV-91	31307.0	49500.0	63	18193.0	50	51478.5
DEC-91	22826.0	38000.0	60	15174.0	53	66652.5
JAN-92	32879.6	48000.0	68	15120.4	57	81772.9
FEB-92	26028.0	38000.0	68	11972.0	59	93744.9
MAR-92	13602.1	40000.0	34	26397.9	55	120142.8
APR-92	0.0	40000.0	0	40000.0	48	160142.8
MAY-92	0.0	48000.0	0	48000.0	41	208142.8
JUN-92	0.0	40000.0	0	40000.0	37	248142.8
JUL-92	0.0	48000.0	0	48000.0	33	296142.8
AUG-92	0.0	36000.0	0	36000.0	31	332142.8
SEP-92	0.0	38000.0	0	38000.0	28	370142.8

Page: PgDn/PgUp   Scroll: ↑↓   Top: ^PgUp   Bottom: ^PgDn   Quit: F3,/,Home

F07. Summary Load Analysis Report. Good for snapshot of load versus capacity, not for interactively adjusting schedules within capacity.

AUTO SCHEDULING - OPTIONS SELECTION

10/01/91

Auto Scheduling Process	(Y/N)	Constraint/Target
Delete Current Supplies	Y	
Balancing	Y	PAB(F) = SS
Cut Phase I	Y	PAB(C) = 0
Cut Phase II	Y	Unrestricted
Add Phase I	Y	PAB(F) = 0
Add Phase II	Y	PAB(F) = SS

Select/2ndpg Quit
Select data

F08. CAS Auto Scheduling. For quick, easy generation of feasible, efficient schedule. Interactive scheduling also provided.

SCHEDULE BALANCING

* Item No: BR-100 Plnr Pry Mltpl Qty   Desc: 3-LINE OFFICE PHONE   PD PAB(F) PD PAB(C)
  DS   S/S Days 10   Inmtry 2400   2400   2400

Adjust supply so that:

A. PAB(F) = 0
B. PAB(C) = 0
C. PAB(M) = 0
D. PAB(F) = SS
E. PAB(C) = SS
F. PAB(M) = SS
G. PAB(F) = Target Inventory
H. PAB(C) = Target Inventory
I. PAB(M) = Target Inventory
J. PAB(F) ≥ 0
K. PAB(C) ≥ SS
L. Supply = Forecast
M. Supply = Backlog
N. Supply = Demand

Period	AB(F)	PAB(C)	S	Chg Qty	Sup Qty
U1OCT1	400	400	P	0	0
U2OCT1	0	1968	P	0	2100
U3OCT1	-198	2278	P	0	2310
U4OCT1	-782	4266	P	0	1988
U1NOV1	-2142	0	P	0	734
U2NOV1	646	4962	P	0	4962
U3NOV1	647	7137	P	0	2175
U4NOV1	1288	9952	P	0	2815
U5NOV1	1562	6530	P	0	1578
DEC-91	2132	8100	P	0	10570
JAN-92	1299	15267	P	0	13167
FEB-92	1265	19233	P	0	13966

Move: ↑↓   Select: ↵   Quit: Esc

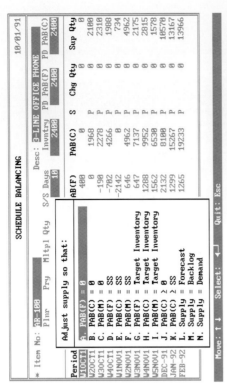

F10. Balance Supply to Demand over horizon of choice. Select from variety of balancing options. Graphical display available as well.

SCHEDULE CAPACITY

* Ld Center: LABOR-1   Description   U/M Type   Text ID
                       OPERATORS   HRS C

Eff Date	R/D	Change	Capacity
01/02/91	R	0.0	2700.0
11/04/91	R	0.0	2000.0
/ /	E	0.0	0.0

Period	Capacity	Req Load	O/S Cap
U1OCT1	13500.0	4405.5	9894.5
U2OCT1	13500.0	4256.5	9243.5
U3OCT1	13500.0	6065.6	7434.4
U4OCT1	13500.0	5151.9	8348.1
U1NOV1	13500.0	4416.8	9083.2
U2NOV1	10000.0	9100.0	900.0
U3NOV1	10000.0	6849.2	3150.8
U4NOV1	10000.0	6849.5	3150.5
U5NOV1	6000.0	4091.5	1908.5
DEC-91	38000.0	22826.0	15174.0
JAN-92	48000.0	32879.6	15120.4
FEB-92	38000.0	26028.0	11972.0

Move: ↑↓, ↵   Accept record: PgDn, ↵   Quit edit: Esc

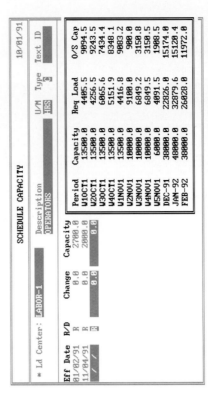

F12. CAS Schedule Capacity. Adjust the capacity for flexible resources, i.e., extra shift of operator overtime.

SCHEDULE BALANCING

* Item No: BR-100 Plnr Pry Mltpl Qty   Desc: 3-LINE OFFICE PHONE   PD PAB(F) PD PAB(C)
  DS   S/S Days 10   Inmtry 2400   2400   2400

Period	SS GOAL	C/O DMND	FORECAST	PAB(F)	PAB(C)	S	Chg Qty	Sup Qty
U1OCT1*	5000	2400	2000	400	400	P	0	0
U2OCT1*	5000	132	2500	0	1968	P	0	2100
U3OCT1*	4857	2000	2500	-198	2278	P	0	2310
U4OCT1*	4348	0	2500	-782	4266	P	0	1988
U1NOV1	4348	5000	2174	-2142	0	P	0	734
U2NOV1	4348	0	2174	646	4962	P	0	4962
U3NOV1	4348	0	2174	647	7137	P	0	2175
U4NOV1	4989	0	2174	1288	9952	P	0	2815
U5NOV1	5263	5000	1304	1562	6530	P	0	1578
DEC-91	5833	9000	10000	2132	8100	P	0	10570
JAN-92	0	6000	14000	1299	15267	P	0	13167
FEB-92	0	10000	14000	1265	19233	P	0	13966

Ret/Beg/End/Next/Prev/Tod1/Graph/Tally/Unzoom/Other/Quit
Modify the current record

F09. For example, interactive Schedule Balancing. Like a Master Schedule Report you can edit. Data columns customizable.

SCHEDULE DEMAND (C/O DMND)

* Item No: BR-100 Plnr Pry Family No S/S Days   Desc: 3-LINE OFFICE PHONE   PD AVL(C) PD PAB(C)
  DS   10   Inmtry 2400   2400   2400

Period	AVL(C)	PAB(C)
U1OCT1	0	0
U2OCT1	0	1968
U3OCT1	0	2278
U4OCT1	0	4266
U1NOV1	0	0

Period	AVL(C)	PAB(C)
U2NOV1	4962	4962
U3NOV1	6530	7137
U4NOV1	6530	9952
U5NOV1	6530	6530
DEC-91	8100	8100

Due Date	Order Number	Quantity	S	T	Order Reference
09/30/91	CUSA121	1400			
10/04/91	CUSA111	1000			
/ /	CUSA232	132			
10/08/91	CUSA121	1500			
10/14/91	CUSA421	500			

Move: ↑↓, ↵   Accept record: PgDn, ↵   Quit edit: Esc

F11. CAS Schedule Demand. Add a new customer order after reviewing product availability. Example of discrete demand, rate-based supply.

SCHEDULE CHANGE BY ITEM 10/01/91

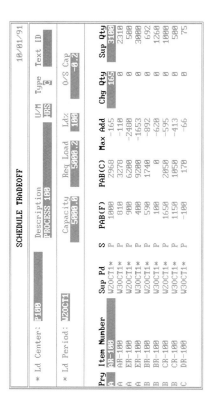

* Item No: AR-100
  Plnr: A Pry: A Mltpl Qty: 1 S/S Days: 10 Desc: C-LINE OFFICE PHONE
  DS   Inventry 2400 PD PAB(F) 2400 Change 0 PD PAB(C) 2400

* Sup Period: W20CT1*
  S P PAB(F) 0 PAB(C) 1935 Max Add 835 Sup Qty 2100

Load Center	Ld Period	Type	Req Load	Sup Ldz	Tot Ldz	Add To 100%
MATERIAL-1	W10CT1	C	420.0	10	33	45472
LABOR-1	W20CT1	C	1680.0	39	32	11554
MATERIAL-1	W10CT1	M	420.0	55	55	22696
P100	W10CT1	C	1890.0	50	83	841
P100	W10CT1	C	1260.0	28	90	835
P100	W10CT1	C	84.0	2	96	3365
PACK	W10CT1	C				
PACK	W20CT1	C	336.0	19	50	10994

Ret Beg/End/Next/Prev/Tally/Unzoom/Quit
Retrieve a record by its key field(s)

F13. CAS Schedule Change By Item. Book against available capacity. In this case, screen shows 835 more units can be made before bottleneck hits.

SCHEDULE TRADEOFF 10/01/91

* Ld Center: P100   Description PROCESS 100   U/M HRS   Type C   Text ID
* Ld Period: W20CT1*   Capacity 5000.0   Req Load 5000.2   Ldz 100   O/S Cap -0.2

Pry	Item Number	S	Sup Pd	PAB(F)	PAB(C)	Max Add	Chg Qty	Sup Qty
A	AR-100	P	W20CT1*	1000	2968	-165	165	3100
A	AR-100	P	W30CT1*	810	3278	-110	0	2310
A	ER-100	P	W10CT1*	900	6200	-2400	0	500
A	ER-100	P	W30CT1*	400	9200	-1653	0	3000
B	BR-100	P	W30CT1*	590	1740	-892	0	692
B	BR-100	P	W30CT1*	100		-628	0	1260
B	CR-100	P	W20CT1*	1650	2050	-595	0	1000
B	CR-100	P	W30CT1*	1150	1050	-413	0	500
C	DR-100	P	W30CT1*	-100	178	-66	0	75

Move: ↑ ↓, ↵   Accept record: PgDn, ↵   Quit edit: Esc   Balance: B

F14. CAS Schedule Tradeoff. Adjust the product mix on a bottleneck resource. Max Add says if we add 165 units of AR-100, others will have to give.

LINE LOADING 02/14/92

* Ld Center: LINE-1   Description PRODUCTION LINE # 1   U/M HRS   Type C   Text ID

Item Number	Sup Pd	Quantity	PAB(F)	0215-1	0215-2	0216-1	0216-2	021792	021792
BUBBL-500	0215-1	3500	500	35.0					
BUBBL-200	0215-2	1000	1000		10.0				
BUBBL-700	0215-2	1300	1300		15.0				
BUBBL-100	0216-1	1000	1300			18.0			
BUBBL->MINT	CHANGEOVER					17.0			
MINT-100	0216-2	500	500				5.0		
MINT-300	0216-2	3000	3075				30.0		
MINT-500	0216-2	1500	50						
FRUIT-600	021792	1500	700					15.0	
FRUIT-300	021792	1500	900					15.0	
	Total Capacity			35.0	25.0	35.0	25.0	60.0	
	Total Load			35.0	25.0	35.0	35.0	55.0	
	O/S Capacity			0.0	0.0	0.0	-10.0	5.0	

Modify/Options/Graph/Unzoom/Quit
Display graph

F15. Line Loading screen from Process Planning module. Sequence production on a line including changeovers.

LINE LOADING

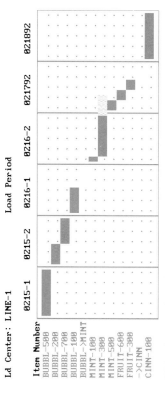

Ld Center: LINE-1

Load Period: 0215-1 0215-2 0216-1 0216-2 021792 021892

Item Number: BUBBL-500, BUBBL-200, BUBBL-700, BUBBL-100, BUBBL->MINT, MINT-100, MINT-300, MINT-500, FRUIT-600, FRUIT-300, ->CINN, CINN-100

F16. Line Loading displayed graphically.

Product Name: Expandable/MRP

Current Version: V4.4	Number of
Release Date: 10/01/91	Installed Sites: 175+

Product Summary:

Expandable/MRP™, an integrated financial, sales, and factory management system (MRP II), features 20 easy-to-use modules aimed at small to mid-size discrete, make-to-order, repetitive, JIT, and batch process manufacturers. Modules include: Inventory, Lot Control, PO, BOM, Standard Costing, Job Scheduling/Costing, Shop Routing, MRP, Master Scheduling, Labor Distribution, GL, AR, AP, SO, Executive Information, Multi-Company, Foreign Currency, Data Dictionary, OnLine Query™, Data Export, and Mass Change Editor.

Vendor Name: Expandable Software, Inc.

Address: 1171 Homestead Road
Santa Clara, CA 95050–5478

Number of Employees: 25

Phone: (408)247-1500 FAX: (408)247-2160

Support Services: Call-in hotline support; remote diagnostics; data conversion; system configuration; installation; on-site training; classroom education (regularly scheduled and on-site); software enhancements and maintenance.

Modifications: Expandable personnel will do limited modifications that do not affect the system's ability to receive upgrades and standard enhancements.

Source Code: User modifications discouraged, but source code is available at $25,000 plus annual maintenance of $3,750.

Full System Product Pricing (in U.S. $)	under $20,000	$20,001 -40,000	$40,001 -60,000	$60,001 -100,000	over $100,000
4 users		X			
16 users			X		
64 users				X	

(all figures are based on approximate U.S. sales price, and are subject to change at any time)

Product Distribution:

Direct sales and support through U.S. regional offices in Santa Clara, CA; Newport Beach, CA; Portland, OR; and Westboro, MA. International sales direct through authorized distributors in Australia, New Zealand, Indonesia, Hong Kong and PRC, Taiwan, and Europe.

Language/Database:

DataFlex object-oriented 4GL and relational DBMS; Database Engine supports client/server model; C; FlexQL SQL report writer; open databases (APIs to third-party databases, e.g., NetWareSQL); SAA/CUA compliant and graphical Windows and Motif interface in 1992.

Operating Platforms:

IBM and compatible PCs, DOS 3.1+, OS/2, Novell NetWare, LANtastic, LAN Manager, LAN Server, Banyan Vines; DEC VAX/VMS, IBM AIX on RS/6000, UNIX and NFS on Sun and selected additional UNIX platforms.

ICIPM   PART MASTER DETAIL - SCREEN 2   COST DATA

```
ICIPM            PART MASTER DETAIL - SCREEN 2          COST DATA

     PART ID: 649N                         TYPE: N  MAKE
 DESCRIPTION: JACK, HYDRAULIC FLOOR ROLLER, 2 TON    UM: EA
 SEARCH NAME: JACK, HYDRAULIC      PLANNER: PP       BUYER: DAL

 LABOR TYPE 1: MFG1          HRS:        0.0400
 LABOR TYPE 2: MFG2          HRS:        0.2200
 LABOR TYPE 3: MFG3          HRS:        0.2200
 LABOR HRS ADDED:     0.4800          CUM:        1.7622

 LABOR COST ADDED:     3.535000       CUM:       13.575000
 MATERIAL COST ADDED:  0.000000       CUM:       23.731520
 OUTSIDE COST ADDED:   2.000000       CUM:        2.000000
 OVERHEAD COST ADDED:  2.767500       CUM:        7.707500
                                STD UNIT COST:    47.094020

                               DATE LAST UPDATE: 10/08/91
 ESC-Exit    F10-1stScreen
```

F04. Part Master Screen 2. Contains part standard cost information. Simplified job system has three labor types per assembly; routing module available.

```
ICIPS            PART STATUS INQUIRY                 V:09-OCT-91 12:46
     PART NAME                PART ID                        ST TY

 JACK, HYDRAULI
 JACK, HYDRAULI
 ASSEMBLY, CAST
 ASSEMBLY, FROM               Select Part Inquiry
 JACK, HYDRAULI
 PLANNING BILL             INVENTORY CONTROL
 JACK, HYDRAULI            PURCHASING
 REPAIR KIT                JOB SCHEDULING
 ASSEMBLY, WHEE            PRODUCT DATA CONTROL
 JACK, HYDRAULI            SALES ORDER
 TEST Q                    MASTER SCHEDULING
 TEST Q                    MATERIALS MANAGEMENT
                           SHOP ROUTING
                           LOT TRACKING

                          ↵-Select         ↑-LineUp      gUp Ctrl-PgUp
 ESC-Exit  F5-                             ↓-LineDn      gDn Ctrl-PgDn
```

F02. Part Status Inquiry. One of four powerful inquiries. Others are Purchasing/AP, Sales Order/AR and GL. All reports are to the screen, print-er, and file.

```
SCRMENU          EXPANDABLE/MRP VERSION 4.4          V:07-OCT-91 13:27

                     EXPANDABLE SOFTWARE, INC.

 MANUFACTURING DATA MANAGEMENT         FINANCIAL DATA MANAGEMENT
 IC -- INVENTORY CONTROL               SO -- SALES ORDER
 PD -- PURCHASING                      AR -- ACCOUNTS RECEIVABLE
 JC -- JOB SCHEDULING/COSTING          AP -- ACCOUNTS PAYABLE
 MM -- MATERIALS MANAGEMENT (MRP)      GL -- GENERAL LEDGER
 MS -- MASTER SCHEDULING               LD -- LABOR DISTRIBUTION
 ML -- MULTIPLE LOCATION               MC -- MULTIPLE COMPANY
 TI -- TAG INVENTORY                   FC -- FOREIGN CURRENCY
 LT -- LOT TRACKING                    EI -- EXECUTIVE INFORMATION
 SR -- SHOP ROUTING
                                       DATA BASE MANAGEMENT
           DESIRED SELECTION?          FQ -- OnLine Query
                                       XX -- UTILITIES

 ESC-Exit   F1-Help    Copyright 1991 Expandable Software Inc.
                       F2-FreeQuest
```

F01. Main Menu. Users enter module initials to go to module menus or a function name to go to a specific function. F1-Help available all screens.

```
ICIPM         PART MASTER DETAIL - SCREEN 1         V:25-OCT-90 18:58
     PART ID: 649N
 DESCRIPTION: JACK, HYDRAULIC FLOOR ROLLER, 2 TON  TYPE: N  MAKE   UM: EA
 SEARCH NAME: JACK, HYDRAULIC        DWG REV: D         ECN: 4256
     PLANNER: PP  PRODUCTION PLANNER  BUYER: DAL, DOROTHY A. LEWIS
 PREFERRED VENDOR:          AUTO PO: N       ABC: A  COMM CODE:
 USER FIELDS 1:          2:          3:          PRODUCT LINE: 649N
 SUBSTITUTE PART:

 MRP FLAG: Y        MPS CODE: E PLAN'D END ITEM
 PLANNING HORIZON: 100    ORDER QTY: 100   MAX. ORDER QTY:      0
 DAYS SUPPLY: 0         FORECAST QTY: 4004  MIN. SALES QTY:     0
 VENDOR LT: 0            RECU LT: 0   KIT LT: 0   MFG LT: 5
 SHIPPING LT: 0         PLAN LT: 4    CUM LT: 69  YIELD: 0.0
                                      SERIAL NO. REQD: N
 WEIGHT: 50.0000    VOLUME: 0.0000        CREATED: 05/30/89
 COMMENT ID:             STATUS: A  ACTIVE     OBSOLETE:
                           COST: 47.094020 LAST UPDATE: 10/08/91

 ESC-Exit   F10-2ndScreen
```

F03. Part Master Screen 1. Contains part data, lead times for MRP/MPS, total cost, etc.

```
MSINS                    MASTER SCHEDULE INQUIRY              U:14-FEB-91 14:37

   PART ID: 649M                          TYPE: M MAKE
DESCRIPTION: JACK, HYDRAULIC FLOOR ROLLER, 2 TON    SEARCH NAME: JACK, HYDRAULIC
UNIT OF MEAS: EA                      SUBSTITUTE PART:
PART STATUS: A ACTIVE
```

PLAN DATE	FORECAST	PROD FORECAST	DEMAND	FIRM/OPEN	PLAN ORDER	PROJ ON HAND	ATP
11-05-91	0	0	2	0	0	533	0
11/25/91	0	0	11	0	0	533	0
11/27/91	400	0	0	0	0	133	0
12/27/91	500	0	0	0	500	133	500
01/25/92	500	0	0	0	500	133	500
02/27/92	700	0	0	0	700	133	700
03/27/92	700	0	0	0	700	133	700
04/27/92	800	0	0	0	800	133	800

```
ESC-Exit                          ↵-Select ↑-LineUp PgUp ↓-LineDn PgDn
```

F05. Master Schedule Detail. A portion of the Master Schedule Detail for a given part. Demand and Planning Time Fence exceptions reported.

```
MMRP1              MATERIAL REQUIREMENTS PLANNING REPORT      U:06-AUG-91 14:19

   RANGE OF PART ID'S? ALL
         PLAN THRU DATE? 12/31/91

   INCLUDE MAKE PARTS?    Y
           PHANTOM PARTS? Y
               BUY PARTS? Y
           EXPENSE PARTS? Y

SELECT ON ACTION MESSAGE?  N

             PLACE ORDER?     Y
          EXPEDITE ORDER?     Y
         EXCESS INVENTORY?    Y

INCLUDE NO DEMAND PARTS?  Y

OUTPUT TO <P>RINTER, <S>CREEN OR <F>ILE?  S

ESC-Exit   F1-Help   F2-PrevQuest   F7-Default
```

F06. MRP Analysis Report Specification. Used for generating specific MRP reports.

```
MMRP                  REQUIREMENTS PLANNING INQUIRY           U:06-AUG-91 15:04

   PART ID: 649M                          TYPE: M MAKE
DESCRIPTION: JACK, HYDRAULIC FLOOR ROLLER, 2 TON    SEARCH NAME: JACK, HYDRAULIC
UNIT OF MEAS: EA                      SUBSTITUTE PART:
PART STATUS: A ACTIVE
```

AT	PLAN DATE	GROSS REQMT	SCHED RECEIPT	PROJ AVAILABLE	PLANNED ORDER	RELEASE DATE	REFERENCE
RM	10/15/91	400		1391	0		EXCESS INVENTORY
RM	11/27/91	400		991	0		EXCESS INVENTORY
RM	12/27/91	500		491	0		EXCESS INVENTORY
RM	01/25/92	500		-9	0		EXPEDITE ORDER
RM	02/27/92	700	100	-709	659	02/23/92	EXP/PLACE ORDER
JC	03/19/92			-609	700		8030 TYPE: S
RM	03/27/92	700		-1309	700	03/23/92	PLACE ORDER
RM	04/27/92	800		-2109	800	04/23/92	PLACE ORDER

```
ESC-Exit                          ↵-Select ↑-LineUp PgUp ↓-LineDn PgDn
```

F07. MRP Detail. MRP Detail inquiry showing a portion of the detail for a given part and the exception messages available.

```
ICIPO               PURCHASE ORDER STATUS INQUIRY            U:29-OCT-90 18:32

   PART ID: 646-7215                      TYPE: B BUY
DESCRIPTION: BOLT, ANCHOR            SEARCH NAME: BOLT, ANCHOR
UNIT OF MEAS: EA                      SUBSTITUTE PART:
PART STATUS: A ACTIVE
```

PO ID	LN	TY	DEL DATE	BAL DUE	QC QTY	SC	S	VENDOR NAME
000010	4	N	08/26/09	144	0	MS	0	ABC CORPORATION
100001	5	N	09/25/90	144	144	MS	0	ABC CORPORATION
100003	3	N	12/13/90	100	0	MS	0	ABC CORPORATION
100006	2	N	11/18/90	200	0	MS	0	ABC CORPORATION
100000	2	N	11/20/90	138	9	MS	0	ABC CORPORATION
100013	1	N	10/18/90	49	0	MS	0	ABC CORPORATION
100014	1	N	12/08/90	10	0	MS	0	ABC CORPORATION
100021	1	N	11/19/90	1	0	MS	0	ABC CORPORATION

```
ESC-Exit                          ↵-Select ↑-LineUp PgUp ↓-LineDn PgDn
```

F08. Purchase Order Status. The status of some open POs for a given part; detail available. A similar report is available by Vendor.

```
POJUP1                  VENDOR PART DETAIL              U:04-FEB-91 15:29

        PART ID: 646-7215                    TYPE: B BUY
                 BOLT, ANCHOR                     EA
                 ORDER QTY: 144       STD MTL COST:    0.125000
      VENDOR ID: ABC001    ABC CORPORATION
 VENDOR PART ID: 9595N               MFG PART ID: 9595NAD     144
 MANUFACTURER NAME: BOLTMAKERS,INC      LOT SIZE: 144
 VENDOR LEAD TIME: 10

      BUY STATUS: A APPROVED           QC FLAG: I   INCOMING QC
    PARTIAL SHIP: P10 PARTIAL, 10% OVER    TAX CODE:
        VAT CODE:                      CURR CODE:
       REFERENCE:                     QUOTE DATE: 03-21-09
 QUOTE UNIT PRICE:    0.110000         QUOTE QTY: 144
                 LAST PO ID: 100071  LAST PO DATE: 10-08-91
              LAST PO PRICE:    0.110000  LAST PO QTY: 50
                    COMMENT:
                            DATE LAST UPDATE: 10-08-91

 ESC-Exit
```

F09. Vendor Part Cross Reference Detail. The detail cross reference between the part number and the vendor/manufacturer. Unlimited references.

```
ICIJS              JOB ORDER STATUS INQUIRY            U:10-JUL-91 11:21

        PART ID: 649N                        TYPE: M MAKE
    DESCRIPTION: JACK, HYDRAULIC FLOOR ROLLER, 2 TON
  UNIT OF MEAS.: EA                 SEARCH NAME: JACK, HYDRAULIC
    PART STATUS: A ACTIVE           SUBSTITUTE PART:

 JOB ID  PRI   TY  DUE DATE  ORDER QTY  BAL DUE  SC  S  REFERENCE

 B001    1.00  S   10-09-90     100       70     MS  0  SO#100085
 B002    1.00  S   10-17-90     100      100     MS  0  SEPT ORDER
 B005    1.00  S   10-16-90      10       10     MS  0  4TH QTR ORDER
 B006    1.00  S   01-21-91     100      100     MS  0  SO#100091
 B007    1.00  S   02-21-91     100      100     MS  0
 B008    1.00  S   03-05-91     100      100     MS  0
 B009    1.00  S   03-21-91     100      100     MS  0  NOV SHIPMENT
 B013    1.00  S   04-03-91     100      100     MS  0  1ST QTR ORDER
 B020    1.00  S   02-11-91      10       10     MS  0  SO#100102

 ESC-Exit                          ←┘-Select  ↑-LineUp PgUp
                                              ↓-LineDn PgDn
```

F10. Job Order Status. The status of some job orders for a given part. Detail is available for job master, schedule, cost, kit list, and shortages.

```
JCIKS               JOB SHORTAGE INQUIRY               U:14-MAR-91 14:45

      JOB ID: B001                      TYPE: S STOCK ORDER
 DESCRIPTION: JACK, HYDRAULIC FLOOR ROLLER, 2   PART ID: 649N
 UNIT OF MEAS.: EA            BALANCE DUE: 70
 ORDER QTY: 100

 OPER  PART ID     SC  SCH KIT   KIT QTY  ISSUED  BAL DUE

   0   646-7214    MS  10-03-90    210      200      10
   0   646-7223    MS  10-03-90    200        0     200
   0   645-7225    MS  03-31-91   2000        0    2000
   0   649N-CWA    MS  10-03-90    200      100     100
  10   139         MS  05-20-91     10        1       9

 ESC-Exit                          ←┘-Select  ↑-LineUp PgUp
                                              ↓-LineDn PgDn
```

F11. Job Shortage Detail. Detailed listing of the parts short on a specific job.

```
SRIRM               ROUTING MASTER DETAIL              U:02-AUG-91 14:34

        PART ID: 649N                              TYPE: M
    DESCRIPTION: JACK, HYDRAULIC FLOOR ROLLER, 2 TON    UM: EA
   ROUTING TYPE: N          ROUTING ID: 649N-BLD    ROUTING REV: CS
 OPERATION CODE: 10           LOT SIZE: 100       PROCEDURE CODE:
 TASK DESCRIPTION: DRILL STEEL PLATE                 VENDOR:
    WORK CENTER: UC01  DRILL PRESS OPERATIONS          TYPE: B
 OPER YIELD PCT: 100.0      CUM YIELD PCT: 100.0
                  QUANTITY IN: 100     QUANTITY OUT: 100
 QUEUE HOURS PER LOT: 0.0000              CUM HRS: 0.0000
 SETUP WORK TYPE: MT   MACHINE TECHNICIAN  OPERATORS: 1.00
    SETUP HOURS: 2.0000                    CUM HRS: 2.0000
   RUN WORK TYPE: DPO   DRILL PRESS OPR.   OPERATORS: 1.00
 RUN HOURS PER PART: 0.1000  EXTD: 10.0000  CUM HRS: 10.0000
  MACH WORK TYPE:                           MACHINES: 0.00
 MACH HOURS PER PART: 0.0000  EXTD: 0.0000   CUM HRS: 0.0000
 MOVE HOURS PER LOT: 4.0000                  CUM HRS: 4.0000
 LEAD TIME IN DAYS: 2.00                    CUM DAYS: 2.00
                            DATE HRS ROLLUP: 09-03-91

 ESC-Exit
```

F12. Routing Master Detail. Traditional routing detail available for work centers, including vendor operations, tooling, and procedures.

IC1BM1   BILL OF MATERIAL DETAIL   U:25-OCT-90 18:57

```
ASSEMBLY ID: 649M                         UM: EA      TYPE: M   ST: A
DESCRIPTION: JACK, HYDRAULIC FLOOR ROLLER, 2 TON       MRP: Y   MPS: E
                                          DWG REV: D    ECN: 4256

COMPONENT PART ID: 646-7215               UM: EA      TYPE: B   ST: A
DESCRIPTION: BOLT, ANCHOR                             MRP: Y   MPS: N
DRAWING ITEM CODE: 0902                   DWG REV:              ECN:

REQUIRED QTY: 1.000000         COMPONENT TYPE: MC MATL COMPONENT
START DATE: 01-15-85               END DATE: 09-17-92
START SN: 53                      END SN:
BILLS TYPE: P  PRODUCTION ONLY
                                  SCRAP FACTOR: 2.0
OPERATION CODE: 10
KIT STORES: MS MASTER
LEAD TIME OFFSET: 5                       REMARK:
                               DATE LAST UPDATE: 10-17-91

ESC-Exit
```

F13. Bill of Material Detail. BOM detail includes effectivity dates, serial number tracking, kit from storeroom, and deliver to operation.

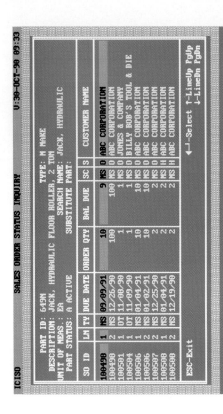

IC1SO   SALES ORDER STATUS INQUIRY   U:30-OCT-90 09:33

```
PART ID: 649M                              TYPE: M NAME
DESCRIPTION: JACK, HYDRAULIC FLOOR ROLLER, 2 TON
                                    SEARCH NAME: JACK, HYDRAULIC
UNIT OF MEAS.: EA           SUBSTITUTE PART:
PART STATUS: A ACTIVE
```

SO ID	LN	TY	DUE DATE	ORDER QTY	BAL DUE	SC	S	CUSTOMER NAME
100498	1	MS	09-09-91	10	9	MS	O	ABC CORPORATION
100501	2	MS	12-26-90	100	100	MS	O	JONES & COMPANY
100504	1	OT	11-08-90	1	1	MS	O	BILLY BOB'S TOOL & DIE
100504	1	OT	11-09-90	1	1	MS	O	ABC CORPORATION
100505	1	MS	01-04-91	10	10	MS	O	ABC CORPORATION
100506	1	MS	01-02-91	10	10	MS	O	ABC CORPORATION
100507	2	MS	12-25-90	2	2	MS	H	ABC CORPORATION
100508	1	MS	01-04-91	2	2	MS	H	ABC CORPORATION
100508	2	MS	12-19-90	2	2	MS	H	ABC CORPORATION

```
ESC-Exit                              ←┘-Select ↑-LineUp PgUp
                                                 ↓-LineDn PgDn
```

F14. Sales Order Status. The status of some open SOs for a given part; detail available. A similar report is available by Customer.

SO1SO   SALES ORDER LINE DETAIL

```
SO ID: 100498      SOLD TO: ABC902    ABC CORPORATION
LINE: 1            SHIP TO: ABC902    TYPE: MS NORMAL SHIPMENT
PART ID: 649M                         DWG: D    ECN: 4256
DESCRIPTION: JACK, HYDRAULIC FLOOR ROLLER, 2 TON    UM: EA
CUST PART ID: 9076                SHIP TYPE: S   STORES: MS
COMPANY ID: 00       DEPT: 0     ACCOUNT: 300    LT:
PRODUCT LINE: 649M               SALES - FINISHED GOODS

REQ SHIP DATE: 10-26-90   PRIORITY: 1.00
SCH SHIP DATE: 01-04-91   REVISED SHIP: 09-09-91         SM REQD: Y
ORDER QTY: 10   REVISED QTY: 10
USD UNIT COST: 0.000000   PRICE CODE: LP   VAT:
UNIT PRICE: 285.000000   DISC: 0.00 TAX:    HOLD:
PARTIAL SHIP: P00 PARTIAL, NO OVER   STATUS: O OPEN
```

LINE AMT	SHIPPED	RETURNED	BAL DUE	LAST ACTION	LAST UPDATE
2850.00	1	0	9	10-22-90	09-11-91

```
ESC-Exit
```

F15. Sales Order Line Detail. Note three shipping dates, revised qty., price code (tables), foreign currency, partial ship, VAT, tax, and hold codes.

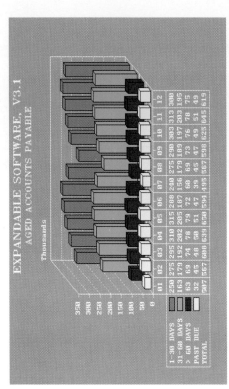

EXPANDABLE SOFTWARE, V3.1
AGED ACCOUNTS PAYABLE

Thousands

	01	02	03	04	05	06	07	08	09	10	11	12
1-30 DAYS	250	275	310	315	288	240	275	290	303	313	300	
31-60 DAYS	163	179	192	202	205	187	179	189	197	203	195	
> 60 DAYS	63	69	74	78	79	80	69	73	76	78	75	
PAST DUE	32	45	48	50	51	47	39	45	47	51	49	
TOTAL	507	567	606	639	650	594	495	567	590	625	645	619

F16. Aged Accounts Payables. One of 17 key business indicators generated by the Executive Information module and charted using Harvard Graphics™.

Product Name: Macola Manufacturing Software

Current Version: V5.02   Number of
Release Date: 10/15/91   Installed Sites: 6,400

Product Summary:

A modular, yet fully integrated PC-based system, Macola Manufacturing Series consists of eight packages. When linked with Macola's award-winning Accounting and Distribution series, it provides full MRPII capabilities. The system is particularly well suited for job shop or repetitive manufacturing environments. The full 17-module system also integrates with a host of vertical market products for enterprise-wide computing.

Vendor Name:	**Macola, Inc.**
Address:	333 East Center St. Marion, OH 43302-4148
Number of Employees:	125
Phone:	(800)468-0834 FAX: (614)382-5999
Support Services:	Four support plan options are available, ranging in price from $75 per module to $3,500 for an entire system.
Modifications:	Available from Macola's custom software division, the MCS Group, or from one of Macola's registered developers.
Source Code:	Source code is available.

Full System Product Pricing (in U.S. $)	under $20,000	$20,001 -40,000	$40,001 -60,000	$60,001 -100,000	over $100,000
4 users	x				
16 users		x			
64 users		x			

(all figures are based on approximate U.S. sales price, and are subject to change at any time)

Product Distribution:

Sold internationally through Macola's network of authorized value-added resellers and consultants.

Language/Database:

Written in Micro Focus COBOL. Btrieve and Micro Focus database file handlers are available.

Operating Platforms:

IBM and compatible microcomputers with a minimum of 640 KB of RAM. Operating systems supported include: Novell, Lantastic, LAN Manager, 3Com, 10Net.

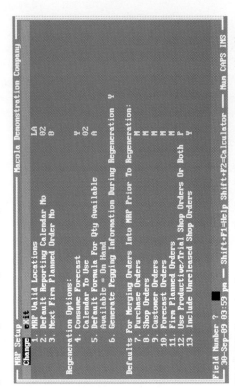

```
┌─ Indented Bill Of Material Inquiry ──────── Macola Demonstration Company ─┐
│ Inquire  exit                                                             │
│ Parent Item No:  PC       Parent Item (Mother Board)           Llc 0      │
│                           Personal Computer                    *Att*      │
│                    11 Levels                                              │
│                                                                  Att A S C│
│                             Quantity U/M Description                 Op    │
│ Lv Seq Component Item       Per Llc                                        │
│                                                                           │
│ 1 10 CPU                    1.00 EA Mother Board For Parent      0 A Y Y   │
│ 2 10 CLOCK                  1.00 EA Central Processing           0 A Y M   │
│                            2       25 Meg Clock For Mother Bo    0 A Y Y   │
│                            2       Clock - 25M                            │
│ 2 20 DATA-BUS               1.00 EA Data Bus/Buffer 25 Meg       0 A Y Y   │
│                            2       Data - Buffer                          │
│ 2 30 MEMMGR                 1.00 EA Memory Manager For CPU Boa   0 A Y Y   │
│                            2       MEM - Manager                          │
│ 2 40 VGA                    1.00 EA Monitor - Rom                0 A Y Y   │
│                            2       Monitor - Rom                          │
│ 2 50 RAM-2MEG               1.00 EA 2 Meg Ram For Mother Board   0 A Y Y   │
│                            2       Ram - 2 Meg                            │
│ 2 60 RAM-ADDRES             1.00 EA Ram Address Multiplexer      0 A Y Y   │
│                            2       Ram - Add - Mult                       │
│ 2 70 RESET-CPU              1.00 EA CPU Reset For Board          0 A Y Y   │
│                            2       CPU - Reset                            │
│ F1 = Next Page                                                            │
│ 30-Sep-89 03:58 pm — Shift+F1=Help Shift+F2=Calculator — Num CAPS INS     │
└───────────────────────────────────────────────────────────────────────────┘
```

F02. This application gives full indented representation of any parent item. It shows all related components in indented format, displaying the quantity per assembly and component description.

```
┌─ MRP Setup ──────────────────────────────── Macola Demonstration Company ─┐
│ Change  exit                                                              │
│                                                                           │
│  1. MRP Valid Locations                      LA                           │
│  2. Default Reporting Calendar No            02                           │
│  3. Next Firm Planned Order No               8                            │
│                                                                           │
│ Regeneration Options:                                                     │
│  4. Consume Forecast                         Y                            │
│     Calendar To Use                          02                           │
│  5. Default Formula For Qty Available        A                            │
│     Available = On Hand                                                   │
│  6. Generate Pegging Information During Regeneration  Y                   │
│                                                                           │
│ Defaults For Merging Orders Into MRP Prior To Regeneration:               │
│  7. Purchase Orders                          M                            │
│  8. Shop Orders                              M                            │
│  9. Customer Orders                          M                            │
│ 10. Forecast Orders                          M                            │
│ 11. Firm Planned Orders                      M                            │
│ 12. Use Productive/Trial Shop Orders Or Both  P                           │
│ 13. Include Unreleased Shop Orders           Y                            │
│                                                                           │
│ Field Number ?                                                            │
│ 30-Sep-89 03:59 pm — Shift+F1=Help Shift+F2=Calculator — Num CAPS INS     │
└───────────────────────────────────────────────────────────────────────────┘
```

F04. MRP Setup is where you tailor the MRP system to your specifications. Regeneration options and merging defaults will determine how requirement and replenishment orders are created.

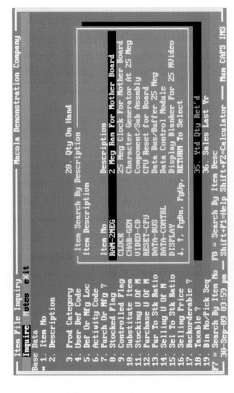

```
┌─ Item File Inquiry ──────────────────────── Macola Demonstration Company ─┐
│ Inquire  notes  exit                                                      │
│ Base Data                                                                 │
│ * 1. Item No                                                              │
│   2. Description                                                          │
│                                          28 Qty On Hand                   │
│   3. Prod Category                                                        │
│   4. User Def Code                                                        │
│   5. Def Or Mfg Loc      Item Search By Description                       │
│   6. Activity Code       Item Description                                 │
│   7. Purch Or Mfg ?                                                       │
│   8. Stocked Flag        Item No      Description                         │
│   9. Controlled Item     RAM-2MEG     2 Meg Ram For Mother Board          │
│  10. Substitute Item     CLOCK        25 Meg Clock For Mother Board       │
│  11. Stocking U Of M     CHAR-GEN     Character Generator At 25 Meg       │
│  12. Purchase U Of M     VIDEO-CD     Component/Sub Assembly              │
│  13. Pur To Stk Ratio    RESET-CPU    CPU Reset For Board                 │
│  14. Selling U Of M      DATA-BUS     Data Bus/Buffer 25 Meg              │
│  15. Sel To Stk Ratio    DATA-CONTRL  Data Control Module                 │
│  16. Selling Price       DISPLAY      Display Blanker For 25 MVideo       │
│  17. Backorderable ?     ↓, ↑, PgDn, PgUp, RETURN To Select               │
│  18. Taxable ?                        35. Ytd Qty Ret'd                   │
│  19. Bin No/Pick Seq                  36. Sales Last Yr                   │
│ F7 = Search By Item No   F8 = Search By Item Desc                         │
│ 30-Sep-89 03:59 pm — Shift+F1=Help Shift+F2=Calculator — Num CAPS INS     │
└───────────────────────────────────────────────────────────────────────────┘
```

F01. Item File Inquiry displays information related to any inventory item. It displays Base, Management, and Manufacturing Data with function key search for Item number and description.

```
┌─ Regenerate Material Plan ───────────────── Macola Demonstration Company ─┐
│ Regenerate  exit                                                          │
│                                                                           │
│ Processing Stage                        Time Begun                        │
│ Material Regeneration Starts            10:29am                           │
│ Summing Initial Quantities Available    10:29am                           │
│ Merging Order Information               10:29am                           │
│ Processing Low Level Code 00            10:29am                           │
│ Processing Low Level Code 01            10:29am                           │
│ Processing Low Level Code 02            10:29am                           │
│ Processing Low Level Code 03            10:29am                           │
│ Processing Low Level Code 04            10:29am                           │
│ Processing Low Level Code 05            10:29am                           │
│ Processing Low Level Code 06            10:29am                           │
│ Processing Low Level Code 07            10:29am                           │
│ Processing Low Level Code 08            10:29am                           │
│ Processing Low Level Code 09            10:29am                           │
│ Processing Low Level Code 10            10:29am                           │
│ Processing Low Level Code 11            10:29am                           │
│ Building Final Output Files             10:30am                           │
│                                                                           │
│ Material Regeneration Finishes          10:30am                           │
│                                                                           │
│ Regeneration Complete                                        Press RETURN │
│ 30-Sep-89 10:30 am — Shift+F1=Help Shift+F2=Calculator — Num CAPS Ins     │
└───────────────────────────────────────────────────────────────────────────┘
```

F03. Regeneration of the Material Plan captures all requirements and replenishments as specified in the MRP Setup. It displays, by time, all available product structure levels used.

F05. This inquiry provides Available To Promise Information for individual inventory items as an aid to order processing and/or sales personnel.

F06. This is the first screen of creating any shop order. It contains the parent item being produced and the scheduling method used to determine the start or due date of the order.

F07. This screen establishes operation details for shop orders. Work center information and operation type are entered for priority scheduling control.

F08. This application allows the manual issuing, return, or scrap of materials. It allows for Serial or Lot item quantities, with batch control per item.

Job Status Inquiry — Macola Demonstration Company

Inquire exit

```
     Job Number          PC-10A    Production Order (PC-10A)
     Shop Order Number    ID-10A
     Shift 1  First Shift          D M X
     Include Detail Types

Material: Oper           Component-Item     Component-Description
Planned-Qty  Uom Issue-Loc  Planned-Cost    Actual-Cost     Mat-Typ  Source
Actual-Qty       Uncosted-Qty
                                  FLOPPY-CNT          Dep-Matl Mat-Typ  Source
   30.00   EA   LA    .00    2,250.00        Floppy Disk Controller
     .00              .00                    Floppy - Control        N      1
                                  KEYBOARD            Key Board For System Computer
   30.00   EA   LA    .00    1,740.00        25 MHZ                  N      1
     .00              .00                    N                       1
                                  PAR-PORT            Parallel Port For I/O
   30.00   EA   LA    .00      540.00        Parallel Port           N      1
     .00              .00                    N                       1

F1 = Next Screen   F10 = Enter New Detail
22-Oct-91 03:02 pm  —  Shift+F1=Help Shift+F2=Calculator  —  Num CAPS INS
```

F09. Jobs may need immediate inquiry. This application displays Status information on operation, material, notes, and outside process details.

Clock Card Processing — Macola Demonstration Company

Add Change Delete List Import exit

```
*1. Employee Number 100     Cooney, Jerry III      Home Dept 100
*2. Pay Period Start Date 09/01/89 *3. Shift 1 First Shift  -- Hours Desc
    Include Detail Types

Date       Type --In-- -Out- Type --In- -Out- Type --In- --Out-
 4. 09/01/89 W  8:00 12:00 Special: W 13:00 17:00  Break: :30  Total:  8:00
    Reg:  8:00 Ovr-T:  8:00 Special:                Break:      Total:  8:00
 5. 09/02/89 W  8:00 12:00 Special: W 13:00 17:00  Break: :30  Total:  8:00
    Reg:  8:00 Ovr-T:      Special:                Break:      Total:  8:00
 6. 09/03/89 W  8:00 12:00 Special: W 13:00 17:00  Break: :30  Total:  8:00
    Reg:  8:00 Ovr-T:      Special:                Break:      Total:  8:00
 7. 09/04/89 W  8:00 12:00 Special: W 13:00 17:00  Break: :30  Total:  8:00
    Reg:  8:00 Ovr-T:      Special:                Break:      Total:  8:00
 8. 09/05/89 W  8:00 12:00 Special: W 13:00 17:00  Break: :30  Total:  8:00
    Reg:  8:00 Ovr-T:      Special:                Break:      Total:  8:00
 9.          Reg:  Ovr-T:  Special:                Break:      Total:
10.          Reg:  Ovr-T:  Special:                Break:      Total:
                              Grand Total For This Period:            37:30

Field Number ?
30-Sep-89 04:01 pm  —  Shift+F1=Help Shift+F2=Calculator  —  Num CAPS INS
```

F10. Employee clock card information such as overtime, holiday, sick, or vacation time may be entered with this application. It also defaults In and Out times from the Shift File.

Labor Transaction Processing — Macola Demonstration Company

Add Change Delete List Import exit

```
* 1. Crew? N  * 2. Employee/Crew No 100   Cooney, Jerry III
* 3. Date         09/02/89    Home Dept 100  Inspection and Quality Control
* 4. Shift 1   First Shift   -- Hours Desc
* 5. Start/End Time 8:00 17:00            Clock Hrs Bal       :00
  6. Break Time              :30
  7. Elapsed Time          8:00
  8. Shop Order No         ID-10A         Subassembly Component
  9. Item No               40             Subassembly Component
 10. Oper No               100            General Assembly Inspection
 11. Work Center           100
 12. Oper Type             I              Machine No  INSP
 13. Oper Complete?        N           18. Machine Hours      8.0000
 14. Indirect Code         IN          19. Qty Complete       0.00
 15. Inspection                        20. Qty Rejected       0.00
 16. Incentive Code                    21. Qty Scrapped       0.00
                                       22. Std No Of Men      2
                                       23. Std Hours Earned   0.00
 17. Labor Grade           B           24. Labor Cost Type    B
     Level B - Skilled                     Inspection & Testing

Field Number ?
30-Sep-89 04:01 pm  —  Shift+F1=Help Shift+F2=Calculator  —  Num CAPS INS
```

F11. Activity against direct and indirect labor are applied using this application, which is also crew sensitive, and especially useful in tracking Employee performance.

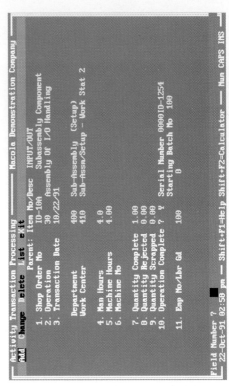

Activity Transaction Processing — Macola Demonstration Company

Add Change Delete List exit

```
     Parent: Item No/Desc  INPUT/OUT
 1. Shop Order No      ID-10A     Subassembly Component
 2. Operation          30         Assembly Of I/O Handling
 3. Transaction Date   10/22/91

    Department         400        Sub-Assembly (Setup)
    Work Center        410        Sub-Assm/Setup - Work Stat 2

 4. Man Hours          4.0
 5. Machine Hours      4.00
 6. Machine No

 7. Quantity Complete  1.00
 8. Quantity Rejected  0.00
 9. Quantity Scrapped  0.00
10. Operation Complete ? Y    Serial Number 000001D-1254
11. Emp No/Lbr Gd      100        Starting Batch No 100

Field Number ?
22-Oct-91 02:50 pm  —  Shift+F1=Help Shift+F2=Calculator  —  Num CAPS INS
```

F12. Activity against shop orders are processed using this application. Completion, rejection, and scrap quantities, along with labor may also be applied.

Work Center Load Inquiry — Macola Demonstration Company

Department 100 Inspection and Quality Control
Work Center 100 Inspection and Quality Control   Start Date 09/30/89

Start Date	Item-No	Order Typ	No	Operation Id	No	Typ	Pri	Due Date	Setup Hours	Load Hours
10/17/89	CPU	SD	CPU-1A	20	CPT2	I	500	10/20/89		30.00
11/15/89	INPUT-OUT	SD	IO-10A	20	3A-I	I	500	11/20/89		30.00
11/24/89	CPU	CP	000004	20	CPT2	I	999	11/29/89		30.00
11/27/89	VIDEO-CD	SD	UID-1A	20	U-3A	I	500	12/01/89		39.00
12/13/89	INPUT-OUT	SD	IO-10A	40	GNW4	I	500	12/20/89		60.00
12/25/89	INPUT-OUT	CP	000006	20	3A-I	I	999	12/20/89		60.00
12/26/89	PC	CP	000001	40	GNW4	I	999	01/01/90		40.00
01/04/90	VIDEO-CD	CP	000008	20	U-3A	I	999	01/10/90		39.00
01/22/90	INPUT-OUT	CP	000006	40	GNW4	I	999	01/29/90		60.00
01/25/90	PC	SD	PC-10A	20	GNW4	I	500	02/01/90		60.00
01/29/90	PC	CP	000002	40	GNW4	I	999	02/01/90		20.00
01/31/90	CPU	CP	000005	20	CPT2	I	999	02/01/90		10.00
02/09/90	INPUT-OUT	CP	000007	20	3A-I	I	999	02/13/90		10.00

F1 = Next Page F10 = Enter New Department
30-Sep-89 04:04 pm —— Shift+F1=Help Shift+F2=Calculator —— Num CAPS INS

F14. This application can be very useful in determining what operations may or may not need rescheduling. The load hours are displayed for each operation, with function key paging controls.

Cost Master File Inquiry — Macola Demonstration Company

1. Item No PC   Parent Item (Mother Board)   Uom: EA
                       Personal Computer

Per 1 Units	Cur U/A	Cur Total	Std U/A	Std Total
2. Man Hours	8.10	42.40	8.10	42.40
3. Material Cost	0.00	275.77	0.00	275.77
4. Labor Cost	111.54	471.49	111.54	471.49
5. Outside Cost	0.00	0.00	0.00	0.00
6. Var Burden	20.03	110.23	20.03	110.23
7. Fixed Burden	47.69	171.67	47.69	171.67
Total	179.26	1,029.16	179.26	1,029.16
8. Manuf-Data	0.00	0.00		
9. Labor Grade				

Last Change: 09/30/89   Last Build: 09/30/89   Last Standard: 09/30/89
Inquiry Only Access - No Changes Allowed   Press "RETURN" To Continue
30-Sep-89 04:02 pm —— Shift+F1=Help Shift+F2=Calculator —— Num CAPS INS

F13. This inquiry screen displays current and standard cost totals of inventory items. Reports that are generated within SPC use this information for analysis and What-If scenarios.

Trial Allocation Inquiry — Macola Demonstration Company

Shop Order No CPU-1A   Parent Item No CPU   Ord Qty 30.00
Order Loc LA   Issue Loc LA   Mother Board For Parent
                                      Central Processing

Component-No Message	Component-Description	Uom	Qty-Planned Stor-Area	Qty-On-Hand Qty-Avail
CLOCK	25 Meg Clock For Mother Board	EA	30.00	.00
Shortage	Clock - 25M		30.00	.00
CPU-30MEG	280 Micro Processor 30 Meg	EA	30.00	.00
Shortage	CPU - 280		30.00	.00
DATA-BUS	Data Bus/Buffer 25 Meg	EA	30.00	.00
Shortage	Data - Buffer		30.00	.00
MEMMGR	Memory Manager For CPU Board	EA	30.00	.00
Shortage	MEM - Manager		30.00	.00
RAM-2MEG	2 Meg Ram For Mother Board	EA	30.00	.00
Shortage	Ram - 2 Meg		30.00	.00

F1 = Next Screen   Return = Enter New Shop Order Number
22-Oct-91 02:59 pm —— Shift+F1=Help Shift+F2=Calculator —— Num CAPS INS

F16. This application displays component items and quantity information. It is especially important in showing component availability for shop orders that are scheduled for release.

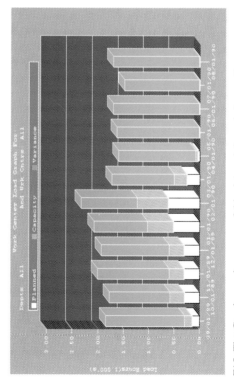

F15. The Graphs can be very useful in determining what operations may or may not need rescheduling due to overload or underloading of work centers. There are five available graphs.

Product Name: MFG/PRO

Current Version:	V6.1C	Number of	
Release Date:	10/18/91	Installed Sites:	450+

Product Summary:

MFG/PRO by qad. inc is a complete manufacturing and distribution management software system including sales order processing and financial management. It is suitable for a wide range of manufacturing types, including process, batch process, repetitive, and assemble to order. Contains processing logic to handle multiple sites, multiple language, and multiple currency in an open systems environment.

Vendor Name:	**qad. inc**
Address:	6450 Via Real, Carpinteria, CA 93013
Number of Employees:	140
Phone:	(805)684-6614
Support Services:	qad. inc has company-owned support offices in selected countries to provide support for MFG/PRO worldwide. These offices are fully equipped training centers. Support is also available through a network of dedicated distributors.
Modifications:	Customization is available from qad. inc and through its distributor network.
Source Code:	Source code is available for an additional charge.

Full System Product Pricing (in U.S. $)	under $20,000	$20,001 -40,000	$40,001 -60,000	$60,001 -100,000	over $100,000
4 users		x			
16 users				x	
64 users					x

(all figures are based on approximate U.S. sales price, and are subject to change at any time)

Product Distribution:

Directly through a network of offices in North America, Holland, Hong Kong, and Sydney, Australia. Also available internationally through a network of licensed distributors.

Language/Database:

PROGRESS, a fourth-generation language and relational database system by PROGRESS Software Corporation.

Operating Platforms:

Runs on all operating systems, networks, and hardware supported by PROGRESS, including UNIX, HP-UX, VMS, ULTRIX, XENIX, and MS-DOS.

nfmenu   qad Demonstration Company — Main Menu   12/02/90

DISTRIBUTION
1. Items / Products
2. Addresses
3. Inventory Control
4. Physical Inventory
5. Purchasing
6. Sales Quotations
7. Sales Orders/Invoice
8. Features & Options
9. Sales Analysis
10. Service/Repair Order
11.
12.

MANUFACTURING
13. Product Structures
14. Routings/Work Center
15. Work Orders
16. Shop Floor Control
17. Repetitive
18. Formula/Process
19. Product Line Plan
20. Resource Plan
21. Forecasting
22. Master Schedule Plan
23. Materials Rqmts Plan
24. Capacity Rqmts Plan

FINANCIAL
25. General Ledger
26. Multiple Currency
27. Accounts Receivable
28. Accounts Payable
29. Payroll
30. Cost Simulation
31.
32.
33.
34. Taxes
35.
36. Manager Functions

Please select a function.   F4 or blank to EXIT.   20

Enter data or press ESC to end.

F02. Functions may be accessed by entering the menu number, using arrow keys, entering the program name, a nickname, or by pressing a preassigned function key (defined by each user).

---

mrpmrpiq.p a   23.13 MRP Summary Inquiry   12/02/90

Item Number: 02-0007   Site: 1000   UM: EA   7MM CARDED PENCIL
Qty On Hand: 2,000.0   Pur/Mfg: M
Buyer/Planner: PL   Order Policy: POQ   Mfg LT: 2   Min Ord: 0
Master Sched: yes   Order Period: 7   Pur LT: 0   Max Ord: 120
MRP Required: no   Time Fence: 0   Ins LT: 0   Order Mult: 0
Plan Orders: yes   Safety Stk: 0   Inspect: no Order Qty: 1,000.0
Issue Policy: yes   Safety Time: 0   Cum LT: 22   Yield: 100.00%

	Past	12-01-90 11/30/90	12-31-90 12/31/90	01-01-91 01/31/91	02-01-91 02/28/91	03-01-91 03/31/91	04-01-91 04/30/91	05-01-91 05/31/91
Gross Reqs	0	0	0	36,960	40,000	0	0	0
Sched Receipts	0	0	0	0	0	0	0	0
Projected QOH	2,000	2,000	2,000	40,000	80	80	80	80
Plan Ords Due	0	0	35,040	40,000	0	0	0	0
Plan Ords Rel	2,000	0	30,960	52,000	0	0	0	0

End of file.

F1-Go F2-Help F3-Ins F4-End F7-Recall F8-Clear F9-Prev F10-Next

F04. MRP summary data may be displayed horizontally. F10 rolls the display buckets forward in time, F9 backward. Daily, weekly, or monthly buckets may be selected for display.

F01. Title Screen. Access to each system session is password controlled. All system functions and selected data fields may also be individually protected by password.

F03. Additional item master information is contained on other screens. Not shown is the costing, pricing, vendor sourcing, and other basic inventory item information.

```
mrmpiq01.p c          23.16 MRP Detail Inquiry                   12/02/90

Item Number: 02-0007          Qty On Hand: 2,000.0        Site: 1000
7MM CARDED PENCIL                          UM: EA      Pur/Mfg: M
Buyer/Planner: PL     Order Policy: POQ    Min Ord: 0    Pur LT: 0
Master Sched: yes     Order Period: 7      Max Ord: 0    Mfg LT: 2
MRP Required: no      Time Fence: 0        Ord Mult: 120 Pur LT: 0
Plan Orders: yes      Safety Time: 0       Order Qty: 1,000.0 Ins LT: 0
Issue Policy: yes     Safety Stk: 0        Yield%: 100.00% Inspect: no
                                                          Cum LT: 22

Due Date  Gross Reqs  Sched Rcpt  Proj QOH  Plan Ords Details
                                            Beginning Available
                                   2,000
01/01/91  32,880                 -30,880    Prod F/C 01-0001
01/01/91                  80       30,960    U/O: 1201B001  ID: 1031
                                             Release Date 12/28/90
01/15/91  1,200                   -1,120     S/O: 1000      Line: 1
01/15/91                4,080       2,960     U/O: 1201B002  ID: 1032
                                             Release Date 01/11/91

Press space bar to continue.
```

F05. MRP details for an item may be displayed in a vertical format. Space bar scrolls to view additional detail information. All requirements are pegged for easy review.

F06. MRP may be executed in either regeneration, net change, or selective mode. After running, fresh exception messages may be displayed on-line by each planner for their review.

```
rprsiq04.p b          20.11 PL Resource Load Detail Inquiry              12/02/90
```

Resource	Description	Start		Day/Week/Month	Per Column		Output
1000	ASSEMBLY/PACK MANROW	12/01/90		M		1	terminal

	Past	12/01/90	01/01/91	02/01/91	03/01/91	04/01/91	05/01/91
	11/30/90	12/31/90	01/31/91	02/28/91	03/31/91	04/30/91	05/31/91
Workdays	0	21	23	20	21	22	23
Capacity	0	336	368	320	336	352	368
Total Load	0	270	225	315	360	450	540
Over/Under	0	66	143	5	-24	-98	-172
Cumulative	0	66	209	214	190	92	-80

```
Press space bar to display graph.
```

F07. Product Line Planning (Resource Requirements Planning) factors production plans, capacity, and load profiles to provide an analysis of over/underloaded resources.

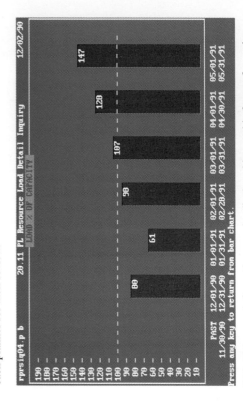

F08. This same information may be displayed in graphic format for easier analysis. Capacity Requirements Planning provides more detailed data on Department and Work Center loading.

sosont.p b | 7.1 Sales Order Maintenance | 12-02-90

Sales Order: 1000 | Customer: 1000 | Ln Format S/M: single

Ln Item Number	Qty Ordered UM	List Price	Disc%	Net Price
3 02-0001	25.0 EA	120.00	0.00	120.00

02-0001 Features

Feature	Mandatory
PENCILS	yes
REFILLS	yes
	no

F1-Go F2-Help F3-Ins F4-End F7-Recall F8-Clear

F10. The Features & Options module assists in properly entering sales orders for configurable items. Pop-up windows, used extensively in MFG/PRO, ease the selection of options.

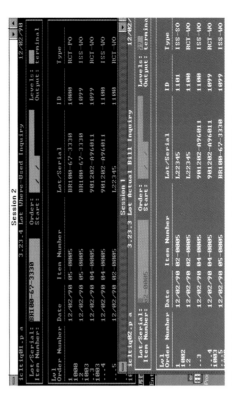

F12. Full Lot/Serial Control is standard in MFG/PRO. Shown here is its capability to track lots completely through the purchase-production-shipping process, in either direction.

---

msmsig.p a | 22.13 Master Schedule Summary Inquiry | 12-02-90

Item Number: 02-0007 | 7MM CARDED PENCIL | MRP Req: no
Site: 1000 | Mfg LT: 2 | Plan Orders: yes | Pur/Mfg: M
QOH: 2,000.0 | EA Pur LT: 0 | Order Qty: 1,000.0 | Min Ord: 0
Order Policy: POQ | Safety Stk: 0 | Yield%: 100.00% | Max Ord: 0
Order Period: 7 | Safety Time: 0 | Time Fence: 0 | Ord Mult: 120

| | Past | 01/01/91 01/08/91 01/15/91 01/22/91 01/29/91 02/05/91 | | | | | |
		12/31/90 01/07/91 01/14/91 01/21/91 01/28/91 02/04/91 02/11/91					
Prod Forecast	0	0 0 0 0 40,000 0
Forecast	0	32,000 0 0 0 0 0
Sales Orders	0	0 0 1,200 0 0 0
Gross Reqs	0	0 0 2,000 0 0 0
Master Sched	0	30,960 0 0 40,000 0 0
Projected QOH	2,000	0 80 80 80 80 80
Avail Promise	0	32,960 0 0 40,000 0 0

F1-Go F2-Help F3-Ins F4-End F7-Recall F8-Clear F9-Prev F10-Next

F09. Master Schedule may be displayed in summary or in detail. This inquiry calculates and displays available to promise for *any* item. Buckets may be daily, weekly, or monthly.

---

mfmenu | qad Demonstration Company | 12-02-90

17. Repetitive

1. Repetitive Schedule Maintenance
2. Repetitive Schedule Inquiry
3. Repetitive Schedule Summary
4.
5. Repetitive Schedule Explosion
6. Repetitive Operation Schedule
7.
8.
9.
10. Cumulative Order Maintenance
11. Cumulative Order Inquiry
12. Cumulative Order Report
13. Repetitive Setup Transaction
14. Repetitive Labor Transaction
15. Repetitive Down Time Transaction
16. Repetitive Rework Transaction
17. Repetitive Reject Transaction
18. Repetitive Scrap Transaction
19. Non-Productive Labor Feedback
20.
21. Repetitive Reports
22.
23.
24.

Please select a function. F4 or blank to EXIT. 2

Enter data or press ESC to end.

F11. The Repetitive module features ease of scheduling, backflush from point-of-use, the ability to modify an automatic backflush, and preserves lot tracking integrity.

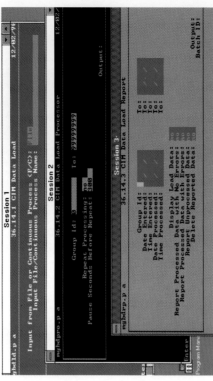

F13. Shown here is the submenu for the Formula/Process module of MFG/PRO. The maintenance of formulas, ingredients, processes, batches, and associated information are supported.

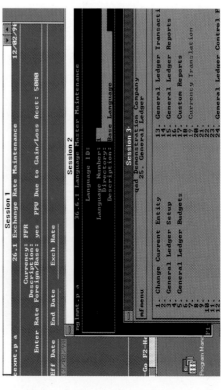

F14. The CIM Interface facilitates transfer of data from external systems into the MFG/PRO database. Field validation rules are still in effect, thereby maintaining data integrity.

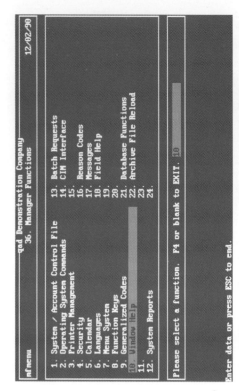

F15. MFG/PRO provides full multicurrency and multilanguage functionality. Subsidiary ledgers, denominated in foreign currencies, may be automatically converted and consolidated.

F16. MFG/PRO enables the System Manager to tailor how function keys, menu structure, help text, codes, value ranges, master comments, and many other system parameters are implemented.

Product Name: Minxware

Current Version: V2.41
Release Date: 09/16/91

Number of
Installed Sites: 175+

Product Summary:

Minxware is a UNIX-based, real-time information system fully integrating sales, customer service, finance, production and engineering for discrete manufacturers. Ease-of-use features include: Informix SQL and 4GL relational tools, context-sensitive help, wildcard search and select, embedded description search, 132-column report compression to screen, multisession windowing on dumb and "X" window terminals, bar-code data collection, laser forms printing, and more.

Vendor Name:	**Minx Software Inc.**
Address:	1762 Technology Drive Suite 224 San Jose, CA 95110
Number of Employees:	70
Phone:	(408)453-6469
Support Services:	Support services include new releases, unlimited phone support, and a full suite of professional services to meet the full range of customer needs.
Modifications:	Most requirements can be handled with the standard report writer or Informix SQL and 4GL. Modifications to source code are also available.
Source Code:	Full source code is delivered with your Minxware license and remains resident on your computer.

Full System Product Pricing (in U.S. $)	under $20,000	$20,001 -40,000	$40,001 -60,000	$60,001 -100,000	over $100,000
4 users		X			
16 users				X	
64 users					X

(all figures are based on approximate U.S. sales price, and are subject to change at any time)

Product Distribution:

Minxware is sold direct in the United States through regional sales offices and through an extensive network of distributors worldwide. Minxware is currently marketed in six foreign languages and 17 countries throughout Europe, Asia Pacific, and Canada.

Language/Database:

Minxware is written in C and is available in native or Informix relational database formats.

Operating Platforms:

Minxware runs on all UNIX platforms. Minxware's source code is completely portable from 386 platforms to mini, micro, and mainframe platforms. Since Minxware can run on any UNIX operating system, hardware options are unlimited.

```
                        Minx Information System

          Copyright (C) 1984-1991 Minx Software, Incorporated

                          All Rights Reserved

                            1-(800)-FOR-MINX




          Enter Database Number (0 - 999) or [RETURN] to Quit
```

F01. Each Minxware license provides up to 1,000 databases to ensure unrestricted operational options. A single database accommodates unlimited divisions and departments. Different databases may be used for "what-if" modeling and other needs.

```
AP> Accounts Payable              MR> Material Requirements Planning
AR> Accounts Receivable           MS> Master Production Scheduling
BM> Bill of Material              OM> Order Management
BT> Background Report Monitor     PA> Project Accounting
CA> Cost Accounting               PI> Physical Inventory
CP> Rough-Cut Capacity Planning   PO> Purchasing
CS> Customer Service              RW> Report Writer
EC> Engineering Changes           SF> Shop Floor Control
GL> General Ledger                SU> System Utilities
IN> Inventory Control             UP> User Programs


              Enter Selection or [RETURN] to Exit
```

F02. Upon selecting a database 0–999, users are delivered to the main System Menu. Users may then move to any module submenu or go directly into any program that has not been password restricted by the system manager.

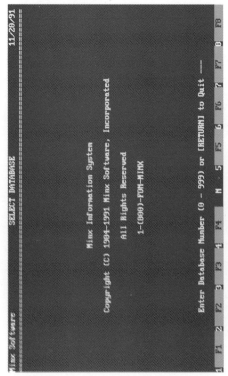

```
 1) Part Maintenance                13) Part Inquiry by Description
 2) Part Inquiry                    14) Product for a Part Maintenance
 3) Location Maintenance            15) Products for a Part Inquiry
 4) Location Inquiry                16) Bill of Serial Numbers Inquiry
 5) Transfer Parts Between Locations 17) Serial Number Where-Used Inquiry
 6) Cross Reference Maintenance     18) Lot Maintenance
 7) Cross Reference Inquiry by Part 19) Lot Inquiry
 8) Cross Reference Inquiry by Vendor 20) Serial Number Location Inquiry
 9) Warehouse Maintenance           RP) Inventory Reports Menu
10) Change Stocking Unit of Measure TR) Inventory Transactions Menu
11) Part Transaction Inquiry        UT) Inventory Utilities Menu
12) Part Description Maintenance

           Enter Selection or [RETURN] to System Menu
```

F03. Maintenance and inquiry screens can be individually password protected. Minxware's comprehensive "Serial and Lot Number" tracking provides cradle to grave serial and lot number accountability.

```
 1) Current Parts Value            14) Vendor Cross Reference By Part
 2) Warehouse Report               15) Vendor Cross Reference By Vendor
 3) Stock Status Report            16) Location Valuation Report
 4) Re-order Recommendations       17) Inventory Posting Journal Report
 5) Parts Catalog (By Description) 18) Extended Part Description Report
 6) Transaction Log                19) Bill of Serial Numbers Multi-Level
 7) Parts Added Through BOM Module 20) Serial/Lot Number Where Used Report
 8) ABC Analysis Report            21) Lot/Serial Trace Report
 9) Inventory Usage Analysis       22) Part's Revision Trace Report
10) Inventory Location Report      23) Part's Tracking Type Report
11) Parts With No or Zero Qty Loc. 24) Checkpoint/Later Tracked S/N In Stock
12) Part Master Report             25) Part's Status Code Report
13) Cycle Count Report             26) Status Code Report
                                   27) Bar Coded Cycle Count Report

          Enter Selection or [RETURN] to Inventory Control Menu
```

F04. Each module provides a complete set of standard reports with broad "select and sort" options. For those with additional reporting needs, Minxware includes a powerful "Report Writer."

```
Minx 2.41              PART'S AVAILABILITY INQUIRY                  11/20/91
MR.4                                                      Database: 241
Part Number: 10021        Safety Stk:      50  Planning Method Code: 0
Description: Connector, Disk Drive    SC: PI REV: a S/UM: EA P/UM: CS

                        ORDER    ORDER            QUANTITY
  ORDER TYPE            NUMBER   QUANTITY  DATE    REQUIRED    BALANCE
Nettable Quantity on Hand                                        1422
Quantity in Inspection    1.00                                   1462
Purchase Order Line: 1     135    20      02-05-91               1462
Sales Order Line: 1        146    20      10-01-91        1      1461
Sales Order Line: 3.00     149            10-02-91        1      1460
Sales Order Line: 1.00     149            10-02-91               1397
Sales Order Line: 2.00     153            10-03-91       63      1397
Purchase Order Line: 1     145            10-09-91      200      1197
Sales Order Line: 1        149    20      11-01-91               1217
Sales Order Line: 2.00     163            11-14-91      237       980
Purchase Order Line: 1     abc    20      11-14-91              1000
Sales Order Line: 1.00                    11-14-91        1       999
Demand Forecast                           11-18-91      100       899
Purchase Order Line: 2     168    800     12-04-91              1699

              Enter (N)ext Screen or [RETURN] to Quit -
 F1  F2  F3  F4  N  5  F5  6  F6  7  F7  8  F8
```

F05. Since Minxware is a real-time system, this "Parts Availability Inquiry" actually performs a mini MRP type calculation in real-time. Using MINXWINDOWS users can access this type of data interactively.

```
Minx 2.41              PART INQUIRY BY DESCRIPTION                  11/20/91
IN.13                             : ncc                   Database: 241
Description Part Number:                           Case Sensitive: No
Starting Part Number: All
Ending Part Number :                                  Match Count: 4

                                              UENDOR  BUYR        S/
  PART DESCRIPTION          PART NUMBER       CODE    CODE SC RU  UM
1- Connector, 3 Pole        10010             acme    sk   P  a   EA
2- Connector, Disk Drive    10021             acme    rs   PI a   EA
3- Connector,4 cond.fem.Board 10022           acme    sk   PI a   EA
4- Connector,RS232          10058             acme    rs   P  a   EA

              Enter Line (1 - 4) or [RETURN] to Quit -
 F1  F2  F3  F4  N  5  F5  6  F6  7  F7  8  F8
```

F06. In this example a user is trying to find detailed information about a particular connector without knowing the part number. By entering only a "piece" of the description, the system has returned four "matches" to choose from.

```
Minx 2.41              PART INQUIRY BY DESCRIPTION                  11/20/91
IN.13                                       P/UOM: EA    Database: 241
Part Number: 10022                          SC  : PI     S/UOM: a
Description: Connector,4 cond.fem.Board                  Rev. : a

Use UOM Conversion: No          UOM Conversion Fact:    1.000000
Last Status     : No            Class Code         : hdur
Last Status Chg : 10/04/88      ABC Code           : C*
Account Number  : 1  -1  -15110 Planner Code       :          45
Buyer Code      : sk            Fixed Lead Time    :
Prime Vendor    : acme          Per-unit Lead Time :     0.000
Routing Part No.:               Yield Factor       :     1.00
Qty In Inspection :  0.000000   Planning Method    :
Qty In SO Staging :  0.00       MRP High Level Code:          0
Quantity in WIP   :  0.000000   Minimum Order Qty  :        250
Qty Issued to WIP :  0.000000   Safety Stock Qty   :         50
Track Part      : At Inv Movement Re-Order Point Qty:        250
Tracking Type   : Serial Tracked Date/Rev Track: Date Tracked
Single Location : No            Commodity Code     :
Nettable QOH    : 100.000000
Non-nettable QOH:   0.000000

              (N)ext Screen or [RETURN] to Continue -
 F1  F2  F3  F4  N  5  F5  6  F6  7  F7  8  F8
```

F07. By selecting the line number "3" from the previous screen the user is now viewing item master, MRP control, and summarized current inventory data for the part in question.

```
Minx 2.41              PART INQUIRY BY DESCRIPTION                  11/20/91
IN.13                                       P/UOM: EA    Database: 241
Part Number: 10022                          SC  : PI     S/UOM: EA
Description: Connector,4 cond.fem.Board                  Rev. : a

ECO Number        :                Last Quoted Cost    :      0.001
Drawing Size      :                Material Cost       :   6.250000
Drawing Ref No    :                Material Overhead   :      0.625
Sales Order Alloc :     0.00       This Level Labor    :      0.000
In-process Alloc  : 12.000000      This Level Overhead :      0.000
No. Days Supply   :        5       This Level O.P.     :      0.000
Period/Date Issues:     0.00       O.P. Overhead       :      0.000
                                   Lower Level Labor   :      0.000
W-T-D Issues      :   0.000000     Lower Level Overhead:      0.000
W-T-D Receipts    : 100.000000     Lower Level O.P.    :      0.000
W-T-D Adjustments :   0.000000     Lower O.P. Ovrhd    :      0.000
                                   Total Standard Cost :   6.875000
Date Cost Updated : 11/18/91       Average Cost        :    414.237
P.O. Qty On Order :     0.00       Labor Hours to Make :      0.000
Matl Safety Code  :                Lot Shelf Life      :          0

              (P)revious Screen or [RETURN] to Continue -
 F1  F2  F3  F4  N  5  F5  6  F6  7  F7  8  F8
```

F08. By selecting "N" for next screen again, the user is now viewing additional statistical activity and detailed cost data for the same part. This "start with summary," "cascade to detail" approach is standard throughout Minxware.

```
                    1) Open Projects
                    2) Project Transaction Log
                    3) Open Project Cost
                    4) Project PIP Reconciliation Report
                    5) Completed Project Cost
                    6) Project Structure Report
                    7) Project GANTT Report


        Enter Selection or [RETURN] to Project Accounting Menu

 F1  F2  F3  4  F4   N   5  F5  6  F6  7  F7  8  F8
```

F10. Reports can be run to any number of local or remote printers. Reports can also be run to disk for import into other software products. *Any* report in *any* module can be run to screen, compressing 132-column output to 80-column terminal display.

Minx 2.41   PROJECT INQUIRY   11/20/91
PA,2   Database: 241
Project ID: 500-1   Revision:

	ESTIMATES	ACTUALS	LOWER LEVEL
PIP Material	1100000.000	0.000	575073.192
PIP Labor Hours	675.00	44.00	393.00
PIP Labor Amount	15000.000	484.000	7955.750
PIP Overhead	35000.000	48.400	16806.910
PIP Outside Processing	2000.000	0.000	32250.000
Material From Stock	0.000	0.000	-10.500
Material Purchases	50.000	0.000	114309.700
Material Overhead	225000.000	0.000	4512.500
Indirect Labor Hours	10000.000	0.000	40.000
Indirect Labor Amount	0.000	0.000	1400.000
Indirect Labor Overhead	0.000	0.000	280.000
Subcontracted Amount	0.000	0.000	
Miscellaneous Charges	1500.000	0.000	826.000
Scrapped Material	0.000	0.000	3315.140

```
            (N)ext, (P)revious, or [RETURN] to Quit -

 F1  F2  F3  4  F4   N   5  F5  6  F6  7  F7  8  F8
```

F12. By entering "N" for next screen the user is now viewing project estimates vs. actuals. Not shown are screens 3 and 4, which include AP and AR Credit/Debit Memo and Deposit information along with Operational, COGS, and actual Shipped data.

```
                1) Project Maintenance
                2) Project Inquiry
                3) Project Transaction Inquiry
                4) Sales Order/Quotation For A Project Inquiry
                5) Shipments For A Project Inquiry
                6) A/R Invoices For A Project Inquiry
                7) Cash Receipts For A Project Inquiry
                8) Purchase Orders For A Project Inquiry
                9) A/P Vouchers For A Project Inquiry
               10) Work Orders For A Project Inquiry
               RP) Project Accounting Reports Menu
               TR) Project Accounting Transactions Menu
               UT) Project Accounting Utilities Menu

         Enter Selection or [RETURN] to System Menu

 F1  F2  F3  4  F4   N   5  F5  6  F6  7  F7  8  F8
```

F09. Project Accounting can track customer contract and other internal projectized activities. By linking a project number to a line item on a PO, SO, Invoice, Stock Location (etc.), actual costs will "flow" into the project with each normal transaction.

Minx 2.41   PROJECT INQUIRY   11/20/91
PA,2   Database: 241
Project ID: 500-1   Revision:

Capitalized/Expensed: Capitalized	Est. Personnel Required :	76
Progress Billing : Yes	Est. Payout (Months) :	12
WO Actual/Standard : Actual	Scheduled Start Date :	01/18/90
Scheduled By : Sr Project Mgr	Scheduled Completion Date:	12/03/90
Master Project ID : 500	Actual Start Date :	01/18/90
Project Manager : Kay Mackintosh	Actual Completion Date :	
Project Type :	Percent Completed :	25%
Project Status :	Closed For Accounting :	
Bill-to Customer ID : cyclops		
Name : Cyclops, Inc. :		
PIP Account : 1 -1 -15310		
COGS Account : 1 -1 -53010		

```
            (N)ext or [RETURN] to Quit -

 F1  F2  F3  4  F4   N   5  F5  6  F6  7  F7  8  F8
```

F11. Projects can be hierarchically linked to "Master Projects" causing cost data to "flow" from lower- to upper-level projects. In this inquiry example the user entered Project ID: "500-1" which reports to Master Project ID: "500".

```
 1) Call Register                    11) Codes Report
 2) Pending Calls Report             12) Service Order Cost Report
 3) Response Efficiency Report       13) Service Order Activity Report
 4) Contract Detail Report           14) Picking Report
 5) Calls For A Contract Report      15) Transaction Report
 6) Site Report                      16) Product Population Report
 7) Site Survey Report               17) Scheduled PM Report
 8) Engineer Detail Report           18) RMA Register
 9) Engineer Activity Report         19) RMA Receipts And Issues Report
10) Engineer Craft Code Report       20) Uninvoiced Service Orders Report

              Enter Selection or [RETURN] to Customer Service Menu ─────

1 F1  2 F2  3 F3  4 F4  N  5 F5  6 F6  7 F7  8 F8  F0
```

F14. By allowing *any* report to be run to screen and then "pivoting" between the report and a maintenance screen to take action, Minxware is moving users toward a paperless environment. Not shown is the MINXWINDOWS screen with up to four sessions.

```
Contractee ID: abc1                    Bill-To Customer: abc
Name     : ABC Products                ABC Products
Address 1: 101 Main Street             101 Main Street
Address 2: Suite 205                   Suite 205
City     : BLOOMINGTON                 ACKWORTH
State ZIP: UI      53004               IA      50001
Country  : U.S.A.                      U.S.A.
Telephone: 600-542-1367                600-542-1367
Telex    :
Fax      : 600-542-1360                600-542-1360
Contact  : Lovena Schmidt              Lovena Schmidt
Last Invoiced Date : 03/08/91
Contract Type Code : 24 Hr.            Note Codes:
Contract Status Code: Open             Invoicing Cycle: Yearly
Contract Start Date : 06/20/90         Currency Code : us dollars
Contract End Date   : 06/19/91
Customer P.O. : 4930246─

                              (A)ccept or (E)dit ─

1 F1  2 F2  3 F3  4 F4  N  5 F5  6 F6  7 F7  8 F8  F0
```

F16. The service contract maintains type and status codes, billing cycles, currency codes (as Minxware supports full multicurrency options), etc. Not shown are screens 2 and 3 displaying product and serial numbers under contract.

```
 1) Call Handling Maintenance        12) Site Survey Inquiry
 2) Call Handling Inquiry            13) Service Engineer Maintenance
 3) RMA Maintenance                  14) Service Engineer Inquiry
 4) RMA Inquiry                      15) Engineer Activity Inquiry
 5) Service Contract Maintenance     16) Product Site Maintenance
 6) Service Contract Inquiry         17) Product Site Inquiry
 7) Site Maintenance                 18) Product Structure Inquiry
 8) Site Inquiry                     19) Transfer A Serial/Lot Number
 9) Survey Item Maintenance          RP) Customer Service Reports Menu
10) Survey Item Inquiry             TR) Customer Service Transactions Menu
11) Create a Site Survey            UT) Customer Service Utilities Menu ──

              Enter Selection or [RETURN] to System Menu ──────

1 F1  2 F2  3 F3  4 F4  N  5 F5  6 F6  7 F7  8 F8  F0
```

F13. As a system selectable option, Site records in Customer Service can be created automatically at time of shipment. This provides transparent serial number traceability into the file and allows maintenance and warranty contract "clocks" to be engaged.

```
Call ID       : 132
Serial/Lot Number: 56702        Desc: UNIX Standard PC
Product Number: 10000           Name: Integrated Business Concepts
Site ID  : ibc1

Address ID : ibc-1              Contract ID   : ibc-1
Contact    : Mary Yang          Contract End Date: 09/28/91
Email      :                    Contract Type  : Labor
                                Warranty End Date:
                                Cust. P.O. Number:

Entered By : bill               Engineer ID  : Harriet H.
Entry Date : 02/06/90  16:21    Name: Harriet Hawthorne
Type Code  : Priority 2         Respond By  : 02/07/90  10:00
Status Code: Closed

Fault Code : 13                 Resolution Code : Onsite Rep
Desc: Hum From Inside Housing    Desc: Onsite Repair
Priority   : 0                  Resolution Date : 02/08/90  17:00
Severity   : 0

                    [RETURN] to Continue ─

1 F1  2 F2  3 F3  4 F4  N  5 F5  6 F6  7 F7  8 F8  F0
```

F15. By manually or auto-assigning a "Call ID" users can track each incident and quickly determine whether a product is under a warranty or service contract. Not shown are screens 2 and 3 for problem and resolution details and assigned technical staff.

Product Name: CIIM

Current Version:	V8.4	
Release Date:	CIIM on Oracle 06/15/91	Number of
	CIIM on Sybase 09/15/91	Installed Sites: 100+

Product Summary:

The CIIM (Computer Interactive Integrated Manufacturing) family of manufacturing, distribution, and financial applications are based on a modern enterprise-oriented, open systems strategy: engineered in CASE, developed in Oracle and Sybase, operates on multiple hardware platforms.

Vendor Name:	**Interactive Information Systems, Inc.**
Address:	3716 East Columbia Tucson, AZ 85714
Number of Employees:	75
Phone:	(602)790-4214
Support Services:	24 hour hotline available, in addition to on-site consulting and training, remote dial-in diagnostics, and monthly call-summary reconciliation.
Modifications:	Available directly from IIS or any of our authorized value added resellers.
Source Code:	Provided with the software at no extra charge.

Full System Product Pricing (in U.S. $)	under $20,000	$20,001 -40,000	$40,001 -60,000	$60,001 -100,000	over $100,000
4 users			x		
16 users				x	
64 users					x

(all figures are based on approximate U.S. sales price, and are subject to change at any time)

Product Distribution:

Direct offices in Tucson, Northern California, Southern California, Cincinnati, Toronto, Sydney, Singapore, and Hong Kong. VARs in Sweden, Finland, Norway, Denmark, Singapore, Mexico, Central America, South America, Brazil, Spain, Belgium.

Language/Database:

Oracle and Sybase

Operating Platforms:

Customers currently operating on: AT&T (UNIX), Sun (UNIX), DEC (VMS and ULTRIX), HP(UX), IBM (AIX), Sequent (DYNIX and PTX), Pyramid (UNIX), SCO 386, 486 (UNIX).

```
                    IMCS Inventory Menu                        IIS
                                               (c) Copyright 1990

       Choice Description
       [+]    1   Inventory Information Transactions
       [+]    2   Shop Order Transactions
       [+]    3   Allocation Transactions
       [+]    4   Issue Inventory Transactions
       [+]    5   Inspect/Receive Transactions
       [+]    6   Inventory Reports
       [+]    7   Accounting/Tracing/Adjustment Transactions
       [+]    8   Shop Calendar Maintenance
       [+]    9   Inventory Movement Transactions
       [+]   12   Serial, Lot Batch, and As-Built Maintenance
       [+]   13   Accounting Transactions

                                                               [X]

Enter Selection: _____
```

F02. From the Inventory Module Menu, users can access the 120 "off-the-shelf" inventory screens and reports through the 15 submenu paths available.

```
CIIM                INVENTORY TRANSACTIONS                  IMCS V8.4
Trans Date  : Oct 24 1991          Inspector    :
User        : dbo                  Rej/Scrap CD:
              CREDIT                             DEBIT
Account Type: INV                  Account Type: INV
Account No  : H-TUC_1-INV          Account No  : H-TUC_1-INV

Part No     : 16RIB                Site Id     : TUC_1
Lot Batch No:                      Serial Begin:
Waiv/Dev/Rej:                      Serial End  :

Order No    :                      Order Type  : SH
Line No     :                      Transaction : NREC
Release No  :                      Source      :
Ship Via CD :

Currency    : US  United States    Quantity    : 25
Unit Cost   :            0.00      Warehouse   : MAIN
Av Unit Cost:            0.00      Bay No : 1       Tier No: 3
Total Cost  :               0      Row No : 2       Bin No : 4
                                   Eng Chg Lvl : 1  Duty Status: NA

[F] [N] [P] [Cl] [Np] [A] [U] [J] [D] [*] [Lp] [x]
```

F04. From this inventory audit screen, a user can query any field. For example, one could review all purchase parts received within a specific date range with a lot number assigned.

```
                   CIIM Main Menu                        IIS
                                       Copyright (c) 1991

       Modu¯ e Choice Description
       [+]  OE    1   Order Entry / Cust / Invoices
       [+]  INV   2   Inventory / WIP / Costing
       [+]  PUR   3   Purchasing / Vendors
       [+]  BOM   4   Bills of Mat / Rout / Work Ctr
       [+]  SFC   5   Shop Floor Control
       [+]  CFG   6   Custom Configurator
       [+]  MS    7   Master Scheduling
       [+]  MRP   8   Material Requirements Planning
       [+]  CRP   9   Capacity requirements Planning
       [+]  GL   10   General Ledger / Profit Analysis
       [+]  AR   11   Accounts Receivable / Sales Analysis
       [+]  AP   12   Accounts Payable
       [+]  SYS  15   System Processes

[F] [N] [P] [Cl] [Np] [A] [U] [J] [D] [*] [Lp] [X]
```

F01. This is the CIIM Main Menu. Any user can access modules (by alpha or numeric choices) or directly access a specific screen by entering its name. Security is user by user for module and submenu access.

```
CIIM           PART COST INFORMATION                  IMCS V8.4

Part Number  : 16RIB                Site Id    : TUC_1
Description  : 16 Pin Ribbon Cable  Site Name  : Tucson Main
Currency Code: US                   Cost Set   : 1
Description  : United States Dollars  Description : Current Inventory
                                     Date Entered: Oct 10 1991

Level Material      :   0.00   Standard Material      :   0.00
Level Labor         :   0.00   Standard Labor         :   0.00
Level Outside Proc. :   0.00   Standard Outside Proc. :   0.00
Level Acquisition   :   0.00   Standard Acquisition   :   0.00
Level Overhead 1    :   0.00   Standard Overhead 1    :   0.00
Level Overhead 2    :   0.00   Standard Overhead 2    :   0.00
Total Level         :   0.00   Total Standard         :   0.00

[F] [N] [P] [Cl] [Np] [A] [U] [J] [D] [*] [Lp] [X]
```

F03. In a quick view, the user can review both recurring or LEVEL, as well as summary or STANDARD, costs. In addition, material burden percentages and 98 simulation cost sets are available.

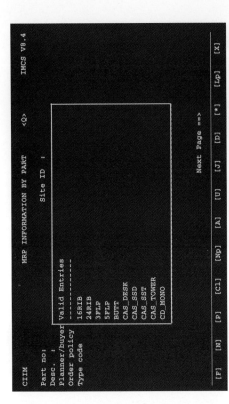

```
 CIIM                    MRP INFORMATION BY PART              IMCS V8.4
 Part no:                          Site ID :
 Desc. :
 Planner/buyer   Valid Entries
 Order policy    --------------
 Type code        16RIB
                  24RIB
                  3FLP
                  5FLP
                  BUTT
                  CAS_DESK
                  CAS_SSD
                  CAS_SST
                  CAS_TOWER
                  CD_MONO
                                              Next Page ==>
 [F] [N] [P] [Cl] [Np] [A] [U] [J] [D] [*] [Lp] [X]
```

F06. A user can review a report, or on this screen, the MRP output for a particular part/contract (site). In addition, hotkeys can jump to other functions. List of Values window for Part Number is shown.

```
 CIIM                 CUSTOMERS SHORT FORM                  CIID V8.4
 Customer Number: CUST101      Sold To Name: JB MFG CORP.
 Home Company   : DEMO         Abbreviation: JB1
                                     Sold to Same Address?:
 Billing Location:   1               Sold to Location:   1
 Dflt Currency : US
 Contact: Jim Jensen             Jim Jensen
 Phone  : 254-6678   Exten:      254-6678
 Addr 1 : 4453 Industrial Way    4453 Industrial Way
 Addr 2
 City   : Tucson     State: AZ    Tucson        AZ    85733
 County : Pima       Country: United   United States
 Cust Class: AAA                 Ship to Same Address?:
                                 Sold To Cust Class :
                          SHIP TO LOCATION
 Ship To Location:   1        Contact: Jim Jensen
 Addr 1: 4453 Industrial Way  Phone  : 254-6678     Exten:
 Addr 2:                      City : Tucson         State: AZ
 Zip  : 85733    Country: United     County:
 [F] [N] [P] [Cl] [Np] [A] [U] [J] [D] [*] [Lp] [X]
```

F08. The first screen of three supported methods for order entry. Other methods support the direct entry of quotes and a quick entry screen. This screen verifies and allows entry of new customers.

```
 CIIM             LOCATIONS BY PART/CONTRACT        IMCS V8.4
 Part Number : HD              Contract     : DEMO
 Desc : Hard_Disk             Contract Ref : Demo_Contr
 Eng Chg Lev : 0
 Type  Warehouse   Bay Row Tier Bin   Lot/Batch    Qty OH
 IN    MAIN        1   2   3   4                    20
                              Total Quantity On Hand : 20
 Char Mode: Replace  Page 1            Count:  1
```

F05. This is a query screen that allows a user to see all inventory locations, lot numbers (if applicable), quantity, and what type of location by part/contract (site)/change level.

```
 CIIM                SALES CATALOG          CIID V8.4
 Catalog Number : IIS-23FLP-TUC_1   Item Type: IP Inventory Part
 Catalog Desc   : 2-3.5 Floppy Drives   Inventory Item: Y
 Part Number    : 3FLP               Weight :
 Site Id
 Inv Unit of    CIIM     CATALOG SUBMENU       CIID V8.4
 Unit of Mea
 Conversion                                              1
 List Price         1. Customer Cross Reference
 Entity Code
 Currency           2. Catalog Price Breaks          Option
 Sales Credi
 Sales Debit        3. Sales Catalog Notes
 Cost Credit                                     t 15 1991
 Cost Debit         4. Catalog Substitution Parts
                   Enter Selection #:
 [F] [N] [P] [Cl] [Np] [A] [U] [J] [D] [*] [Lp] [X]
```

F07. This entry and query screen is where the external (catalog #) to internal (part number/contract (site)) relationship is made. In the bottom block are unlimited customer-specific part number ties.

```
IMCS Purchasing Menu                              IIS
                                       (c) Copyright 1990

    Choice   Description
    [+]  1   General Menu
    [+]  2   Requisition Menu
    [+]  3   Order Menu
    [+]  4   Receipt/Inspection Menu
    [+]  5   Allocations Menu
    [+]  6   Purchasing Inquiry Menu
    [+]  7   Report Menu
    [+]  9   Purchasing Cancel, Close, and Reopen Processing

Enter Selection: _____                                     [X]
```

F09. This Purchasing Module Menu allows access to the 67 screens and reports available "off-the-shelf" in CIIM. Unique features include multiple currencies, purchasing allocations, and quality inspection.

```
CIIM                         ORDER RECEIPT                        CIID V8.4
                     (PURCHASE ORDER SEARCH ASSISTANCE)

Order No   Cd Line RL  Vendor No  Part No   Site ID      Mailed
PO102      1   1    1  VEND102    HDWRE     TUC_1         Y



          Qty due at Dock   Due Date      Vendor Name Ch Flag Challenge Qty
                     50      Nov 17 1991   Inter'l     N            0

[F] [N] [P] [Cl] [Np] [A] [U] [J] [D] [*] [Lp] [X]
```

F10. This Purchasing Receipt screen allows query on any field to speed the receiving process. By pressing the "NEXT BLOCK" function from a given purchase order line, the receiving process is initiated.

```
CIIM              PURCHASE ORDER RECEIPT              IMCS V8.4
Order No: PO102      Order Code: 1  Line No:  1      Release No: 1
Part No: HDWRE            Site ID: TUC_1             Receipt No: 1
Buy Qty Recv'd: _____    Qty Scrap: _____  Qty Shop QC:
Inv Qty:              Date Recv'd: Oct 29 1991 4:22:53:020PM
Receiver:            Copies: 1    Pack List No:
Carrier Name:                     Dock Reg. No:
Freight Bill No:                  Tag No:
    VENDOR & PART INFORMATION _____ LOCATION _____
Part Desc: Misc Hardware Kit      Qty to Location:
Vendor No: VEND102  Name: Inter'l Waiv/Dev/Rej:
Mark For:                         Lot/Batch No:
Department:          Due Date: Nov 17 1991   Expir. Date:
Buyer Code:    Name: Test Buyer      Serial No:
Demand Ord: Demd CD: Demd No:      Duty Status: NA  ECL: 1
Demand Release:  Demd Sequence:    Warehouse:
Buy Qty Due:      50  Buy U/M: KIT     Bay No:
Invntry Qty:      50  Inv U/M: KIT     Row No:
Insp CD  Sample% Sample Qty Conversion Fact   Tier No:
  0    0     0         0          1            Bin No:

[F] [N] [P] [Cl] [Np] [A] [U] [J] [D] [*] [Lp] [X]
```

F11. Purchase Order Receipts, page 2.

```
CIIM                   BILL OF MATERIAL DISPLAY                 IMCS V8.4
Date       : Oct 29 1991                 Site Id    : TUC_1
Parent Part No: CAS_SSD                  Site Name  : Tucson Main
Description : Assembled Desk Top Case    Unit/Meas  : EACH
Serial Begin : CASD-0000001              Eng Chg Order:
Serial End :                             Eng Chg Level: 1
Lot/Batch No :                           Maint Level : NA    Severity: 0
Structure Type: P   Purchase Type

      Component Part  Line  Qty/Assm   Phase In    Serial Begin
Level Description     Item  UOM        Phase Out   Serial End
1     CAS_DESK        1     1          10/16/91    CASD-0000001
      Desktop Case          EACH
1     FAN             2     1          10/16/91    CASD-0000001
      Cooling Fan           EACH
1     HARDWARE        3     1          10/16/91    CASD-0000001
      Misc Chassis          EACH
1     KEYLOCK         4     1          10/16/91    CASD-0000001
      Security Key          EACH
                                                   Next Page ==>
[F] [N] [P] [Cl] [Np] [A] [U] [J] [D] [*] [Lp] [X]
```

F12. Date effective Bills of Material by date applicable, part number/contract, by level are displayed.

```
CIIM                                                    IIS

        Cost Transactions

        Choice Transaction    Description
  [+]     1    cstrol           Complete Cost Roll
  [+]     2    pcstrol          Partial Cost Roll
  [+]     3    bomcstmov        Part Cost Set Move
  [+]     4    bmwcstmov        Work Center Cost Set Move
  [+]     5    partcost         Part Cost
  [+]     6    matcost          Material Cost


Enter Selection:                      (Module, Choice, or Transaction) [X]
```

F14. Numerous costing options available within the Bill of Material Module provide individual or mass updates by routing and/or part, simulations, and a very simple facility to change your active cost sets.

```
CIIM                    MASTER SCHEDULE LEVEL 1              IMCS V8.4

  part.no: 5FLP                 Site ID : TUC_1
  Descr.: 5.25" 1.2 Mb Floppy Drive   Name  : Tucson Main
  Planner/Buyer      :          Order policy : A
  Prod plan grp      :          Finish leadtime:        0
  Demand  timefence  :          Cum.  leadtime:         0
  Planning timefence :          On hand   :             0
  Lot size           :          Allocated :             0
  Safety stock       :          Last run  :             0



  [F]  [N]  [P]  [Cl]  [Np]  [A]  [U]  [J]  [D]  [*]  [Lp]  [X]
```

F16. This Master Production Schedule view screen details the period by period (user defined) status of a forecasted item (including the appropriate breakout from LEVEL 0 or parent).

```
CIIM                      ROUTING ADD                      IMCS V8.4

  Part Number : CAS.SSD          Site Id   : TUC 1
  Desc: Assembled Desk Top Case  Site Name : Tucson Main
  Lot/Batch No:                  Eff Code  : EA
  Phase In  : Oct 16 1991        Operation No:      300
  Phase Out                      Op Overlap : N
  Struct Type : M                Op Desc    : Sub Contract to Vend
  Serial Begin: CASD-0000001
  Serial End  : CASD-9999999
  Maint Level : NA   Severity Level: 0   Occur Rate :         1

  Source          : Vendor Contract    Mach Std Setup Time:        0
  Work Center No  : CASE  Alt:          Mach Run Time Code :        3
  Machine Number  :                     Mach Std Run Factor:        8
  Tool Number     :                     Move Time          :        8
  Manifct Eng Plan By:     Date:        Efficiency Factor  :        1
  Qual Eng Plan By:        Date:        Std Lot Quantity   :       10
  Shop Ord Rtg Revisn:                  Op Material Burden :        0
                                        Incremental Cost   :        0

  [F]  [N]  [P]  [Cl]  [Np]  [A]  [U]  [J]  [D]  [*]  [Lp]  [X]
```

F13. Entry or view routings from this screen, including operation by operation (tied to work centers) structure types, effectivity dates and codes, etc. Labor can be tied to operations also.

```
CIIM              OPERATIONS BY ORDER                      IMCS V8.4

  Status  Order Code  Order No  Release  Seq No    Priority
    2         M          11                          99999

     Part No       Contract        Start Date  Due Date    Orig Qty
  A033816            NT            02-OCT-91  02-OCT-91        5

                                                              L D C
  Op  Ext.                  Work     Start  Remaining Allowed A I A S
  No. No.   Description     Center   Date   Qty Due  Hours   P R P T
                                                             N F I S
  10    Assemble            A      02-OCT-91  5      .1
  ___  ___  _____  _____  _____  ___ ___ _____  _____
  ___  ___  _____  _____  _____  ___ ___ _____  _____
  ___  ___  _____  _____  _____  ___ ___ _____  _____
  ___  ___  _____  _____  _____  ___ ___ _____  _____
  ___  ___  _____  _____  _____  ___ ___ _____  _____

  Order Labor Information                       ==> Page 2

        Char Mode: Replace  Page 1             Count: *1
```

F15. Resident within the CIIM Shop Floor Control Module, you can view the status of a given shop order by status, by operation (including overlap, capability, direction, capacity), etc.

12

Implementing an *HI/MIS*

This chapter presents proven methodologies to use in the process of implementing an *HI/MIS*. These methodologies are designed to accomplish a quality implementation in the least amount of time that is practical while making the most efficient and effective use of relatively few resources.

The following topics related to the implementation process are discussed:

1. Implementation project planning
2. Resource and time requirements
3. Establishing priorities
4. Formation of the project team
5. Product training
6. Developing operational procedures
7. Utilizing the pilot technique
8. Evaluating system cut-over alternatives
9. Handling emergency situations
10. Evaluating the results of the implementation
11. Using outside consultants

IMPLEMENTATION PROJECT PLANNING

Planning the project is an essential first step to a successful *HI/MIS* implementation. A look at the track record for failed or suboptimal system implementations shows that relatively few are due to product factors. Less than 5 percent are due to hardware problems, such as underpowered equipment or frequent downtime. Under 20 percent are a result of software problems, such as selecting the wrong product or significant defects in the code.

The majority (over 75 percent) of the failed or suboptimal implementations are due to human factors. It is these factors that can be managed successfully by careful planning at the beginning of the implementation project.

Following are examples of some of the nonproduct or human factors that impact implementation success:

- The end user community will make or break an implementation. Poor attitude or a lack of motivation in the company's user community will ensure a problematic implementation.

- Insufficient commitment by the company's management to the project foreshadows eventual implementation problems. This manifests itself in several ways. One common problem occurs when management does not allocate sufficient resources to implement the system properly. A lack of *perceived* management commitment can also cause the project to lose momentum and stall. Management needs to be visibly supportive of the new system, so that skeptical or reluctant users will get the message and work diligently on the implementation.

- Inadequate training of key implementors, MIS personnel, and the end user community will significantly impair the implementation.

- Mistakes in choosing implementation alternatives can also undermine the project's success. All sophisticated, highly functional systems will offer the company a wealth of choices in optimizing how the system will serve them. Small mistakes in making these choices lead to a suboptimal system. Large mistakes can lead to a dead end and stall the project.

- Trying to get the system on line faster than the organization can adjust to the necessary changes leads to frustration and resistance in the end user community. A more severe problem can occur if, in the rush to bring the system on line, the existing systems and procedures are prematurely abandoned. Without a period of parallel processing or adequate testing of the new system, the company faces a potential breakdown of system operations.

These human-factor causes of implementation problems can, through careful planning and preparation, be controlled. The tasks necessary to implement the *HI/MIS* in the shortest practical time can be coordinated and managed. A reasonable estimate of the resources necessary to implement the new system can be projected. Senior management, with the task list, time line, and resource requirements in hand, can make an informed decision whether to commit wholeheartedly to the project. The company is thereby ready to take a coordinated, realistic, managed approach to implementing the *HI/MIS*.

Expended Time Budget

There are several important elements in the project plan for implementing an *HI/MIS*. A key part of planning involves laying out the expended time budget. The budget estimates the amount of time that specified internal personnel must dedicate to each of the implementation tasks. This provides the basis for building a staffing schedule for the project.

As part of the process for ensuring buy-in, the expended time budget should be discussed, individually and in advance, with the key internal personnel. This will help them gain the proper expectation for how much of a time commitment they will be asked to make on the project. The expended time budget must also be reviewed to ensure that its demands on personnel time are realistic. If the relationship of expended time to elapsed time will cause 80-hour work weeks, a modification of plans is in order. Management should also review the time commitments of key personnel to ensure that these personnel are not diverted from other high-priority tasks for unacceptable periods of time.

Management must commit to provide the internal personnel resources projected by the expended time budget. A clear understanding and expression of the commitment should be obtained. The commitment is for the aggregate number of personnel hours required for the project, which will certainly be large and may impact other company goals. Also, the commitment is for specified key personnel whose individual schedules must be freed up to enable them to work on the project. Management commitment on both of these points is necessary to avoid subsequent scheduling conflicts that will hamper the implementation project.

Elapsed Time Budget

The objective of the elapsed time budget is to project the time milestones for implementing each of the key areas of functionality and for completing the entire project. This enables the company to see when particular areas will become functional and whether the activities associated with the project conflict with other business priorities. For example, do the milestones conflict with a routine shutdown period, extremely busy time of the year, or another problematic time period?

Also, management can then assess whether the timing for a particular area becoming functional should be adjusted in order to meet certain company goals. The elapsed time budget is important for ensuring that the implementation project is coordinated with other company activities and is consistent with strategic company objectives.

Responsibility Assignment to Individuals

All personnel involved in the performance of a project task should be identified. Further, it is important to identify not just who will be working on a project task, but who will be *responsible* for the task.

While a task may involve several people, it is best to assign one individual with overall responsibility for the successful completion of the task. The responsible individual will not necessarily perform the bulk of the work involved in the task. But the individual designated as responsible should be one who can be relied upon to coordinate the work of others and ensure that their assigned task is completed on time.

Predecessor/Successor Task Relationships

Project tasks are often interrelated. Frequently, being able to perform a given task is dependent upon the earlier completion of other tasks. These tasks share a predecessor/successor relationship. An important part of the project planning process entails identifying these predecessor/successor task relationships.

Once these relationships are identified, the project team can lay out the optimal sequence of tasks that completes the implementation process in the shortest practical time. A lack of adequate attention to these predecessor/successor relationships will cause the project to take longer than necessary. Completely ignoring these relationships can cause more severe problems. To illustrate this risk, consider the following example:

The Purchasing Department has worked very hard and is right on time with their tasks to implement the new system in their area. They have developed procedures, trained the users, and are now ready and anxious to load the open purchase orders and start using the new system.

At this point, the purchasing team realizes that in the new system, the entry of basic vendor information is controlled through the accounts payable module. This vendor information must be loaded prior to the loading of the open purchase orders. However, the accounts payable module is not scheduled to become functional for another two months.

Concerned about the impact that this delay will have on implementing the system in their area, Purchasing asks if Finance can expedite their implementation of accounts payable. They learn that accounts payable will actually not be able to meet its two-month implementation milestone.

It seems that Finance ran into an unexpected delay early in the process of implementing accounts payable. The accounts payable module requires default chart of accounts numbers that are controlled within the general ledger module. Unfortunately, the new general ledger system, with a revamped chart of accounts, is not scheduled to come on-line until close to the company's next fiscal year end, which is six months away.

Obviously, things can be done to overcome the implementation obstacles facing the company in the above example. But, there will be some delay while the project team and user community scramble to compensate for poor planning. With good planning, the project team could have avoided the frustration and near chaos that can ensue in these types of situations. It is prudent to give proper attention to predecessor/successor relationships during the planning process.

Checkpoints

Checkpoints should be planned into the implementation process at natural intervals. Checkpoints serve as opportunities for the project team, the users, and management to gain a perspective on how well the project is progressing. The quality and timeliness of the implementation should be reviewed along with a preliminary analysis of whether the projected benefits from the project are being realized. If changes in the project plan are called for, they should be incorporated before pushing on toward the next checkpoint.

An example of a natural place for a checkpoint in a project might be the successful implementation of basic Inventory Control. The project team and users will know that this milestone has been reached when they can begin to rely on the inventory quantity information in the system as an accurate reflection of the actual physical quantities found in the stockrooms and production areas. This particular place is also a good candidate for a checkpoint since further implementation of functions such as MRP and Master Scheduling are fundamentally dependent on working, accurate Inventory Control.

Checkpoints are also valuable opportunities for motivating the people involved in the project. Implementing a full MRP-II system is a large project that will realistically span a significant length of time. By breaking the process up into phases or stages, it becomes much easier for the project team, users, and management to see the progress actually being made.

The users and project team members are being asked to climb a mountain. The climb will seem easier if it can be taken one plateau at a time. And the ascent will be much more enjoyable if the climbers are permitted to pause for a moment at each plateau, to admire the view and appreciate what has been accomplished. Because providing a sense of accomplishment is important in keeping the project team and users motivated, management may want to utilize the opportunity afforded by the checkpoint to recognize their accomplishments and reinforce the significance of their work for the company.

The checkpoints should be spaced frequently enough to accomplish the objectives enumerated above. But, the interval between checkpoints should be large enough to ensure that they retain their meaning as major accomplishments. Spacing the checkpoints too frequently can also result in an over-control situation where the project team feels that they cannot accomplish the project tasks without the constant supervision and approval of management. As a rule of thumb, three to five major checkpoints during the course of a full MRP-II implementation project seems to work well.

RESOURCE AND TIME REQUIREMENTS

What will a typical implementation require in terms of resources and time? This is a very difficult question to answer. The first thing to realize is that there is no such thing as a *typical* implementation. All implementations represent a unique set of variables. These include the hardware, the software, the specific implementation objectives, the company itself, the nature of its processes, the involved personnel, the business environment, and many other internal and external factors. While it is a difficult task to realistically estimate these requirements, it is a necessary one and an integral part of the overall implementation planning process.

Estimating the Expended Time Budget

The amount of time that the company's personnel will need to expend in the implementation project depends on several factors.

Project Objectives

One key factor is the intended level of sophistication of the system being implemented. If the intent is to implement a full MRP-II system with comprehensive, highly sophisticated functionality, such as Capacity Requirements Planning and extremely detailed Shop Floor Control, expect this to require a relatively high level of resources. A more modest set of objectives, such as accurate Inventory Control and Order Processing, would require significantly fewer resources.

Complexity of the Company's Operations

The complexity of a company's operations can dramatically impact the required implementation resources. A company with multiple manufacturing processes, multiple production planning methods, and multiple product distribution channels that operates in a multisite, international environment will usually require more resources than a simpler single-product line, single-site company.

Nature of the Company's Existing Systems

All existing companies have a system. The system may be formal or informal, and it may be automated, completely manual, or a mixture. But if the company is operating, there must be some sort of system in existence. The only exceptions are start-up companies and those entering a new area (such as manufacturing operations) for the first time.

In increasing order of difficulty, the three situations an implementation team can be faced with are:

- An existing automated system
- No system at all
- An entrenched manual system

Converting from an existing automated system usually requires the least amount of resources. In this situation, operational procedures should already exist that can be adapted to the new system. This is still a challenge, but it should be relatively easier than the alternatives.

If the data in the existing system is of adequate quality, it can be converted and transferred to the new system using an automated process. This can significantly reduce the data development and loading requirements.

A possible negative in converting from an existing automated system is that some users may exhibit a bias towards the old system. No matter how good the new system is, the old system will probably perform a few functions in a superior manner. A few timely reminders of the additional advantages and benefits that will be provided by the new system can help maintain a positive attitude towards its implementation.

A somewhat more difficult situation occurs when there is no current system in place at all. This is often called "going from nothing to something." It is a challenge. Operational procedures do not exist and therefore must be developed from scratch. All of the fundamental questions must be addressed, perhaps for the first time. How is a customer order processed? How are incoming material receipts controlled? Who is responsible for the ownership and ongoing maintenance of data? Many times these questions have to be answered in the abstract, in order to prepare the system to support operations that will not commence until sometime in the future.

Another challenge is that little or no existing base data will be available. Bills of material, routings, engineering information, cost data, planning parameters, and a wide range of additional fundamental data may need to be developed.

The most difficult of all situations is posed by the company that has an entrenched manual system. This category includes purely manual systems and those augmented with minor home-grown spreadsheet and database applications. The problem is that the operational procedures are often obscure. In other words, they are very specific or unique to the company. Usually, the longer the manual systems have been around, the more esoteric they become.

Unfortunately, these manual procedures can be very difficult to simulate in an automated system. As an illustration, consider the user who cheerfully recounts: "It's so simple in our manual system. I look for the yellow stick-em on the order acknowledgment. If it's stuck on the top right corner, I know it's been approved. If it has a red checkmark on it, I call to confirm. A blue one means I should fax a copy. So how do I do that on this dreadful new system?"

In this situation, it is reasonable to expect that the company and the user base will take extra time to adapt to the new automated system.

Complexity of the Software

Another factor affecting the amount of time expended to implement the system will be the complexity of the software. Even *HI/MIS* products can vary widely in their relative complexity. A complex software product can take significantly more resources for training, installation, and support than does a less complex product. The more features and alternatives available, the more time will be needed in configuring the software for optimal use.

But keep in mind that there is a difference between a product being complex and a product being capable. An overly simple product may lack important capabilities. When this occurs, significant implementation time will be needed to develop acceptable workarounds for the software's deficiencies.

Related Tasks

Additional work often needs to be accomplished as part of the overall implementation effort. Often, this additional work can significantly add to the required resources. Common examples of this situation include the need for new or adjusted part number coding and for other types of fundamental base data to be formulated or adjusted. This might include adjustments to the company's chart of accounts, vendor coding, customer coding, or cost structure data.

Bills of material are worthy of separate mention. Even when they do exist their accuracy is quite often insufficient to enable material planning to run successfully. Depending on the complexity of the manufacturing environment, achieving a high level of bill of material accuracy may be a significant project of its own for certain companies.

Personnel Experience and Knowledge Base

A project team that includes individuals with significant prior experience implementing or at least operating an integrated manufacturing system will likely be more efficient and require less expended time. The team will be able to select the optimal choices more quickly and accurately. For example, if Marketing has extensive prior experience with how an automated system can be used to process an order through the quotation, approval, booking, release, and ship cycle, they have an advantage.

Similarly, an important factor is whether an understanding of the fundamental concepts being implemented already exists within the company. For example, is there a clear understanding of Master Scheduling, the basic logic of Material Requirements Planning, or the normal flow of closed-loop MRP? If these concepts are new to the company, the expended time budget should include adequate training for all the involved personnel.

Occurrence of Problems, Surprises

This last category of factors affecting expended time requirements covers the items that cannot be planned for specifically. But a realistic budget will recognize that it is normal for a number of problems and surprises to arise during the course of the implementation process.

A common situation is overestimating the quality of the base information currently available. For example, initial estimates may indicate that the bills of material for a company are 99 percent accurate. Then, the first attempt is made at running MRP. Upon analyzing the results, the company is surprised to learn that in reality, there are errors on perhaps 50 percent of the bills.

Personnel issues can also be expected to occur. Some project team members or key users may run into problems devoting their committed amount of time to the project. Also, involved personnel may begin to exhibit unexpectedly negative attitudes about the project, the project team, or the new system. Left untreated, these issues can deteriorate and cause the project to fall behind schedule or even to fail. Accordingly, time must be expended to work these problems out as the project goes forward.

Problems or surprises related to the software can also cause more time to be expended than initially planned. For example, the project team may unexpectedly discover that the software does not adequately meet a specific need. The team would then have to expend additional time in developing a reasonable workaround to accommodate the needed functionality. If significant bugs in the software occur, it will require extra time to work through their solution. In addition, planned modifications to the software may not be delivered on time or, when received, may be found to be poorly designed or buggy.

This is not an exhaustive list of problems and surprises that can occur. Anything is possible. The project team should have the attitude that problems and surprises *will* occur and that the team will handle them and achieve success. The project plan should also allow for these occurrences and contain sufficient budgeted time for their resolution.

Benchmark for Typical Expended Time Budget

With all the factors listed above affecting the course of the implementation project, the total amount of expended time required to implement an *HI/MIS* can vary widely. But, if we construct the hypothetical typical implementation, a benchmark for expended time can be given.

For benchmark purposes, a typical implementation is defined as one where:

1. The project objectives are moderately aggressive.
2. The company's operations are of average complexity.
3. The company already has an existing automated system.
4. The software to be implemented is an *HI/MIS* product of average complexity with fully adequate capabilities.
5. Only a moderate amount of related tasks must be accomplished.
6. The company has fairly experienced and knowledgeable implementors and users.
7. A reasonable number of small problems and surprises occur during the implementation.

Based on field experience, this average implementation can be expected to require in the range of 1,500 to 2,500 total person-hours to complete. This is equivalent to approximately one person-year of work. This general estimate of required time has been labeled a benchmark. But it should not be considered a benchmark in the sense that a company wins by completing their implementation in less expended hours than the benchmark amount.

Successful implementation is not a black and white issue. There are many shades of gray. The test of a successful implementation should not simply be that all of the software modules are up and running. There is the issue of quality. How *well* are the modules running in the functional areas? To what degree are they providing the expected benefits?

The implementation of a new system also provides an excellent opportunity to improve the company's operational procedures. The opportunity exists to *not* simply automate inefficient wasteful practices, but to take the time to examine *why* these practices exist and eliminate or at least streamline them before automating.

The implementation process should not be viewed as a race. The first one across the finish line is not necessarily the winner. The true challenge is in achieving a quality implementation, one that fully accomplishes the intended objectives and provides substantial benefits to the company for many years. Therefore, it is prudent to make the proper investment in resources to do the job right.

Estimating the Elapsed Time Budget

The estimate of calendar time that will elapse before the implementation project is completed depends primarily on the rate at which resources are utilized. An automobile trip can serve as a useful metaphor. Let's assume that this particular trip will be 2,000 miles in length (2,000 person-hours of expended time). This length is fairly constant; not much can be done to significantly change it.

But the car can travel at very different speeds. The faster it goes, the sooner the passengers will arrive at the intended destination. To go faster, the driver simply increases the flow of fuel to the engine. So a fundamental question is— How much "gas" will management give to the project? One person part time? Or, 10 people full time? The elapsed time of the trip is dependent on the answer to this question.

In addition, the elapsed time of the automobile trip depends on whether problems are encountered along the way, such as:

- Highway construction
- Mechanical breakdowns
- Passengers who insist upon frequent stops
- A poor roadmap for getting from here to there

Similarly, the elapsed time of a system implementation will depend on whether problems are encountered along the way, such as:

- Delayed construction of needed modifications
- Hardware breakdowns or software bugs
- Personnel who impede progress
- A poor project plan for getting from here to there

According to conventional, traditional wisdom, companies have been told to expect the implementation of an MRP-II system to take 18 months. Further, this is considered an optimistic amount of elapsed time, predicated on having a high level of management commitment and no problems being encountered.

This "classic" timeframe poses a serious problem to many companies. Some simply do not have the luxury of one and a half years to complete their implementation. An example is a start-up that has no system at all but is beginning to produce product now and will begin shipping product within a month. Other ex-

TABLE 12-1 TOTAL EXPENDED TIME, RATE OF RESOURCE UTILIZATION,
AND ELAPSED TIME

Project	Total Expended Time	Resource Utilization	Elapsed Time for Completion
The mythical typical project.	2,000 hrs	4 people, each dedicated half time	6 months
Quick implementation required; a start-up company situation; objective is to put basic functionality in place; implementation of more sophisticated modules will be accomplished later.	1,000 hrs	2 people full time plus 2 people half time	2 months
Full implementation of all functionality; replacement of entrenched manual system; complex operating environment.	6,000 hrs	1 full-time project manager plus 2 people dedicated half time	18 months

amples are companies facing imminent failure of their existing systems and those that are forced to respond more immediately to competitive pressures.

Too much elapsed time can be a problem for all companies. Longer projects, by nature, are more likely to fail. Over time, they loose momentum as people toil with no immediate results, and the normal turnover in staff introduces new people with different priorities into the projects.

The project plan should call for the shortest realistic elapsed time. It is prudent for management to allocate the level of resources required to complete the project within this elapsed time. The mathematics of the relationship between total expended time, rate of resource utilization, and resulting elapsed time is illustrated in Table 12-1.

ESTABLISHING PRIORITIES

What tasks should be worked on first? To answer this question, the critical path for the implementation project should be determined. The *critical path* is the particular sequence of tasks that will enable the entire project to be completed in the shortest practical amount of time. The path is dependent on the predecessor/successor relationships between tasks and the elapsed time required to complete each individual task.

The process of manually isolating the critical path can be time-consuming (and error prone). There are several currently available, inexpensive project management software products that do an excellent job of automatically calculating a project's critical path.

All tasks found to be on the critical path should logically be assigned a high priority. A delay on one of these tasks will delay subsequent tasks and therefore the project in its entirety. This is contrasted to tasks not on the critical path, where a delay in their completion will not necessarily delay the whole project.

By following the critical path, the amount of time that people will be waiting for predecessor tasks to finish will be minimized. The project will therefore reach its end point in the shortest possible time. However, while completing the entire project in the shortest possible elapsed time is important, there are other factors to consider in establishing priorities. If a company's current system is failing in a particular functional area, then the tasks necessary to address that area must be given priority.

As an example, consider a company implementing a fully integrated system. They have correctly determined that their project's critical path chains through the manufacturing modules. For the entire project to complete in the shortest possible time, immediate tasks on this critical path should be given priority. But the company's current system is experiencing increasing problems in the Accounts Receivable area. The problems are becoming severe enough that there is real concern that the current system will soon fail. The Accounts Receivable functional area must be given priority. It may be possible for work in this area to proceed concurrently with progress in the manufacturing areas. But even if critical path tasks will be delayed, the situation dictates that Accounts Receivable work will come first.

Another important factor in setting priorities is to begin realizing benefits from the new system as soon as possible. Areas with the largest payback opportunities should be positioned for early completion. The benefits from system implementation are often substantial. For example, consider a medium-size company that will achieve improvements in their bottom-line operating results of $25,000 per month upon successful implementation of the system within a particular area. With each month that passes, the company permanently loses its opportunity to make this additional $25,000. It therefore makes economic sense to start this benefit flow at the earliest possible date.

It is also a good practice to identify areas that have an immediate, visible payback and target them for early completion. The early achievement of a milestone that produces visible benefits will motivate the people involved in the project to continue their implementation efforts. Establishing an aura of success around the project is also important for garnering the continued support of senior management while they await completion of the large, longer term payback items.

FORMATION OF THE PROJECT TEAM

Because of its role as the leader of the implementation, the project team is a key factor in determining the level of success ultimately achieved. The team is responsible for formulating the original implementation plan and then managing its execution. It sets the detailed schedules, works with senior management to ensure that necessary resources are available, identifies problems facing the project, and works to resolve them so that the project stays on schedule and within its budget.

The implementation project team is often made up of the same members who composed the earlier evaluation/selection team. The same qualities that made the members the best candidates for the evaluation and selection process tend to also qualify them as the best candidates for leading the implementation process. Also, there is a natural motivation for the same members to work hard to ensure that their earlier evaluation and selection decisions are validated.

Many of the same factors considered earlier in the formation of the evaluation and selection team still apply. (Please see Chapter 10 for a discussion of these factors.) They include:

- Cross-functional representation
- Project team size
- Selection criteria for individual team members
- Time availability
- Structure of the team

Time availability should be given particular consideration in forming the implementation project team. This factor is even more likely to turn into a problem during the implementation process than it was during the evaluation/selection process.

The project team should meet at regularly scheduled intervals. Periodic meetings are an important tool for staying coordinated and for controlling the implementation process. It is also helpful if written minutes or records are made of decisions reached, open issues to be resolved, and new assignments of responsibility.

PRODUCT TRAINING

One method to maximize the effectiveness of product training is to divide the process into two phases. In Phase 1, the vendor is used to train the trainers. These trainers are the company's internal personnel. They will be used to train the remainder of the company's user population later in Phase 2.

The personnel receiving direct training from the vendor should be key personnel from each of the functional areas. These personnel may or may not also be members of the project team. The project team members should also receive training, although it may be limited to basic or overview training.

In Phase 2 of training, the company's internal trainers now teach the product to the users in their functional areas. Importantly, they do more than just train the users on the product. Phase 2 of training should not begin until after the procedures have been developed and (hopefully) documented. In this way, the users can be trained on both the software product itself and on exactly how it will be used within their area.

It is also beneficial if Phase 2 user training can be scheduled after base data has been developed and loaded to the new system. This will enable the users to begin actively using the system soon after training. A common mistake is to train all the company personnel too early in the process. By the time the system is ready to be started in a functional area, the users will have forgotten the bulk of their training.

DEVELOPING OPERATIONAL PROCEDURES

Operational procedures define *how* the software will be used. A byproduct of the process of developing these procedures is that many implementation issues and decision alternatives will be brought to the surface. The careful thinking through and documentation of exactly how the system will work in a particular functional area is a valuable process in itself, since it leads to optimal use of the system.

Fully developed and documented procedures are very helpful in training users on a new system. But the value of documented procedures extends beyond just the initial implementation of a system. Smaller companies in particular find written operational procedures helpful in quickly training new personnel. Larger companies tend to have more people doing the same task and can somewhat rely on these personnel to train new personnel. But smaller companies do not have this luxury. A good set of documented procedures can provide these smaller companies with a means to keep a functional area operating in the event of personnel turnover.

The operational procedures need not be elaborate or overly formal. The value of documented procedures is the thought that goes into the process of their development and their value as a training tool. Their particular form is of much lesser importance.

Over-documenting is a waste of precious implementation project resources. Actually, the thought of volumes of antiquated procedures manuals gathering dust on everyone's shelves seems contrary to an *HI/MIS* approach. But a simple set of procedures, especially for use during the implementation and initial use of the new system, has definite value. The company may decide to discontinue updates to some or the majority of the documented procedures at a later date, once the system is settled in and stable, when many people have solid knowledge on its operation.

It is best to develop operational procedures as early as is practical in the implementation process. Since part of their value is in bringing implementation issues to the surface, the project team will want these issues identified earlier as opposed to later. It is also beneficial to have the procedures available for Phase 2 of product training (see above section).

UTILIZING THE PILOT TECHNIQUE

The term *pilot* has a few different definitions. In definition 1, the pilot is a technique where the system is phased in one area at a time. This allows problems to be isolated and fixed before truly going live in all parts of the operation. For this to work, an operating area must be separable. For example, to avoid loading the entire parts master list, an operating area is selected that exclusively uses only a manageable subgroup of the company's total parts.

The advantage of this approach is that it spreads the workload. If the implementation of all areas at one time is too much for the company to undertake, this approach may be appropriate. Also, if parallel processing is required, it may be more feasible to duplicate the data input resources for just the one area of the company undergoing the pilot. Then, after the system has been proven in at least this one pilot area, the confidence level may be high enough to implement in the remaining areas without the need to process the entire company's business in parallel.

One concern in using this approach is that the various operating areas of a company can be quite different. Proving the system in just one small area does not necessarily mean that it will work in all others. It is a good idea when selecting an area for pilot to choose one that is as representative as possible of the full range of the company's operations.

In definition 2, the pilot is a technique where a small group of people (probably comprised mainly of the project team members) simulate the company's environment by testing various setup alternatives and a full range of transactions against a trial or pilot copy of the system. The purpose of this pilot is to test and validate different options for implementing the system. This type of pilot is more common and usually even more valuable than the type of pilot described in definition 1. But these approaches are not mutually exclusive. In some situations, it can make sense to use both types of pilot in conjunction.

This pilot technique (definition 2) works best when an entire business cycle is simulated. For example, the project team could begin the simulation by assuming that a new product is being introduced. The remainder of the cycle might look like the following:

1. Engineering and planning data are entered
   (a) Add item master information
   (b) Add bill of material information
   (c) etc.
2. Product demand is forecast
3. Master schedule of production is developed
4. Material requirements planning (MRP) is run
5. Raw material requirements are examined
6. Purchase orders are generated
7. Materials are received
8. Product is built
   (a) Open work order
   (b) Kit and issue materials
   (c) etc.
9. Product is shipped
10. Customer is billed
11. Financial results are reported

It's best to pick the most representative product(s) or product line(s) for simulation. Each of the functions in the business cycle should then be performed for a *manageable* number of transactions.

As the participants in the pilot complete each step, they must constantly be evaluating the effectiveness of the system. They need to ask themselves, "Is the system providing me with the information I need to do my job? What problems do

I see? Is this the best method to use in performing this function? What notes or operational procedures will need to be communicated to the users to get them to use this part of the system successfully?"

The participants will usually need to progress through the cycle several times. It will take a few times just to get the system to work at all. Then at least a few more times to determine how to use it optimally. The pilot process may take from a few to several weeks to complete, depending on the complexity of the system and the company's operations.

A major benefit is that, at the end of the pilot process, the project team knows exactly *how* the software can be used successfully in each of the company's operational areas. The team is then in a position to implement the system confidently, knowing how it will be used to meet the users' requirements and understanding fully the mechanics of how the system operates.

The company also benefits since the project team has the opportunity to test various implementation alternatives to find the optimal way to use the system to meet the company's needs. The team will also experience the wrong ways to operate the system and find troublesome software bugs and other problems before the system is brought up live for use throughout the company. Additionally, the pilot avoids the waste of resources that often occurs when live data is developed and loaded, unforeseen problems are subsequently encountered, and the data has to be redeveloped and reloaded.

Probably the people best suited to conduct the pilot are the members of the project team, based on their extensive knowledge of the operational areas of the company. The team members should have already been trained on the software by the vendor and should, therefore, be able to put the system through its paces.

The pilot should be scheduled after implementation planning and after initial training has been accomplished. Development of the operational procedures should await the results of the pilot, since the experience and knowledge gained during the pilot will most likely affect many of the procedures.

EVALUATING SYSTEM CUT-OVER ALTERNATIVES

Parallel processing is one alternative method to cut-over from one system to another. This method consists of continuing to run the old system for a period of time while at the same time running the new system. The major advantage of running both old and new systems in parallel is that the old system can be relied upon as a backup. If a serious problem is encountered in the new system, it will therefore not cause a major disruption of business. Parallel processing minimizes the risk to the company while the new system proves its reliability.

The major disadvantage of parallel processing is that it requires almost a doubling of resources to implement. Users must provide information to both old and new systems during the period of parallel processing. In some situations this doubling of input requirements can be automated, with original entry to one system being translated and fed electronically to the other. But considerable programming effort is typically required to code the translation, interface, and error-checking routines to perform this function.

Although it requires significant additional resources, parallel processing is prudent for certain applications (functional areas) where a system failure would pose serious problems for the company. Accounts receivable is often used as an example of this type of application. Most companies cannot afford to have a failure in this area for any extended period of time. The failure could mean a significant loss of cash flow, potential permanent loss of revenue, and, in an extreme case, the very existence of the company could be at risk.

The success of a parallel processing period is measured primarily by comparing various balances and summary output reports from the two systems. For example, immediately after a billing/payment application cycle, the new aggregate accounts receivable balance from the old and the new systems are compared. They should agree perfectly, or they should at least be able to be reconciled perfectly by adjusting for known differences in how the two systems are being operated.

If there are any differences, the detail level records in the system can then be checked against each other. In the accounts receivable example, this could be accomplished by producing a detailed listing of open items by customer and verifying that there is the expected one-to-one correspondence between systems.

The parallel processing can be discontinued after the necessary confidence level has been reached. By that time, all system transactions should have been validated, including period-ending procedures. The necessary confidence level will justifiably come earlier if the software being implemented is off-the-shelf and has already been proven successful at many other sites. However, even with a proven software product with this track record, the company would be prudent to allow additional time if any new functions have been added to the standard product or if any modifications were performed.

It's normal to target a timeframe for the completion of the parallel period, such as two months, in the implementation project plan. But the company should remain flexible and be prepared to adjust the schedule based on the actual experience during the parallel period.

Another alternative to system cut-over is often called the *cold turkey approach.* This method entails an immediate shut-down of the old system (or at least a discontinuance of entering new information into it) and a reliance solely on the new system. After a specified cut-over date, the company operates exclusively on the new system, with no parallel processing period at all.

Cutting over cold turkey offers the major advantage that no duplication of resources is required to operate the old system. The major disadvantage to this approach is that it is risky, and the stakes being gambled are high. One might be wagering the future of the company on the premise that the system will work right and that the users will be able to operate it successfully from the very start. Cold turkey does not provide the safety net of the old system being operated in parallel as a backup.

Cold turkey is appropriate for certain types of situations. One possible example might be in replacing a manual purchasing system. If the new system can at least be relied upon to print the new purchase orders on two-part paper, it could fail in all other aspects (e.g., keeping track of cash commitments and interfacing to inventory control) and the company would still not be any worse off than with the manual system. In the event of a failure with the new system, the operation of the manual system could be replicated by using the retained hardcopies of the original purchase orders. Thus, a backup safety net still exists.

Cold turkey is also appropriate when the company's old system has failed or reached the breaking point. In this situation, there is really no decision to be made; the new system must be the solution and be made to work correctly immediately. The decision can also be forced in the situation where the company simply does not have the resources available to support two systems. A cold turkey cut-over is then the only feasible, although risky, option.

The implementation project team does not need to choose either the parallel processing or the cold turkey approach as the exclusive method to use for the entire system. The team can elect to mix the two approaches, using parallel processing in certain functional areas, the cold turkey method in other areas, and perhaps a combination or hybrid of the two methods for a third group of functional areas.

For each given functional area, the project team should evaluate which cut-over method is most appropriate. The likelihood and consequences of a failure in the initial usage of the new system should be evaluated. This evaluation includes the risks to the business, the level of confidence that exists relative to the soundness of the new system, and the adequacy of the contingency options that are available. Whenever the cold turkey method is selected for a functional area, the project team should be able to articulate a contingency plan than can be implemented in the event the new system initially fails.

The project team should incorporate the plans for cut-over into the overall implementation plan. This ensures that the time lines and resource requirements in the system-wide implementation plan reflect the significant activities associated with the system cut-over efforts.

HANDLING EMERGENCY SITUATIONS

Unfortunately, implementation projects are sometimes undertaken by companies more as a response to an emergency than as a consequence of planning and foresight. For example, start-up companies are notorious for waiting much too long to address their information system needs. Another all-too-common occurrence is a failed implementation of one system, which leaves little time to do the job right with a replacement system. Similarly, the imminent failure of or collapse of a company's existing system will create an emergency. In situations like these, the new system needs to be implemented (literally) yesterday.

There are some accelerated methods that can be used in these situations. The first step is to identify the company's mission-critical functions and then to focus all implementation efforts on getting these functions properly supported. These mission-critical functions are typically the basic ones essential for the survival of the company, such as:

- Billing for what has been shipped
- Collecting for what has been billed
- Protecting the company's assets by knowing
  - What inventory is owned
  - Where it is
  - Where it went

The project team should focus all efforts on implementing and stabilizing this basic level of functionality. It may be best to not attempt to initially achieve a truly optimal implementation, even though the cost of change in the future will be high and some opportunities may be permanently lost.

Obviously, management should dedicate additional resources to the project in order to meet the emergency time deadlines. There are no magic answers. The mathematics of the relationship between total expended time, rate of resource utilization, and resulting elapsed time (see Table 12-1) still hold true. The company must therefore set the project goals lower (at least initially), concentrate on the basics, and apply more resources.

Simply shortcutting the required implementation steps is not the most prudent course of action. The implementation steps discussed earlier in this chapter should still be performed, but their performance will need to be accelerated or compressed as the emergency situation dictates.

EVALUATING THE RESULTS OF THE IMPLEMENTATION

The results of the system implementation should be evaluated in order to ensure that the company is obtaining the expected benefits. During the course of the implementation, the project team, users, and management should stay aware and focused on the original intentions for acquiring and implementing the new system.

In the heat of battle it's quite easy to lose sight of the original intentions in implementing the new system. The project team and the users become so wrapped up in just getting the system working and in solving problems that they often forget why they originally undertook the project. It's easy to lose focus.

The evaluation of the results of the implementation can begin by simply making a list of the expected benefits. This should be a realistic set of objectives that is reflective of the expectations of both the functional area personnel and management. It is important to also decide *how* the benefits will be measured. For the numbers to be useful and credible, the method of measurement must be chosen carefully.

A few examples of clearly defined statements of expected benefit would be:

- 90 percent reduction in parts shortages
- 15 percent improvement in on-time delivery performance

These benefits are straightforward enough and sufficiently quantifiable to be understandable by everyone in the company. There will still be a challenge in properly making the periodic measurements and it's unavoidable for some judgmental issues to enter into the process.

One technique to make the measurements as true and representative as possible is to try and filter out extraneous effects on the factor being measured. For example, assume that an expected benefit has been identified as:

- 35 percent reduction in work-in-process inventory

In this case, expressing the value of work-in-process inventory levels as the number of days sales (instead of in absolute dollars) will somewhat filter out the natural effect of changing sales/production volumes.

It is realistic to expect the benefits of a system implementation to take a while to accrue. Generally, the more profound the expected benefit, the longer it will take to realize. But it is also important to at least target a reasonable time frame, for example:

- 10 percent total inventory reduction at the end of *2 months*,
- 30 percent reduction at the end of *4 months*,
- etc.

The evaluation of derived benefits should certainly begin soon after the project completes. Ideally, this measuring/evaluation activity should have been taking place *during* the project, particularly after key checkpoints. Since the more substantial and pervasive benefits will take time to accrue, the evaluation process should go on for a good period of time after project completion. A regular measurement/evaluation/analysis/corrective-action cycle performed at three-month intervals seems to work well.

The implementation project team will probably bear primary responsibility for evaluating the benefits. Finance may assist the team in validating the measurements to ensure that the data are recording real changes and that the perceived results are credible.

The project team should report the results to management so that the company is informed and can evaluate the return on its investment in the new system. Based on results, a commitment of additional resources may be appropriate to modify or improve the implementation to obtain increased benefits.

USING OUTSIDE CONSULTANTS

Evaluating the Consultants' Competence

Prior experience is one key element of competence. The prospective consultants will ideally have significant experience in:

- The implementation of manufacturing-oriented systems
- The company's industry
- Working with companies of the same size and organizational character
- The chosen software and associated products

In verifying the consultants' experience and capabilities in these areas, the company should talk with clients who have previously used their services. Consultants who have delivered quality service to clients willingly provide references.

When evaluating a consulting firm, a company should determine which specific individual(s) will be performing the services. The quality of the firm is less important than the quality of the individuals who will actually be assigned to do the work. These individuals should be met with directly and the company should seek assurance that these same people will provide the services.

There are a few acid tests that can be used to verify that prospective consultants possess the necessary level of competence. Listen carefully to see whether the consultants can explain the technical implementation and software functionality issues in language understandable to the layman. This is a good indication that the consultants actually do understand the issues well and do not resort to buzzwords to gloss over holes in their knowledge.

Similarly, see if the prospective consultants can explain their recommended approach to the implementation process and issues such as project planning, resource requirements, the pilot technique, and parallel processing without resorting to predeveloped slides or diagrams. This is a good indication that they actually do understand these issues and have experience in providing these types of services.

The Consultants' Role

The most appropriate role for the consultants is to serve as advisory, nonvoting, members of the project team. They should be viewed as a resource or tool available to the project team. The consultants should not cast votes in decision-making processes. They should not dictate the performance of implementation tasks or the choice of implementation alternatives. The team members and the users are going to take ownership of the implemented system. Therefore, they should be the ones to direct the implementation and be the final decision makers.

Some consultants prefer to work in a different role. They will take over the implementation process, run the system initially for the client, then after some number of months will attempt to turn the system over to the client. This is referred to as a *turn-key implementation* and is almost always a mistake.

The project team members and the other company personnel know more about the company, its operations, and its business needs than outside consultants could possibly learn during the life of the project. Consequently, the team can do a better job than the consultants in choosing implementation alternatives and adapting the products to fit the company's needs. Moreover, the turn-key approach does little to obtain the necessary buy-in from the user community for the newly implemented system.

Where Consultants Can Be Useful

Qualified consultants can actually be useful in many places throughout the process of implementing an *HI/MIS*. The following discussion suggests how they could potentially be used.

Perhaps the first place to consider using consulting assistance is in the original formation of the implementation project team. (Please refer to Chapter 10 for a discussion of how consultants can assist in this area.) One of the most important places to seek outside assistance, especially if there is not a wealth of relevant experience within the company, is in developing the overall implementation plan. Consultants can help recognize the predecessor/successor relationships of tasks, help determine realistic resource requirements and timeframes, and can help identify priority tasks.

Consultants can be of benefit in conducting and facilitating the pilot by helping to develop the "script" for simulating the company's business cycle. As issues develop during the pilot process, they can help suggest workarounds and improved alternative methods to try. They can also ensure that the participants in the pilot are really putting the software through its paces and are simulating a realistic operating environment.

Often, outside assistance is appropriate in developing operational procedures. Consultants can help in the development of these procedures by suggesting a framework for their expression and by ensuring that the finished procedures are complete and suitable. Some consulting groups may have boilerplates or at least a library of similar procedures to facilitate the process. All consultants, based on experience levels, will have some idea of normal or best industry practices that can be incorporated into the company's new operational procedures.

Consultants can assist in the development of base data. Advice can be given on ways to establish the new data, such as recommendations on the optimal bill of material structuring. Advice can also be given on the content of specific fields, such as the parameters used to control the MRP process. Some consulting groups may also be able to assist in the conversion/loading of base data by providing the technical assistance to automatically perform the transfer of data from the old to the new system.

Consultants can often assist in the training of end users, especially if generic training is required on fundamental concepts such as MRP-II and Master Scheduling.

The experience of competent consultants can be of particular value in deciding on which functional areas to parallel. They can assist by helping to identify and evaluate the related risks, confidence levels, and fallback alternatives available. When it is apparent that the time is right to cut-over to the new system (and discontinue use of the old system), the consultants can assist by making a rational, independent appraisal of the stability of the new system.

Finally, consultants can be effective in evaluating the quality of the implementation. They can assist the company in doing this for themselves by recommending measurement techniques to test for the achievement of the expected benefits. On an ongoing basis, they can help to correctly interpret and evaluate the results of the measurements, isolate the causes of differences, and suggest actions to make improvements and obtain increased benefits.

SUMMARY

The methodologies described in this chapter have enabled companies to implement *HI/MIS* successfully. They are designed to effect a quality implementation in the shortest feasible time while making efficient and effective use of relatively few resources.

A concise list of the primary steps in the implementation process is presented below. Before taking the first step, the company should consider using outside consultants and, if appropriate, engage them for assistance as early as possible in the process.

- Form the project team.
- Plan the implementation project.
  - Establish reasonable expectations for resources and elapsed time.
  - Determine the project priorities.
  - Choose the approach for system cut-over.
  - Assign responsibilities.
  - Designate project checkpoints.
- Accomplish phase 1 product training.
- Utilize the pilot technique.
- Develop operational procedures.
- Develop and load base data.
- Accomplish phase 2 product training.
- Initiate system use.
- Process in parallel.
- Cut-over to new system.
- Evaluate the results of the implementation.

Index